History and the Triune God

History and the Triune God

Contributions to Trinitarian Theology

Jürgen Moltmann

SCM PRESS

Translated by John Bowden from the German
In der Geschichte des dreieinigen Gottes.
Beiträge zur trinitarischen Theologie,
published 1991 by Christian Kaiser Verlag, Munich

© Jürgen Moltmann 1991

Translation © John Bowden 1991

British Library Cataloguing in Publication Data

Moltmann, Jürgen
History and the triune God:
contributions to trinitarian theology.
I. Title
230

334 02513 3

Printed in Great Britain by
Clays Ltd, St Ives plc

To Dumitru Staniloae,
my fatherly friend,
who encouraged and stimulated me
in thinking about the Trinity

Contents

Preface

The articles collected here were written in the ten years after the publication of my book *The Trinity and the Kingdom of God* (1980). In them I have attempted to interpret the 'social doctrine of the Trinity' developed there in connection with the history of salvation and the human experience of God. At the same time I have been concerned to see the Trinity in connection with the future of history and the human expectation of God. So the articles have been collected from two perspectives. In 'The History of the Trinity' I attempt to understand the meaning of 'I believe in God, the Father, the Son and the Holy Spirit, the triune God'. In 'The Trinitarian View of History' I then attempt to grasp the divine dynamic of history. Part I is a contribution to the theology of the Trinity itself; Part II contains theological discussions with theologians and philosophers who have become important to me. Theology is dialogical. In dialogues one can clarify and sharpen one's own position. Because one is also in dialogue with people who are no longer in a position to reply, and because every age must grapple with the thinking of previous ages, I have taken the liberty of calling these theological arguments 'conversations' too. Part III is a brief sketch of my own theological career which I was asked to provide in 1985. It is an attempt to take account of the past and future and to demonstrate the continuity of my theology in the context of the very different challenges of our time.

I have worked through and revised some of these articles so that they are no longer identical with the form in which they were first published. That is particularly the case with I, 2 and II, 1.

Tübingen, 30 August 1990

Books by Jürgen Moltmann

To avoid unnecessary repetition in the text and notes, publication details of the main works by Jürgen Moltmann mentioned or cited regularly are given below in chronological order of publication; the date of the original German is in brackets. Elsewhere they are referred to simply by title or short title.

Theology of Hope. On the Ground and the Implication of a Christian Theology (1964), SCM Press and Harper and Row 1967

The Crucified God. The Cross of Christ as the Foundation and Criticism of Christian Theology (1972), SCM Press and Harper and Row 1974

The Church in the Power of the Spirit. A Contribution to Messianic Eschatology (1975), SCM Press and Harper and Row 1977

The Trinity and the Kingdom of God. The Doctrine of God (1980), SCM Press and Harper and Row 1981

God in Creation. An Ecological Doctrine of Creation, The Gifford Lectures 1984-1985 (1985), SCM Press and Harper and Row 1985

The Way of Jesus Christ. Christology in Messianic Dimensions (1989), SCM Press and Harper and Row 1990

The Open Church (1977), SCM Press 1978 (US title *The Passion for Life. A Messianic Lifestyle,* Fortress Press 1978)

The Future of Creation (1977), SCM Press and Fortress Press 1979

Introduction

Some Questions about the Doctrine of the Trinity Today

The doctrine of the Trinity has become important in the last ten years because it is the way in which the distinctive feature of Christianity is formulated. Dialogue with other religions is not helped if Christians relativize that which is distinctively Christian and give it up in favour of a general pluralism.[1] Who would be interested in a dialogue with Christian theologians who no longer want to advocate Christianity clearly? In theological dialogue with Jews and Muslims, Christians will learn to understand and interpret the doctrine of the Trinity in a new way because they will also learn to understand themselves anew in new relationships, but they will not relativize this doctrine or give it up.[2] In serious dialogue each side must show a profile. Those who give up their own position in favour of a supposedly higher truth are neither capable of dialogue nor worthy of dialogue. Attempts to achieve a monotheism which is capable of commanding a general consensus along the lines of 'the God who is always greater' by giving up confession of Jesus as Son of God and the doctrine of the Trinity come to grief on the distinctive features of Judaism, Christianity and Islam and the differences between them.

In recent years the following questions have become important to me in the doctrine of the Trinity: 1. the concept of trinitarian fellowship; 2. the question of masculine and feminine metaphors; 3. the further development of the trinitarian theology of the cross, and 4. the perspectives of a trinitarian view of history.

1. The social doctrine of the Trinity

My impression is that the idea of a 'social doctrine of the Trinity' has gained ground in contributions to the doctrine of the Trinity over the last ten years. 'The psychological doctrine of the Trinity', the description given by Michael Schmaus to Augustine's doctrine of the Trinity, has faded into the background. Many people felt that the trinitarian doctrines of the transcendental subjectivity of God put forward by Karl Barth and Karl Rahner were inadequate, though they did not dispute the value of these doctrines. The idea became established that the triune God is a single communion or fellowship which is formed by the three divine persons themselves. The unity of the triune God is no longer seen in the homogeneous divine subject nor in the identical divine subject, but in the eternal *perichoresis* of Father, Son and Spirit. This insight has far-reaching consequences for the hermeneutics of the history of salvation and human experiences of God; for the doctrine of the image of God in human beings and the conception of a creation which corresponds to God; for the doctrine of the unity and the form of the church as the 'icon of the Trinity'; and not least for the eschatological expectation of a new, eternal community of creation. The monarchical, hierarchical and patriarchal ideas used to legitimate the concept of God are thus becoming obsolete. 'Communion', 'fellowship', is the nature and the purpose of the triune God.

Fortunately this idea is not new. It has a prior history in Catholic theology, even if it does not go down very well with the Roman hierarchy. Michael Schmaus understood the doctrine of triunity as a 'perfect doctrine of communion'.[3] According to M.J.Scheeben, 'the divine persons form this unique and exalted society, a society whose members are equal, related and bound together in the most perfect way and which is therefore the unattainable, eternal and essential ideal of all society'.[4] This tradition has been investigated again by Wigand Siebel, *Der heilige Geist als Relation. Eine soziale Trinitätslehre,* Münster 1968.[5] Nor does Orthodox theology have any problems in understanding the unity of the triune God as 'community'. The great Cappadocians already understood it in this way. The friendly and affirmative reviews of my book by the Greek Orthodox theologian Christos Yannaras[6] and the Romanian Orthodox theologian Dumitru Staniloae[7] indicate a new convergence of the doctrines of the Trinity in the Eastern and Western churches which could prove even more fruitful than the resumption of the discussion over the *filioque*. Anglican theology has constantly reflected on the idea of the trinitarian community of God. That is already evident from the fine article by S.H.Ford, 'Perichoresis and Interpretation: Samuel Taylor Coleridge's Trinitarian Conception of Unity', *Theology* LXXXIX, January 1986, no.727, 20-3, and the new studies by the British Council of Churches, *The Forgotten Trinity*, 1. *The Report of the BCC Study Commission on Trinitarian Doctrine Today;* 2. *A Study Guide on Issues Contained in the Report of the BCC Study Commission on Trinitarian Doctrine Today,* London 1989. There is an admirable summary in J.O'Donnell, SJ, 'The Trinity as Divine Community', *Gregorianum* 69.1, 1988, 5-34; and C.M. LaCugna and J.O'Donnell, 'Returning from "the Far Country": Theses for a Contemporary Trinitarian Theology', *Scottish Journal of Theology* 41, 1988, 191-215.

The triune God is community, fellowship, issues an invitation to his community and makes himself the model for a just and livable community in the world of nature and human beings.[8] According to this view it is the 'communion of the Holy Spirit' which guarantees the unity of the church, and not monarchical centralism. 'The church is the people united by the unity of the Father and the Son and the Holy Spirit,' said Cyprian.[9] It was Leonardo Boff who in the base communities of Latin America rediscovered this form of the fellowship of the triune God and made it the foundation first of his ecclesiology and then also of his doctrine of God. In *Church, Charism and Power. Liberation Theology and the Institutional Church,* Crossroad Publishing Company and SCM Press 1985, 58ff., he contrasts the form of church communion according to John 17.21ff. with the hierarchical form of the church. This involved him in disciplinary proceedings with the Congregation of the Doctrine of Faith in Rome and he was disciplined with an ominous 'penitential silence'. His book *Trinity and Society* (1988) was vigorously criticized because it took over my thesis that 'the Trinity is our true social programme' and based its proposal for a 'communitarian church' on the social doctrine of the Trinity. I regard Leonardo Boff's ecclesiological and trinitarian theses as being ecumenical and Catholic in the best sense. They could be called 'dangerous' only by an authoritarian religious system in which the people is made dependent and kept in tutelage. The social doctrine of the Trinity gives Latin American liberation theology a theological depth and practical aims for church and society. A human society is becoming visible in which personality, sociality and nature are brought into equilibrium and people are becoming capable of surviving with one another and with nature.

2. Gender roles in the Trinity

Feminist theology has urgently raised the question of masculine and feminine metaphors for the deity and in particular for the persons of the Trinity. Because images of God, as images of what Tillich called 'our ultimate concern', always have the effect of legitimating human conditions, it goes without saying that there should be criticism of patriarchal and androcentric images of God by women who for centuries have been passed over, humiliated and at men's beck and call, but who are now becoming aware of their own worth. That needs no further discussion here.

In the first wave of the feminist criticism of religion the images of 'God the Father' and 'Lord God' were criticized and rejected as projections of male domination. Mary Daly attempted to understand the Godhead 'beyond God the Father' with neutral ontological concepts which she had taken over from Paul Tillich.[10] These ontological concepts of 'supreme being', the 'depth of being' and 'being beyond being' are also helpful in the context of the ecological crisis which human, i.e. male-dominated, culture has brought upon nature, because they are not as anthropocentric as purely personal conceptions of God. Personal and historical conceptions of God are not in fact adequate for understanding

God as the mystery of human beings *and* nature.

In a second wave of feminist criticism of religion, an attempt was then made to balance out the images of God in masculine and feminine terms.[11] For this, exegetical research offered feminine conceptions for the presence and earthly activity of God. While Yahweh is imagined as Lord and King, as Saviour and Judge, in Israelite experiences of God his activity on earth is primarily described in feminine metaphors: the *ruach* of Yahweh, the *ʰokmah* of Yahweh, the *shekinah* of Yahweh.[12] According to the kabbalistic tradition, as Gershom Scholem has demonstrated, 'the feminine side of the Godhead' lies in the *shekinah*.[13] According to the early traditions in Syria and the so-called 'Gnostic' communities, in both being and activity the Holy Spirit hides the motherly mystery of God, as Elaine Pagels has shown.[14] The apocryphal Gospel of the Hebrews calls Jesus the 'Son of the Holy Spirit': 'My Son,' says the *ruach* of Yahweh, 'in all the prophets I was waiting for you to come and that I might find rest in you.'[15] The Acts of Thomas call the Holy Spirit, in the feminine,[16] 'the mother of creation' and 'our compassionate mother'. The Syrian church fathers called the Holy Spirit 'our mother' for two reasons. First, the Paraclete comforts as a mother comforts her children, and secondly, believers are 'born' anew from the Holy Spirit. So the Spirit is their merciful mother, just as the Spirit is the essential mother of the firstborn Son Jesus. This idea of the motherly office of the Spirit of God entered the mystical piety of both East and West through the fifty homilies of Makarios.

But is it enough to introduce the femininity of the Spirit into the Trinity? Does not the femininity then always remain subordinate to the Fatherhood and the Sonship in the Godhead? By these feminine metaphors for the Spirit is not femininity simply co-opted into a world of masculine concepts, without being able to change it? And does not the addition of the motherly power of origin to the fatherly power of origin make human emancipation towards autonomy completely impossible? If God is called 'Father and Mother' (as by John-Paul I), the rule of God is patriarchy and matriarchy at the same time. No room is left for human freedom.

The next step in the feminist criticism of religion was therefore to discover the feminine side in each person of the Trinity.[17] In respect of God the Father this follows without difficulty from the biblical combination of fatherliness and mercy. According to the Hebrew expression for mercy, the 'merciful father' is the 'motherly father'.[18] In connection with the Holy Spirit one need only go back to the original *ruach Yahweh* to discover its feminine side. When the Nicene Creed calls the Spirit 'Lord and giver of life', it means the 'Lord who frees' and the mother 'who brings to life'. But the truly surprising discoveries have been made in connection with the idea of Christ as the 'perfect human being'. According to Gal.3.27-29, all those who are baptized into Christ have 'put on Christ'.[19] But in Christ there is 'neither Jew nor Greek, bond nor free, not man and woman'. All are one in Christ and heirs of the coming kingdom of God according to the promise. Why does Paul say that the new person in Christ is 'not man *and* woman'? Evidently here a *tertium genus,* a third kind, of humanity is to come into being, transcending the sexes. In Christ not only is the Fall done away with but also the creaturely division of the human being, Adam, into man, *ish,* and woman, *ishah* (Gen.2.21ff.) is overcome and the pre-sexual unity of human beings restored. Is Christ the 'new' (Rom.5.14) or 'last Adam' (I Cor.15.45), the trans-sexual person? Does the kabbalistic Adam-Cadmon myth correspond to this? Does that mean that the new creation of human beings in Christ is of an androgynous kind? Is the creation itself to be corrected through Christ?[20] 'Not man *and* woman' in fact sounds like an androgynous interpretation of baptism. Since the Nag Hammadi discoveries, this can also be demonstrated in the so-called 'Gnostic' communities. The image of Jesus typical of nineteenth-century liberal Protestantism always also saw behind the 'sinlessness' of the Redeemer the harmonious union of male and female characteristics, i.e. the union of *animus* and *anima.*[21] But can an androgynous personality be the solution to the question of gender? Is it not an individualistic solution to this question: each perfect in him/herself, neither needing the other? As Christians, do human beings really become androgynous through the *imitatio Christi*? Is not being a woman or being a man a special and different charism of the Spirit which distinguishes us and brings us to life?

Last but not least, the trinitarian notion of communion has attracted feminist theologians,[22] since the problems which gave rise to feminist theology were not the difference between the sexes as such, nor fatherhood as such, but the claims to domination which were associated with fatherhood in the patriarchal society, and the claim that maleness was true humanity, which led to an androcentric culture. The trinitarian notion of the mutual *perichoresis* of the three divine persons is in fact an expression of communication which is free from domination. The divine persons are there with one another and 'together are worshipped and glorified', as the Nicene Creed says. They have everything in common apart from their personal characteristics. The divine persons are there for one another: the Father for the Son, the Son for the Father, the Spirit for the Father and the Son. They achieve this perfect representation of one another. So ultimately they are also there in one another: *'Propter hanc unitatem Pater totus est in Filio, totus in Spiritu Sancto; Filius totus est in Patre, totus in Spiritu Sancto; Spiritus Sanctus totus est in Patre, totus in Filio'* ('Because of this unity the Father is fully in the Son, fully in the Holy Spirit; the Son is fully in the Father, fully in the Holy Spirit; the Holy Spirit is fully in the Father, fully in the Son'), as the Council of Florence says.[23] They interpenetrate each other mutually to such a degree that they exist in one another and indwell one another mutually. 'I am in the Father, the Father is in me', says the Johannine Jesus (John 14.10). The fellowship of the triune God is thus the matrix and the sphere of life for the free community of men and women, without domination and without subjection, in mutual respect and mutual recognition. It is the matrix and the sphere of life for the community-in-creation of all living beings and things, since 'fellowship' is the recognizable meaning in the formation of structures of matter and life. Feminist theology has made 'mutuality' one of its basic terms.[24] Mutuality can clearly be recognized in the trinitarian perichoresis, in which it takes on a richer significance than in the I-Thou philosophy of Martin Buber, from which it is derived. According to John 17.21f., the character of the primal image in the Trinity does not lie either in the paternal monarchy or the matriarchy of the Spirit, nor in any way does it lie in individual persons, but in the relationships of fellowship between the persons. The level of relations in the Trinity at which the eternal *perichoresis* can be recognized is the element in God from which analogies are to be formed.

3. The trinitarian theology of the cross

In my book *The Crucified God* I came upon a trinitarian theology of the cross by reversing the soteriological question 'What do the suffering and death of Christ mean for us?' so that it became the theological question 'What do the suffering and death of Christ mean for God?' My answer was: the Father's pain over the death of the Son. If God 'was in Christ', as Paul says in II Cor.5.19, and if the Father is 'in the Son' and the Son 'in the Father', as the Gospel of John stresses (14.10ff.), then through the crucifixion of Jesus, the Son of God, the Father of Jesus Christ is also drawn to share in the suffering. Therefore he is not 'the one who causes suffering',[25] but 'the one who suffers with'. It is one divine passion which leads to the pain of the Father, the death of the Son and the sighing of the Spirit: the passion of love for lost creatures. I have therefore replaced the metaphysical axiom of the essential impassibility of the divine nature with the essential passion of the eternal love of God (*The Trinity and the Kingdom of God*). Paul Fiddes has taken that up and spoken of 'the creative suffering of God'.[26] This conception corresponds to talk of the essential *mercy* of God. The doctrine of the essential impassibility of the divine nature now seems finally to be disappearing from the Christian doctrine of God. In this way it is becoming possible to see the cross on Golgotha in the heart of the triune God, so as to perceive the revelation of God in the crucified Jesus.

The mediaeval image of the Trinity in the Western church presented by the 'mercy seat' shows pictorially what is involved (for details see p.56 below). Certainly this was originally intended to depict the acceptance of the atoning sacrificial death of the Son by God the Father, as this is celebrated in the mass. But the painters often reflected on the Father's face the pain of the Son's death on the cross. We can therefore, conversely, read the images of the mercy seat as the surrender of the Father through the Son in the Spirit.

The silence about the Holy Spirit causes certain difficulties for the trinitarian interpretation of the event of the cross. Lyle Dabney investigated the pneumatology of the cross in his Tübingen dissertation.[28] He found the presence of the Spirit in Jesus' 'Abba' prayer in Gethsemane and in the intercession of the Spirit 'with unutterable sighs' for the Christ dying forsaken by God.[29] His thesis is that 'the Spirit is the presence of God in the absence of the Father'.

Another problem area opens up in connection with the 'theology of the atonement'. In my works on the trinitarian theology of the cross I myself have always stressed the christology of solidarity, in order to point to the solidarity of God with the victims of injustice and violence in the solidarity of Christ with them. There were also contextual reasons for this: those who have to exist in the shadow of the injustice of the perpetrators cannot very well offer 'reconciliation' to the victims and those who have to exist with the recollection of their suffering. They cannot even pray for reconciliation without having previously bowed down before the victims. If there is reconciliation for the perpetrators, it can come only from the victims. Therefore my christology was both consciously and unconsciously orientated on the victim 'who bears the suffering of the world ... ' However, it is right that from such a christology of solidarity for the victims an atoning christology for the perpetrators should also emerge: 'Who bears the sin of the world ... ' I have always hinted at that but never developed it myself.

From the sphere of the theopoetical and theodramatical theology of Hans Urs von Balthasar,[30] the Catholic theologian Norbert Hoffmann SSCC has worked on this theme in two important books: *Sühne - zur Theologie der Stellvertretung*, Eisiedeln 1981, and *Kreuz und Trinität. Zur Theologie der Sühne*, Einsiedeln 1982. While he unnecessarily contrasts the christology of atonement with Karl Rahner's christology of solidarity, he has succeeded in depicting the atoning death of Christ as the trinitarian revelation of the atoning God and in discovering in 'Christ who died for us' the eternal 'God is for us'. 'Only with the doctrine of the Trinity is the historical truth of the cross given theological illumination' (*Kreuz und Trinität*, 52). I certainly cannot follow all the author's speculative trains of thought. But his theology of atonement has stimulated me to develop a christology of atonement from the christology of solidarity (I, 5), to liberate the Reformation doctrine of justification from its one-sided orientation on the perpetrators and interpret it in terms of both victims and perpetrators: God's righteousness is a righteousness which executes justice and puts things right.

4. The trinitarian view of history

Trinitarian thought seems to move in eternal circles and, like liturgical doxologies, to love repetitions. Historical thought since modern times has been committed to a linear approach, seeing progress from the past through the present to the future. Connections between the two arise from the conversion of the salvation-historical Trinity into a trinitarian conception of salvation history, of the kind that already happened in the early Middle Ages. The famous and at the same time controversial model here is Joachim of Fiore (II, 1). He cannot be said to have 'dissolved' the Trinity into a salvation history with an eschatological determination, but he does introduce a historical dynamic which seeks to reconcile human history eschatologically with the eternal history of God. My discussions in Part II of this book with Thomas Aquinas, Karl Barth and Ernst Bloch keep revolving round this point: if the historical knowledge of the triune God discloses reality as history with an eschatological goal, then it makes sense to assume a movement from the initial creation through historical reconciliation to eschatological consummation. Past − present − future are then not three ongoing unfoldings of an eternity beyond time, but are directed towards a future in which this time is consummated and ended. The kingdom of nature, the kingdom of grace and the kingdom of glory are not three aspects of the one kingdom of God, but three stages on the way to its consummation. Therefore the two-stage theology of nature and grace or creation and covenant is not enough. There is a further movement to the new creation of all things in glory.

The Italian theologian Bruno Forte, in the tradition of southern Italian historical thought in the line of Joachim of Fiore, Giordano Bruno, Giambattista Vico and Benedetto Croce, has called his doctrine of the Trinity *Trinity as History − The Living God − God of the Living*. He follows the Trinity as history by developing a trinitarian conception of history which points to the 'trinitarian home' (I Cor.15.28). I am aware that my thought is very close to his, though in his work I miss any discussion of secular views of history and the definite negation of the negative in real history.

For some time now, American and English process theologians have been concerned to reconcile their process thought with trinitarian thought. If the triune God is called the 'God who is rich in relationship', then there is a degree of convergence with the concept of God as 'divine relativity', which is found in Charles Hartshorne. Norman Pittenger, *The Divine Triunity*, Philadelphia 1977, sought to reinterpret the traditional doctrine of the Trinity in terms of process philosophy. There has been a series of articles on this question from the school of Schubert Ogden and John Cobb.[31] The gulf between a deliberately 'natural' process theology and a traditional doctrine of the Trinity grounded in revelation is, however, still deep. So too is the gulf between a view of history with an eschatological openness and a view of history which derives from the understanding of nature as process. The interconnections are all the more important when they resist the division of reality into human history and non-human history, since the ecological crisis of nature, and with it the apocalyptic endangering of human history, has arisen from this division.

W.Pannenberg, *Systematische Theologie* I, Göttingen 1988, 283ff., has developed his doctrine of the Trinity from the idea of the 'reciprocal self-distinction of Father, Son and Spirit as the concrete form of the trinitarian relations' (335ff.). That leads to the idea that the divine persons not only constitute their personality mutually, but also constitute the Godhead (347ff.). Because Pannenberg maintains the 'monarchy of the Father', he dispenses with the idea of communion or fellowship in the divine *perichoresis* and instead of this takes up the monarchy into the relationships within the Trinity. It is not completely clear to me why he has to maintain the idea of monarchy.

I

THE HISTORY OF
THE TRINITY

1

'I Believe in God the Father'

Patriarchal or Non-Patriarchal Talk of God?

1. The dethroning of the Father God

'I believe in God the Father Almighty, maker of heaven and earth.' So Christians have confessed in the Apostles' Creed for almost two thousand years. When they do so, are they confessing the God of a patriarchal society, the rule of fathers over their families and men over public life, or are they joining in the unique Abba mystery of Jesus of Nazareth, who brought the kingdom of God near to the poor, the forsaken and sinners? Are they confessing the absolute dependence of all transitory being on the heavenly Father of all, or are they joining in the glorious freedom of the children of God which Paul heard in the cry 'Abba' from those who are filled with the Spirit of Jesus? This is the question. Is the God of the Bible only a further manifestation of the age-old deity of patriarchy, or is 'the Father of Jesus Christ' another God: a God who leads women and men into the shared freedom of the messianic time in which there will no longer be matriarchy and patriarchy, because the rule of one human being over another has come to an end? If we put the question like this, we are already expressing an intention to seek a non-patriarchal way of talking of God the 'Father' which is in accord with the gospel and which liberates men and women. With this theological intent is associated, finally, a practical interest in a non-patriarchal fatherliness and a masculinity which is liberated for open, human identity.[1] The feminist protest against patriarchy in heaven and on earth must also involve males in turning from domination to community.

1

'I can no longer call God "Father". I can no longer pray the "Our Father",' say some women, who discover how much the patriarchal domination of males in church and state, religion and politics, has banished them to the role of the dependent, childlike woman who has yet to come of age, and how much the language of patriarchal culture with its masculine stamp has alienated their world of experience, feeling and expression from their own, human self.[2]

In the last resort, human forms of domination have always sought their legitimation in religion, and indeed have found it there. Images of God are worshipped with ultimate devotion. They support the existence and the community of those who worship them. Knowledge which supports existence may not be put in doubt. Whatever is anchored in religion and legitimated by religion is therefore unshakeably firm. Crimes against religion were regarded as the most serious. Anyone who mocks and blasphemes the gods puts the basis of a society in question. So in some circles the feminist protest is regarded as 'blasphemy'.

In our culture, religious worship of God as 'Lord and Father' has legitimated both the rule of the father in the family and the rule of the 'father of the land' in the state, just as it has legitimated the fatherly rule of male priests and pastors in religion. If the religious images of a religious community and the idea of the fundamental values of a community are determined purely by males, then women can find meaning for their life only by way of masculinity, and have to participate in the life of religion and society as men conceive it. The feminist protest against religious patriarchy is a vital part of the liberation of women to be themselves. Without it the liberation of males from the distortions of patriarchy will also be impossible.

What conceptions in Christianity alienate women? Not just the conception of God as 'Lord and Father', not just the idea of the significance of Jesus in male functions like those of prophet, priest, king, lord and judge, but even the way in which since Paul congregations have been addressed as 'Dear brothers'. The intention has been inclusive, but the effect has been exclusive. So too has the view, also dominant since Paul, that those who are children of God in faith have 'sonship': of course this has been meant inclusively, but it has proved alienating. Are women to become 'brothers', or will they be excluded from the 'brotherhood' of believers? Are women to feel like 'sons' before God the Father or are they to be subordinated to the 'sons of God' as their heads? Nowadays this masculine terminology is only rarely used in an exclusivist way, but inclusive terminology is just as discriminating. Any inclusive language is basically imperialistic. It takes others over, and does not allow them to be themselves. So Christianity faces the critical question whether this masculine-sexist language and this patriarchal way of thinking can be stripped away, like the garb of a particular time, or whether it stands or falls by them. Does Christianity also offer possibilities with which women can identify?

But of course there is another side to the dethronement of the patriarchal

2

image of God. Is protest against it still meaningful in a society which in legal, socio-political and cultural terms is already in process of leaving behind it the personal patriarchy of the male – so-called 'fatherly authority'? Is not feminist protest perhaps killing only gods who are paralysed and already dying? If, as Alexander Mitscherlich already prognosticated in 1963, we are 'on the way to a fatherless society', then the de-patriarchalizing of the image of God is a change of consciousness which, while necessary, is still only following upon the changes in real conditions.[3] The modern industrial society is developing into a 'fatherless society' because authority is no longer perceived and responded to in personal terms, but is becoming increasingly bureaucratic and anonymous. That means that it is exercised irresponsibly and 'with limited liability'.[4] In a world which is no longer ruled over in sovereign fashion by potentates and patrons, but chairpersons and boards of directors, committees and computers, protest against father figures can easily become anachronistic, since the father figures themselves are. By now Oedipus has long ceased to have a father. The objectivifation of political, social and family authority in modern societies can hardly be described any longer in the personal terms characteristic of former times. Only in the churches and in the world of religious ideas do the old conditions and the obsolete images persist.

If we look at the situation in modern families, we only rarely see the 'master of the house' who controls everything and whom all weakly obey, because the male has already long since disappeared from the family. He works outside the home and is no longer in a position to dominate wife and children, simply because he has no time for them. Nowadays we do not find many almighty fathers living with their families; the tendency is, rather, for them to have no power. This remark does run counter to the fact that there are many kinds of masculine brutality in marriage and the family, to which shelters for women bear a lamentable and shameful witness, but goes some way towards explaining it.

What does the feminist protest against God the Father and the power of patriarchy mean for such men? They feel their actual powerlessness and react against it first with aggression, as do all those who are attacked; then with depression, as do all those who cannot defend themselves; and lastly with resignation, as do all those who have to give in. However, that can lead to males not only giving up the arrogant, high-handed power which they cannot exert in any case, but also losing any capacity to join in or readiness to take responsibility. The growing irresponsibility of men towards their families and children and masculine regression into childish games of narcissitic self-concern are sorry side-effects of the depatriarchalization of modern society. So it is necessary to develop a non-patriarchal way of talking about God the 'Father' in heaven in order to encourage people in his name to have courage to adopt a masculinity which does not lay claim to domination and a fatherhood without loss of power

3

and feelings of powerlessness, since there is nothing wrong with becoming and being a father.

Even more important, however, is the question of the significance of the move towards a 'fatherless society' for the development of awareness and independence in children. For Sigmund Freud, the super-ego owes its origin to the identification of the child with the father.[5] Ego-consciousness is then developed by this super-ego. What kind of consciousness-forming takes place if there is no father, and children have only their mothers to react with? Recent clinical research shows that the result is a 'melancholy type' (H.Tellenbach).[6] One can also attribute the origin of male 'machismo' to an unresolved bond to the mother. The 'structural triad' of mother, child and father is an essential part of the successful humanizing of men and women, even if the biological triad may not be. 'The father is an indispensable part of this structure.'[7] That is evidently just as true of the development of daughters as it is of the development of sons.

2. The religion of patriarchal domination

'Patriarchy' is understood to be a male order covering authority, possessions and right of inheritance which at the beginning of the historical age slowly but surely suppressed and displaced the former matriarchal forms of life.[8] With patriarchy goes a particular religion which legitimates and stabilizes it: the numinous power is represented by male images, usually of the father, and communicated through male kings and princes. Regardless of the kind of male images by which the divine was grasped, these images made it the origin of the father's authority in the family, the ruler's political power and the priest's authority in religion.

Wherever the religion of patriarchy established itself, there was a tendency towards monotheism in religion and the development of monarchical rule in politics. The one God in heaven was matched by the one ruler on earth. If this monotheism was represented in exclusive terms, the political rule which corresponded with it tended to be imperialistic: one God – one law – one world. The correlate of this was: one ruler – one will – one humankind.[9] The religious legitimation of the one ruler was always derived from his being a 'son of God' or being *par excellence* 'in the image of God'. The early political religions in Persia, Babylon and Egypt already display such structures; they are embodied in ideas of a Christian theocracy in Rome, Byzantium and Moscow, and in the age of absolutism they recur once again in the court of the French Sun King and in lesser European residences. For all the difference in time and culture, the hierarchical match between political and divine rule remains. There was nothing Christian about this idea. In so far as it was represented in historical Christianity, it is a Christian form of the religion of patriarchal domination. Genghis Khan, too, legitimated his Mongol rule of the world, by which the cultures of peoples

4

from Korea to Hungary were destroyed, in this way: 'In heaven there is none but the One God, and on earth none but the one ruler Genghis Khan: the Son of God.'[10] Ironically this was his answer to the delegates of 'Christ's representative' in Rome.

However, monarchical monotheism was matched not only in political rule but also in 'fatherly authority' in the family. Almost everywhere we still find traces of matriarchal cultures in the worship of the 'Mother of all', 'Mother earth', the 'Mother of all living beings'.[11] This matriarchal cult had a pantheistic character, and the divine was understood as eternally-fertile life: the individual phenomena of life arise from the great motherly stream of life and return to it, to be born from it anew. In the all-embracing, unconditional love of the three-dimensional goddess which fills heaven, earth and the underworld, life and death are one. Rituals of birth and burial often still show something of this old idea.[12] More recent researches into matriarchy keep indicating that this pantheism of life was the religion of matriarchy. By contrast, monarchical monotheism can be designated the religion of patriarchy. At Greek temple sites like Delphi and Olympia one can still see how Zeus 'the father of all', with his Olympian gods, displaced the 'earth mother' Gaia and her chthonic powers. In Delphi the priests of Apollo are said to have killed the snake through whom the earth mother spoke to the Pythia, and then to have established their own temple on the site after doing penance for this religious crime. In this way, in principle the rule of the male was also legitimated. The divine no longer spoke to the people through the snake and the woman, but through the spirit and the man.

The position of the father in the family as priest of the household derives from this. It also provided the legitimation for a male hereditary succession of authority and possessions. The male understood himself as the one who gives the seed of life. The old matriarchal, matrilinear succession was replaced by the patrilinear hereditary succession of property from father to son. And in order in turn to guarantee this, proof of paternity had to be given in each case, which was impossible without the imprisonment of wives in their families. The consequence was that women were deprived of their rights and enslaved.

Even now, democratically elected prime ministers of the states of Southern Germany like to be addressed as 'father of the state' (the land).[13] This anachronism points to the derivation of political power from the authority of the father of the household, which is remarkable, but typical of pre-modern Europe. The Roman father of the household (*paterfamilias*) was a monarchical ruler in the family. He had unlimited and lifelong authority over all those who by law belonged to the family group.[14] Even adult sons continued to remain subject to the *patria potestas*. That was evidently singular in the Mediterranean area. 'But what was remarkable and unheard-of for modern sensibilities was that his authority included rights over punishment and death. He had the power of life and death, the *vitae necisque potestas,* over all members of the household.'[15]

Certainly there were many attempts to temper the absolute power of the Roman master of the house by taking note of the tradition of the elders and the virtues of humanity, but until the time of the Christian emperors his monarchical position in the family remained.

The Roman father of the family had a religious parallel in the ancient Roman father gods and later the Father of the gods, since he functioned as their domestic priest. 'Pater' was an old Roman cult name for the great gods. It is also an element of the name Jupiter. The cultic community subordinated itself to the authority and the protection of the father god. Because this cultic community was co-extensive with the political community, the political ruler was regarded as the priestly king or the priestly father. As Pontifex Maximus, he took the position of the father of the house in the political community. The 'family of the state' was under the authority of the 'father of the state'.[16] But only in the year 2 BC was the emperor Augustus granted the official title of a 'father of the land' (*pater patriae*). From the time of Augustus this then became a common title for the Roman emperors. This title first echoes the expectations of peace and protection entertained by the emperor's subjects, so that many ancient lists of rules for princes reserve for Caesar the virtue of *clementia* and the need to care for his people, while on the other hand the power over life and death is also transferred to him. His rule is to be fatherly, but his fatherhood is also unlimited rule: he is *pater omnipotens*.

It has rightly been pointed out that at the beginning of the so-called 'Constantinian era' Roman ideas about the father were transferred to the Christian God through a work by Lactantius, entitled *On the Wrath of God*.[17] This fusion of the Christian and the Roman concept of God gave Christian history in Europe a fundamentally patriarchalist stamp: the one God is 'Lord' and 'Father' at the same time. The political and family rule which is legitimated by him and is to be exercised in his name is the rule of the fathers. Lactantius was concerned to give prominence to the biblical language about the wrath of the God who judges and thus at the same time to the role of lord in the Roman image of God the Father of all, in place of the philosophical picture of the gentle, gracious God which had been disseminated, e.g., by Seneca. The loving God and the wrathful God are not two different gods, as Marcion had claimed, but the one God's roles as Father and as Lord. On the basis of this double structure, God is 'to be feared and loved'. Because he has the power of father and lord (*duplex potestas: pater et dominus*), human beings are at the same time his children and his servants (*filius et servus*):

> We are all bound both to love him, because he is our Father; and to reverence him, because he is our Lord: both to pay him honour, because he is bounteous; and to fear him, because he is severe: each character in him is worthy of reverence. Who can preserve his piety and yet fail to love the parent of his

6

life? Or who can with impunity despise him who, as ruler of all things, has true and everlasting power of all? If you consider him in the character of Father, he supplies to us our entrance to the light which we enjoy; through him we have entered into the abode of this world. If you contemplate him as God, it is he who nurtures us with innumerable resources.[18]

It is easy to see how this Roman twofold concept of God as Lord God and God the Father has influenced the Christian image of God in the West. In the name of the one who 'is to be feared and loved above all things', his commandments were taught and obedience to him was inculcated. He is the 'Lord over life and death', as we say at funerals. So he has the true power of life and death over all human beings. But is this the God whom Jesus addressed in so intimate and familiar a way as 'Abba' and taught his followers to call upon? If 'Lord' and 'Father' are fused in the picture of God, then are not 'Yahweh' and 'Jupiter' fused, so that the Lord who liberates from slavery (first commandment) and the high Lord of heaven who rules inscrutably over all things can no longer be distinguished? Church prayers which begin, 'Lord, our God, dear Father in heaven . . . ' seem to be referring to one and the same divine person with their 'Lord' and 'Father', whereas the doctrine of the Trinity, following the model of the apostle Paul, distinguished critically between Fatherhood as the property of God and liberating rule as the role of Christ, and spoke of God as the 'Father of our Lord Jesus Christ'.

The transference of the model of the father of the household to political rule, which was natural in the Roman cultural sphere, was disseminated in Christianity mainly through the political interpretation of the fourth commandment (the fifth as the Bible counts them) in catechetical instruction. This instilling of a patriarchal idea of authority and a sense of being subjects had a deep influence on an illiterate people.

In the history of the interpretation of the Decalogue not only is there an analogy between the rule of a household and the rule of the state, but the authority of the state is derived from the authority of the father of the household. Luther's exegesis of the fourth commandment in the 'Greater Catechism' of 1529 became normative for Lutheran countries:

> While speaking of this commandment, we must further mention the various kinds of obedience to all who are over us, command us, and rule us. For all authority has its root and source in parental authority. For where a father is unable to bring up his child alone, he takes a teacher to teach him; if he is too weak, he takes his friend or neighbour to help him; when he departs this life, he gives authority to others who are chosen for the purpose. So he must also have servants, men and maids, under him for the household, so that all who are called master stand in the place of parents, and must obtain from them authority and power to command. Wherefore in the Bible they are all

called fathers, because their office bestows on them the office of a father, and they ought to bear a fatherly heart to their people. In the olden times the Romans and others called the master and mistress of the house *patres et matres familias*, that is, house-fathers and house-mothers. So also their princes and magistrates are called *patres patriae*, that is, fathers of the whole land, and it is a great shame for us would-be Christians that we do not call them so, and honour them accordingly.[19]

We must certainly note that here Luther puts the family office of the fathers and mothers of the house side by side, with equal rights.[20] But in the transference to political power the *matres* fall by the wayside. Moreover Luther restored the unity of family, political and religious patriarchalism, which had often already been broken in the Middle Ages. That all other authority extends from 'the authority of parents' indicates his particular idea of the priority of the family to the state in natural law. But according to Luther's interpretation there is no starting point for criticism of the power of the family and of political power, and for the right to resist.

Calvin interpreted the fifth commandment in a similar way, but added that one should and may obey parents only 'in the Lord':

Hence if they spur us to transgress the law, we have a perfect right to regard them not as parents, but as strangers who are trying to lead us away from obedience to our true Father. So should we act towards princes, lords and every kind of superiors.[21]

The difference between Luther and Calvin indicates a first ambivalence in the political function of the religious concept of Father: 'God the Father' can be used as the legitimation of the authority of the father of the house or of the land, so that believers become obedient and reliable subjects as true children of God. But 'God the Father' can also be used as *criticism* of the power of the father of the house or of the land, so that believers become the true guardians of the authorities. If God reveals his power directly through the natural authorities mentioned, then only obedient affirmation is possible. But if he reveals it through Moses and through Jesus, i.e. through scripture, then for Christians the guardian's office of criticism and the duty to resist in an emergency become matters of divine right.

The transition from the 'political patriarchalism' of Luther, which can be called 'ancient paternalism', to modern absolutism can be seen in Jean Bodin.[22] Bodin was a teacher of Roman law in Lyons. In his *Les six livres de la République* (first published in 1576) he laid the foundations for an absolutist understanding of the power of the state by referring to the rights of the Roman father of the household. As for Luther, so for Bodin the family is the source and origin of community, because community derives from the association of the

8

family. So the right rule over the household is the model for supreme authority in the community. The father of the family exercises right rule over the house as master of the house. To him is due the law of life and death - here Bodin goes back to old Roman law. The corresponding state authority must therefore have the 'right of life and death' over the citizens and is liable to give account to no one but God, the omnipotent source of its earthly power. In his definition of the supreme power of the state, Bodin does not so much stress the aspects of the father and of protection so much as those of the master and of power: '*Majestas est summa in cives ac subditos legibus soluta potestas* ('Majesty is the supreme power over citizens and subjects, which is above the laws').'[23] The supreme authority of the state is not subject to the laws which hold generally, but is bound only by the law of God and the law of nature, from which it derives its power. The principle '*princeps legibus solutus*' ('the prince is above the laws') soon became a detached slogan and led to an absolutist state authority which transcended the law. Nor was this absolute sovereignty to be limited by an appeal to God. The Huguenot attempt to tie the unlimited power of the ruler to God's goodness and law through his being 'in the image of God' came to grief because the depiction of divine omnipotence and glory proved more attractive, as the Versailles Court tangibly showed.

Both theories of the state, political patriarchalism and religio-political absolutism, disappeared with the French Revolution. Along with 'freedom' and 'equality', 'fraternity' took the place of 'fatherhood'. Democracy no longer recognized any political father-authorities. In the case of the ideology of the 'father of the land', the logic of transference was rejected with hard words: the father is certainly there before the son, but the nation is always there before the prince. The prince derives his existence from the nation, and not *vice versa*.[24] And Immanuel Kant proclaimed, very much along the lines of the French Revolution, the transition from 'fatherly rule' to the 'rule of the fatherland' by deliberately using motherly metaphors:

A government which was established on the principle of good will towards the people like that of a father towards his children, i.e. a paternalistic rule (*imperium paternale*), one where the subjects are compelled to behave in a merely passive way as children who have not come of age, who cannot distinguish what is truly useful or harmful for them, so that, if they are to be happy, they must look only to the judgments of the chief head of the state and, be he so willing, merely to his goodness, is the greatest conceivable despotism (a constitution which deprives subjects of all freedom, so that they have no rights at all). A government which is not paternalistic but patriotic (*imperium, non paternale, sed patrioticum*) is one which can be conceived of only for people who are capable of laws, which also govern the beneficence of the ruler. That manner of thinking is patriotic in which all

9

individuals in the state (the supreme head of that state not excluded) regard its common substance as the motherly womb, or the land as the fatherly ground, from which and on which they themselves have sprung into being and which they also must leave behind as a dear pledge, simply to protect its rights through laws which are willed by all, and in which individuals do not think that they are authorized to subjugate this land to use unconditionally at whim. This right of freedom pertains to the members of the commonalty as human beings, so far as they are beings who are capable of having rights.[25]

The mythology of the German Enlightenment can also be understood not least in the light of the central European tradition of political patriarchalism: 'Enlightenment is the departure of human beings from the tutelage which they have imposed upon themselves. Tutelage is the inability to make use of one's understanding without the guidance of another.' This is the programmatic statement which Kant made in 1783. The conceptual world of 'immaturity' and 'tutelage', 'coming of age' and 'emancipation', derives from family life and describes the process by which children grow up. When the problem of the generations thus described is transferred to public life as in Kant, when he speaks of the 'guardians of the people' and enlightened 'courage' in the 'public use of reason', then Enlightenment remains under the influence of political patriarchalism. The philosophy and theology of the coming of age of modern man[26] can hardly be translated into the language of other peoples who have different traditions of Enlightenment and democracy, as do, for example, Anglo-Saxon countries. The committed struggle to 'come of age' is a fight within patriarchy, just as the will for 'emancipation' always presupposes 'fatherly authority',

A people does not 'come of age', since it was never 'not of age'. A people can be ruled over and oppressed. Then it frees itself and takes its destiny into its own hands. A 'world' does not become a 'world come of age', because a world was never a child. So talk of an 'age of emancipation' is wide of the mark. The application of metaphors from individual development to the history of culture and of the world presupposes an 'education of the human race' which there never was.

3. 'Abba': 'The Father of Jesus Christ'

Statistically, God is called 'Father' 11 times in the Old Testament, but according to the New Testament he is addressed as 'Father' by Jesus himself 170 times. With the exception of his dying cry on the cross, following Ps.22, 'My God, why have you forsaken me?', Jesus always addressed God only as 'Abba', and spoke of him always only as 'my Father'. That is no coincidence, but points to the revelatory name of God which Jesus proclaimed along with the advent of the kingdom of God. Several strata can be distinguished in this revelatory name. The function of the revelation of God the Father as 'Abba' in the life and conduct

10

of Jesus can also be recognized clearly.

A. *'Abba'*. It is a comparative novelty and a feature of the message of Jesus that he addressed God with this familiar, intimate and tender word, which was used by children.[27] It is Aramaic and simple, very like the 'Mama, Papa', with which children may still address the person in whom they have basic trust. In using such words they are expressing their trust in the ground and security of their being. In the original pattern of their feelings, it does not matter whether mother or father is being addressed. If we went back to the origin of the child's basic trust as expressed in the word Abba, then we would tend to come upon the mother rather than the father. When Jesus addresses God himself by this name, the accent is certainly not on the masculinity of the Father God or on the exalted nature of the Lord, but on the unprecedented intimacy of Jesus' own relationship to God's divine mystery. The name Abba reveals the inner heart of the relationship between Jesus and God. So this Abba nearness of God also reveals the real nearness of the kingdom of God by which Jesus lived and acted.[28] 'The kingdom of God is at hand' means 'Abba, my dear Father', and *vice versa*: one can address God like this only in the presence of his liberating and healing kingdom. Jesus's Abba is the God who in a motherly way 'has mercy' on the forsaken and one day 'will wipe away all tears from their eyes' (Rev.21.4).

What is the function of the recognition of Abba, and prayer to him, in the life of Jesus? We do not know when and on what occasion Jesus received his revelation and mission. One might think of his baptism. At all events, his mission is a messianic mission, as is shown by his preaching (Luke 4.18ff.). He begins with the proclamation of the messianic age, the eschatological sabbath in the dawning of the kingdom of God. The signs and wonders that he does are the signs and wonders of the messianic turn of the ages. In the messianic age God himself is near.[29] Jesus lives in this nearness, he prays in it, and in it he understands himself as Son. Not as a 'Son of God' (Ps.2.7), but as the 'Son of the Father', as the Son of Abba. Matthew 11.27 puts it like this: 'All things have been delivered to me by my Father; and no one knows the Son except the Father, and no one knows the Father except the Son and any one to whom the Son chooses to reveal him.' The experience of God denoted by 'Abba' stamps Jesus' experience of himself as the Son of this Father. The consequences in his conduct can still clearly be recognized from the accounts: he leaves 'his own', his mother and his family, and entrusts himself completely to the guidance of Abba, his heavenly Father. In Mark 3.32-35, there is an account of his abrupt repudiation of his mother Mary and his brothers:

> And a crowd was sitting around him; and they said to him, 'Your mother and your brothers are outside, asking for you.' And he replied, 'Who are my mother and my brothers?' And looking around on those who sat about him, he said, 'Here are my mother and my brothers. Whoever does the will of God

11

is my brother, and sister, and mother.'

The verdict of his family on him is like that of the Pharisees: 'He is beside himself' (3.21). This is not just a rejection of his mother and his brothers, but a formal separation from his family. Such a separation from his mother was and is unheard-of: a Jew is one who has a Jewish mother. By breaking with his mother Jesus is breaking with the sequence of Jewish generations and the promise. Shalom Ben-Chorin has rightly seen this as a deliberate breach of the fifth commandment.[30] This will also have been the impression of the just men among the Jewish people at the time of Jesus. If we follow Ben-Chorin's reference, we come to Deut.21.18-21: a 'stubborn and rebellious son' is to be handed over by his parents to the elders for the punishment of stoning. They are to say to the elders, 'This our son is stubborn and rebellious, he will not obey our voice, he is a glutton and a drunkard' (v.20). The chapter ends with the comment, 'a hanged man is accursed'. So the New Testament account of Jesus is full of allusions to this chapter in Deuteronomy about the fifth commandment.

What does Jesus put in place of family ties and the tie to the sequence of generations in the history of the promise? He recognizes a new community among those who do the will 'of my Father in heaven' (Matt.12.50). These are the poor people (*ochlos*), not the people of God (*laos*), and this is not God's will in the Torah, which had been known since Moses, but God's messianic will which is revealed by Jesus – hence Jesus' reference to 'my Father'. In the metaphorical sense, this messianic community which is drawn into Jesus' Abba relationship embraces not only 'brothers and sisters' but also 'mothers'. Behaviour in it is not only brotherly and sisterly, but also motherly. Those who follow Jesus, women and men, will rediscover in the messianic community everything that they left behind in their natural families: brothers, sisters, mothers, children – but not fathers! That is often overlooked because it is so remarkable:

> Jesus answered and said. 'Truly I say to you, there is no one who has left house or brothers or sisters or mother or father or children or lands, for my sake and for the gospel, who will not receive a hundredfold now in this time, houses and brothers and sisters and mothers and children and lands, with persecutions, and in the age to come eternal life' (Mark 10.29-30).

There is to be abundant earthly recompense for all that one has renounced, but not for the father. But that means that 'there may no longer be patriarchal rule in the new family, but everyone will just be mothers, brothers and children before God, the Father'.[31] Why not? 'Call no man your father on earth, for you have one Father, who is in heaven' (Matt.23.9). The Abba-nearness of God evidently fills and permeates this new messianic community to such a degree that the function and authority of the earthly fathers vanishes. Patriarchal rule in the church of Christ therefore explicitly goes against belief in the fatherly nearness of God.[32] In this respect the messianic community which Jesus gathers round himself is a 'society of contrast': it goes against the patriarchal society of that time. But it does not go against the mothers, fathers, sisters and brothers in person: whoever does the will of the Father in heaven is a member of this new, messianic community. So later Jesus' mother, too, is to be found in the community: not as a mother but as a believing sister (Acts 1.14).

Here we can recognize a further consequence of belief in God the Father: it does not affirm the authority of the human father, as in Luther's exegesis of the Decalogue. Nor is it just critical, as in Calvin's exegesis of the fifth commandment. Jesus' attitude to the fifth commandment is devastating for any human paternal authority because of the way in which he acts: because God is *the* Father, Jesus' community is 'the end of the fathers'.[33]

The divine 'Abba' mystery breaks through that which ties Jesus to his origin and points him wholly towards the future of the messianic kingdom. Under the guidance of Abba, Jesus goes into the social and religious no-man's-land of a still unknown future, namely the kingdom of God, his Father.

In Romans 8.15; Galatians 4.6, Paul cites Jesus' Aramaic cry of prayer, 'Abba, beloved Father', as a cry of prayer in the Christian community. It was presumably the prayer cried out by the charismatics. Those who believe in the Messiah Jesus are brought into his intimate relationship to God: like Jesus and with him they speak to Abba, the beloved Father. The consequences are analogous: in fellowship with the 'firstborn' among many brothers and sisters, believers understand themselves to be 'children of God'. Like Jesus, and as his disciples, they break with the archaic powers of origin in family, class and culture and live from the future of the messianic kingdom. Therefore in the messianic people of God the cry 'Abba' becomes the supreme expression of freedom.

B. *'My Father'*. When Jesus is not addressing God but talking about him, he does not speak of Abba, but more formally of 'Father'.[34] In this way he introduces a certain distance into talk of God. The masculine definition of the Father, which was unimportant in the cries of Abba, is also affected. Jesus speaks in the third person of God, but always and exclusively of 'my Father'. The God whose nearness and whose kingdom he proclaims is above all else 'his' God. He is not a universal 'God the Father in heaven', nor always already 'our Father', but with strict exclusiveness the Father of this Son Jesus, the Messiah of his kingdom. When Jesus calls God 'my Father', the fatherliness and the kingdom of this Father is revealed by none other than this Son Jesus. What is to be understood as 'fatherliness' and what as the 'rule' and 'kingdom' of this Father is defined solely by the Son. 'Whoever sees the Son, sees the Father' (John 14.9). This rules out all other approaches to the Father: only through the community of the Son Jesus do men and women come to 'his Father'. However, this exclusive possessive excludes any patriarchalism and ensures that only the messianic interpretation is the correct one. One does not come to the Father of Jesus Christ through family, political and religious authorities, but only in fellowship with the Son and in the Spirit of the messianic age. To stress it even more strongly: the God whom Jesus proclaims as 'my Father' is first of all only his God; not our God nor the God of our Father. Only through the proclamation of Jesus and the way in which he turns towards other men and women does his God become their God and his Father our Father.

To what people does Jesus turn to bring them into fellowship with his Father? The addition to the claim of an exclusive revelation in Matt.11.27 is typical and applies to the whole gospel: 'Come to me, all who labour and are heavy laden, and I will give you rest. Take my yoke upon you and learn from me; for I am gentle and lowly of heart.' Through the way in which Jesus turns to the poor and the forsaken, the Father of Jesus becomes the real 'Father of orphans and widows', as he could already be called in the Old Testament (Ps.68.6).

C. The *'Father of Jesus Christ'*. This is the formula which is used above all by Paul when he speaks of God. Usually the formula is more precise: 'The Father of our Lord Jesus Christ' (Rom.15.6; I Cor.1.3; II Cor.11.31; Eph.3.14, etc.). If we analyse this theological formula, we discover that the exclusive relationship of Jesus to his Father is retained. God the Father is defined through Jesus himself, through his messiahship (Christ) and through his Lordship (Kyrios). The Father of Jesus Christ is Jesus' Father and the Father of no one else. We come into communion with the Father of Jesus through the Lordship of Jesus over us: if Jesus becomes our Lord, then his Father also becomes our Father, and we become children of his Father. According to Paul, the 'Lordship of Jesus' which creates this connection consists in the messianic sending of Jesus which brings the kingdom of God, in the priestly surrender of Jesus by the Father for the reconciliation of the world, and in the royal exaltation and transfiguration of the Jesus who is raised from the dead. In the field of force of the Lordship of the Messiah Jesus, the Father of Jesus becomes our Father, and Father over all (Rom.1.7; Gal.1.1; Eph.4.6). At the end of this horizon, as it extends, he is then called the 'Father of glory' (Eph.1.17), because only the kingdom of glory, in which all princedoms, authorities and powers, and death are abolished, fully corresponds to him.

D. *Summary*. 1. The later theological formula that God is 'the Father of our Lord Jesus Christ' exactly preserves Jesus' talk of 'my Father', and this in turn preserves the 'Abba' mystery of Jesus which is the liberating nucleus of his messianic message. The praxis which makes this formula possible is not the formal addressing of God as Father but the familiarity and intimacy of Jesus' prayer 'Abba'. However, this discovery goes against the earliest Christian process of tradition. Matthew added the phrase 'in heaven' to the 'Our Father' and thus introduced a distance into the 'Abba'-nearness of God. Paul is still aware that in Rome and in Galatia the Christian communities address God as 'Abba'. But soon afterwards this address in prayer must have disappeared from Christian worship and have been replaced by more distant forms of address. Whereas the Hebrew words Amen and Hallelujah were taken over and have kept their place to this day, along with 'Abba', remarkably the earliest Christian 'Maranatha' also disappeared.[35] That is certainly no coincidence. It indicates that the fatherly nearness of God denoted by 'Abba' and the imminence of the kingdom from which Jesus exercised his influence belong together. With the delay of the parousia, the spatial and temporal distances were evidently perceived again. The bishop bridged this distance as 'father of the community' and at the same time increased it. However, this process can also be followed in the opposite direction. Anyone who wants to get to the source must swim against the stream of tradition.

2. From Jesus' 'Abba' to the formula 'the Father of Jesus Christ' it is clear that in a Christian, i.e. messianic way, God can be understood as Father only in trinitarian terms, and not patriarchally. The formation of a doctrine of the Trinity was always also an attempt to express this child-relationship without ideas of patriarchal rule. The doctrine of the Trinity is a critical doctrine of God in a specifically Christian sense. The doctrine of the Trinity binds the child to the father and the father to the child and thus draws God the Father into the lifestyle and fate of Jesus. By contrast, wherever thought is patriarchal, in terms of the Father God, its essential tie to the Son Jesus is broken or the Sonship of Jesus is denied. But if the Sonship of Jesus is disputed, then Abba, the Father of Jesus, is also disputed. The dissolution of the doctrine of the Trinity leads to both an Islamicization of the concept of God and a humanistic interpretation of Jesus. And if 'God the Father' is detached from Jesus, then literally all that is left in the concept of God is the role of Lord; then this notion of God can be used as the legitimation for any kind of rule on earth which seeks to be 'by the grace of God' in order to evade control by citizens.

3. However, the New Testament shows no unanimity over the practical consequences of belief in God the Father: there is the ethic of the apostolic family codes, which is an explicitly patriarchal family ethic; and there is the ethic of discipleship of Christ in the Synoptic Gospels which, as I have shown, is an anti-patriarchal ethic of contrast. The Christian family ethic was grounded in the traditional hierarchical derivation: God is the head of Christ, Christ is the head of the husband, the husband is the head of the wife (I Cor.11). But the ethic of discipleship is focussed on the life and messianic sending of Jesus. Its criterion is the Sermon on the Mount: 'Be perfect, as your Father in heaven is perfect' (Matt.5.48). That is the motivation for the command to love one's enemy. The images which Jesus uses here, of the 'sun which rises on the good and the bad' and the rain 'which falls on the just and the unjust', are primal

matriarchal images for the divine mystery of life.

According to the theological argument so far, the ethic of discipleship is the true consequence of the revelation of the Father of Jesus Christ. The ethics of discipleship matches the trinitarian understanding of the Father. By contrast, Jesus is essentially superfluous for the Christian patriarchalism of the household codes, even if all that the community does is to be done 'in the Lord'. In terms of content they say almost nothing that has not already been said by Jewish wisdom and the Stoic-Cynic diatribe.

4. Life in immediate proximity to God

The 'Abba' mystery of Jesus denotes the nearness of the kingdom of God which he proclaims, and this openness of the kingdom to the poor, the abandoned and the bowed-down is expressed most strongly by his intimate way of addressing God as 'Abba'. Women evidently felt this immediately in their dealings with Jesus. They were physically healed, raised up, esteemed and free when they were near him. But his nearness was the nearness of the messianic kingdom and the intimate nearness of God in him. God's rule and kingdom were experienced as saving and liberating. Intimate converse with Jesus' Abba will have been understood as the joyful centre of the nearness of the kingdom. Here there are possibilities for women to identify with Jesus, the kingdom and the Father. But to achieve that, it is necessary to keep going through the strata in the concept of Father which I have described, so as to get back to this true nucleus of Christian talk about God.

The way through the strata of patriarchal talk of God and the patriarchal oppression of women deposited in the centuries of historical Christianity must first surmount the rules of masculine sexist language and replace them with Christian messianic language. If according to Paul there is not 'man and woman' in Christ, but all 'are one and joint heirs of the kingdom according to the promise' (Gal.3.28,29), then this must also be expressed in language. Masculine rules of language must be regarded as non-Christian. However, one cannot alter language arbitrarily. Language is handed down and moulded by a community. The church of Christ is such a community. To the degree that it adapts itself to the forms of particular societies, it loses the liberating power of the gospel. To the degree that it can present in its own community the liberating effects which go out from Jesus and his gospel and can live in contrast to the society around it, it will be recognizable as the church of Christ.

In patriarchal societies this experience of freedom first of all brought about a modification of the image of God and subsequently a tempering of the authority of the Father so that it became a patriarchy of love. To the degree that God was emphasized as Father, Christian patriarchalism came into being, i.e. a paternalism toned down by mercy and love from above: however, to the degree that the mercy and the unconditional love were put first, a fundamental criticism

16

of the rule of the father developed, i.e. a de-theocratizing of the concept of God and a democratizing of the authority of the male.

The difference between the Father God and Lord God of a patriarchal society and the Father of Jesus Christ was and is Jesus himself. Anyone who is orientated on him and with him cries 'Abba' has broken with the laws and the power-re-lationships of patriarchy. The domination of the father and the subordination of wife and children is replaced by the messianic community-in-solidarity of the female and male friends of Jesus, and in that community power is distributed fairly.

In the modern 'fatherless society' this experience of faith brings into being a non-patriarchal fatherliness: a fatherlines without claim to domination and rights to property, in communicative and participatory love, love which is merciful and ready for responsibility. In a depersonalized and therefore increasingly irresponsible society, the experience of God, the merciful Father, leads men to a non-patriarchal fatherliness. It makes them capable of taking responsibility for children, without relying on claims to authority and rights over property. It makes them capable of discovering motherly characteristics in their fatherliness. They are therefore ready at all times to become friends with their children; they do not love themselves in their children, but rather love their children in themselves. They are therefore ready to let their children come and become themselves, to go along with their children, to be there for them and to keep open their possibilities for the future and their capacities to change, as they change themselves. Finally, such fathers do not seek the prolongation of their responsibility to all eternity, but look to the time when their representative function, which is temporarily necessary, becomes superfluous. They do not always want to be there *for* their children, but simply want to take responsibility for their children so that one day they can enjoy life *with* their children.

Males must also overcome the distortions of patriarchalism in order to become complete persons. In the course of this they will certainly also discover the characteristics and the advantages of the old, long-past matriarchy which is now still present only under the surface. This is not the way back to an irresponsible land of childhood. The true future of human beings lies beyond patriarchy and matriarchy. What will this future look like?

The visions are there in concrete promises: a community of human solidarity, communication free of domination, an open society. This future is only betrayed in patriarchy and only hindered in a 'fatherless' bureaucratic society. Women and men, mothers and fathers, will only enter into a 'just, participatory and responsible' human society if first patriarchy and then also the fatherless society have been done away with. In principle that already happens in the motherly love which Jesus manifested in the Father and put into practice through his own behaviour towards the poor, the sick and the sinners. This is the love which does not seek its own to confirm itself, but which seeks the other and the lost to save

17

it. It is communicative and creative love, which makes the unjust just, the ugly beautiful, and the divided whole. It is the divine love which goes beyond the love of father and mother, by determining both. Matriarchy and patriarchy can find their limited meanings in history by helping to contribute to the formation of that messianic community of people in which this love permeates all things.

2

The Motherly Father
and the Power of His Mercy

1. Whose Father is God?

There are two different bases for the use of the name 'Father' for God: 1. the patriarchal world-view and 2. the trinitarian understanding of Christ. In the biblical traditions the name 'Father' is used for God both metaphorically, as an expression of the goodness and providential care of his rule, and also in a literal sense to denote his relationship to his 'only-begotten' Son, the 'firstborn'. The Apostles' Creed twice calls God 'Father': once where he is said to be 'the Almighty, maker of heaven and earth', and the other time in connection with the exaltation of his Son, Jesus Christ, after he had been given up, 'to the right hand of God, the Father almighty'. The twofold use of the name Father in the Bible and the double mention of the Father in the Apostles' Creed has led to a theological ambiguity in the concept of God the Father. Is God to be called 'Father' because he is the almighty creator and lord of all things? Or is he to be called 'Father' because he has brought forth his 'only-begotten Son', Jesus Christ, who as the 'firstborn' became brother of us all? In the first instance the perspective is upward, from the dependence of creatures and servants, and seeks in the face of the feared Lord God those features of the 'Father of all' which invite trust. The name Father here is not meant literally, but in a metaphorical sense. In the second instance the perspective focuses on the 'firstborn' among many brothers and sisters, who has said of himself, 'He who sees me sees the Father' (John 14.9). His Father becomes 'our Father' only through his brother-hood with us; only in fellowship with him do we experience that sense of being children of God by virtue of which, like Jesus, we may call, 'Abba, beloved Father.' Here the name Father is meant literally, because the relationship with God is understood as a generative one. In the first instance the name Father is a way of expressing kindly rule; in the second it denotes the fundamental relationship of love. When he is understood as 'Lord God' in heaven, the Father cannot suffer, since all things come from him and he is dependent on no one. But understood as 'Father of the Son', the Father is passionately involved in the fate of the Son: where the Son is, there too is the Father; when the Son suffers, the Father suffers with him; when the Son rejoices, the Father also rejoices: the Son is from him, but he is also dependent on the Son, for they are one in their mutual love. Thus neither can be without the other, for the Father is in the Son and the Son is in the Father (John 14.10f.), and so by virtue of their mutual indwelling they are 'one', as the Gospel of John puts it. So whose Father is God? Is he the 'Father of all' and as such also the 'Father of Jesus Christ' and 'Our Father'? Or is he the 'Father of the Son Jesus Christ' and as such also our Father, and the fatherly creator of all? Our understanding of the 'Lordship' of God depends on our answer to this question.

2. The patriarchal Lord God

The patriarchal social order gives the male all authority in the family: the father is the lord and owner of his wife (or wives) and his children.[1] He is free, and they are not. As *paterfamilias* he has full rights over his family, and is its highest authority. Because he begets the children, they belong to him, not to his wife. He is the head of his wife and of the family. They have to serve him and honour him.

At the next social level, the 'fatherland' is ruled politically by the supreme head of the land, the prince, the *pater patriae*. The 'father of the land' represents the patriarchal family relationships on a political level. Internally, he must rule strictly and benevolently; externally he must rule with greatness and power. Those who are ruled by him see themselves as his 'subjects'. He has full rights over them, while they have none over him. But the expectation is that he will not withhold his 'grace' from his obedient 'children of the land'.

On the religious level the people which has not come of age is looked after ecclesiastically through pastors and spiritual 'fathers'. The patriarchal family relationships are also copied in church structures, from the 'children of the parish' to the pastors, to the bishops and the patriarchs and finally to the 'holy father'. Authority and laws come from above; obedience, dependence and tutelage prevail below.

Ultimately these pyramids of family, politics and church point to the supreme authority in heaven from which they receive their legitimation, the Lord God, the Father of all. As lord and proprietor of the world God possesses fullness of power, and gives legitimation to all authority in heaven and on earth. Therefore he must be feared and loved above all things. This patriarchal ordering of the world – God the Father, holy father, father of the land, father of the family – is a theistic order, not a trinitarian one. This father religion produces in the individual that super-ego against which atheistic rebellion rises up, has risen up and must rise up, calling for freedom and its own responsibility, since 'where the great world-ruler is, freedon has no space, not even the freedom – of the children of God'.[2]

20

God is rarely called Father in the Old Testament. Where the name appears it is used as a synonym for 'Lord' and expresses the relationship of Israel to its God, whom it confesses as creator of the world, as the Lord of history and as the covenant God who has chosen Israel (Deut.32.6; Isa.63.16; Jer.31.9). The covenant relationship was understood in such an intimate way that the covenant God could be designated 'Father' and the covenant people 'only son'. Hosea even speaks of an intimate relationship of love. Therefore Paul also recognizes that Israel has 'the sonship' (Rom.9.4). However, no gender-specific fixation of God is really meant, although at the same time Israel had patriarchal ordinances: the Decalogue is a male-orientated code. However, the image of God is expressed by both sexes (Gen.1.27), and the image of the mother is also used to express God's mercy (Isa.66.13). As the Lord, God acts in a 'fatherly' and 'motherly' way, especially towards Israel, his 'firstborn son' (Ex.4.22).

In the New Testament, the patriarchal order is above all to be found in the Pauline theology of the 'head': 'the head of every man is Christ, the head of a woman is her husband, and the head of Christ is God' (I Cor.11.3; cf. also I Cor.3.22f.; Eph.5.23; Heb.12.5-10). The theology of the head presupposes a hierarchical gradation of relationships between head and body. Even though these are also modified by Christ's role as a servant, they are nevertheless maintained and are further stabilized by it. The 'head' theology, too, is theistic, not trinitarian, in conception. According to it the image of God is expressed in the male in a way in which it cannot be found in the female, 'since man is the beginning and end of the woman, as God is the beginning and end of all creation'.[3]

3. The birth of the Son from the Father

The trinitarian understanding of the Father appears in the synoptic saying, 'No one knows the Son except the Father, and no one knows the Father except the Son and anyone to whom the Son chooses to reveal him' (Matt.11.27). Johannine theology represents an interpretation of this saying in so far as it stresses the exclusive unity of the Father and the Son: 'He who sees me sees the Father' (14.9), for 'I and the Father are one' (10.30). God the Father is the Father of his only Son Jesus Christ. His Fatherhood is determined exclusively by his relationship to the Son. Therefore his Fatherhood becomes manifest only in the history of the Son and is experienced in fellowship with the Son through the Spirit, who liberates and creates new life. So anyone who wants to understand God in trinitarian terms as Father must forget the conceptions of the patriarchal Father-religion and look to the life and message of the firstborn brother Jesus Christ. In Christian understanding, the name Father is a theological, indeed trinitarian name, not a general religious, political or cosmological idea. If God becomes 'our Father' through the Son and for his sake, then he can be called 'Abba, beloved Father' (Rom.8.15; II Cor.3.17), only in the Spirit of Sonship, i.e. in the Spirit of freedom. The freedom of the Spirit in practice distinguishes the Father of Jesus Christ from the world patriarch of the Father-religion.

The ambiguity in the concept of father is removed when there is a clear distinction between the creation of the world and the begetting of the Son. Literally speaking, no Father-relationship between God and his creatures arises out of creation. From creation and providence God is known only as 'Lord', if he can be known at all from world history.

Only in the relationship to his Son can God literally be called 'Father'. Therefore belief in God the Father begins from the knowledge of the Son and his mercy, and not from his incomprehensible omnipotence. As the Father of the Son, God creates heaven and earth. Through the doctrine of the Trinity God's name of Father is indissolubly tied to Jesus the Son. The doctrine of the Trinity does not divinize Christ, but it 'christifies' God, since it draws the Father into the destiny of the Son.

If the Son has come forth from the Father alone, then this process must be imagined both as 'begetting' and as 'birth'. But that fundamentally changes the image of father: a Father who both begets and gives birth to his Son is not just a 'male' Father. He is a motherly Father. He cannot be understood to have a single sex, masculine, but must be understood to be bisexual or transsexual. He is the fatherly Father of his only begotten Son and he is at the same time the motherly Father of his only-born Son. It was the orthodox dogmatic tradition which made its boldest statements at this point. According to the Council of Toledo in 675, 'We must believe that the Son was not made out of nothing, nor out of some substance or other, but from the womb of the Father, that is, that he was begotten or born from the Father's own being.'[4]

The basis for this image of the motherly Father presumably lies in Old Testament traditions of the mercy of God. *rchm* denotes both the womb (*rechem*) from which life is born and that passionately painful feeling of mercy (*rach^{a}mim*) located in the feminine body which is capable of giving birth.[5] In extended parallels the reference is to the gut, the entrails, which can become cramped in pain. Having mercy is characterized as a motherly feeling, but what is meant is not soft-heartedness nor any feeling of bliss, but that creative love which is like the pangs of birth. So having mercy means more than just being compassionate and being affected by the suffering of others. Having mercy also goes beyond solidarity. Having mercy denotes the pain of bringing the dead to life, of liberating the prisoners and loosing those who are bound. The translation of *rach^{a}mim* into the Latin *misericordia* shifts the focal point to the heart as the human centre. The misery of others goes to a person's heart, and the heart burns in participatory and sharing love. The elements of strong involvement are kept, but the lifegiving power of mercy is lost. If according to the statement of this ancient council the Son comes forth from the Father's womb – 'born of God before time' – then he is the child of the eternal mercy of the Father, and the

22

Fatherhood of God is none other than this life-giving mercy. If we say with the New Testament 'God is Love', then we say it in the sense that God is life-giving mercy. If we call this love of God inexhaustible and creative, then it is also the source of all life which gives birth and inexhaustibly has mercy.

The further consequence of these bisexual statements must be the repudiation of patriarchal theism: the theism of the 'heavenly Father' was and is the religion of patriarchy, just as presumably the pantheism of 'Mother earth' was the religion of earlier matriarchy.[6] With its affirmations about the motherly Father and the lifegiving mercy of God, the Christian doctrine of the Trinity represents a first step towards surmounting the one-sidedly masculine metaphorical language in the understanding of God, but without going over to matriarchal conceptions. It is its true intention to lead to a community of women and men without subordination and without privileges. In fellowship with the firstborn brother of humankind, women and men are one and all heirs of the promise (Gal.3.28f.). Only a human fellowship liberated from sexism and class rule can become the radiant image of the triune God.

4. The pain of mercy

In the older forms of the doctrine of the Trinity, the image of the loving father was combined with that of the inflexible ruler, because the starting point for the doctrine of God was God's essential impassibility. By contrast, more recent studies of the doctrine of the Trinity[7] begin from the passion of Christ and reject, along with the picture of the inflexible sovereign Lord, the axiom of God's impassibility: the deepest ground for the passion of Christ is the pathos of God who for eternity is love. So the Father cannot remain unaffected by the suffering and death of his Son. This leads to the reacceptance of the statements of theopaschism and patripassianism which were rejected earlier. Is theological patriarchalism overcome by a recognition of the 'suffering God'?

When Abraham Heschel was developing his 'theology of the divine pathos'[8] in order to interpret God's passion for Israel and his suffering with Israel, he had to sketch out a bipolar concept of God: God is free and not subject to any fate, yet through his pathos God is committed to Israel in the covenant. He is enthroned in heaven, yet dwells with the lowly and the humble. Through his 'indwelling' (shekinah), the Almighty shares all the sufferings of his people. 'God himself divides himself in two. He gives himself away to his people. He suffers with them in their suffering . . . '[9] This Jewish conception of theopathy presupposes a 'self-distinction' of God. God's omnipotence is here seen in his comprehensive power to suffer.

This idea was also developed by Anglican theology[10] as the 'passibility of God'. The omnipotence which God possesses and reveals in his Son is the omnipotence of suffering love, which has mercy with compassion. On Golgotha the eternal being of God becomes manifest: God is love. Love is capable of suffering. The capacity of love to suffer finds its fulfilment in self-sacrifice. So self-surrender is the eternal being of God. 'In the end it is always the Cross. God - not indeed the Almighty, but God the Father, with a father's grief and a father's helplessness, in which the power of love is contained. God – glorious, suffering, crucified.'[11]

The Spanish philosopher of religion Miguel de Unamuno expressed the conception of the 'grief of God' (*congoja*) in a striking way.[12] In Christ's agony, the pain of the whole world is laid bare, and at the same time the 'grief of God' is also manifested. The 'Christ of Velazquez' not only portrays the agony of Christ but also throws upon it a reflection of the endless suffering of his Father. God reveals himself as one who suffers. In suffering he displays his compassion. 'He covers all pain with his own immeasurable pain.' But as one who suffers he also calls for our compassion.

Finally, we find in Nikolai Berdyaev a developed trinitarian theology of the 'tragedy in God'.[13] He understands the story of human freedom as the passion story of God, who must suffer because he wants his creatures to be free. It is a single movement, which originates at the centre of the Trinity and is completed on Golgotha: the passion of God is the tragedy of human freedom.

If we take up this idea and develop it more precisely in a trinitarian sense, we can say that in sending his Son into this sinful world the Father opens himself to the fate of death in a world which is in process of closing itself off. With the surrender of the Son to death on the cross the infinite pain of the Father begins. On the cross the Son suffers death in being forsaken by the Father. But the Father suffers the death of the Son, and in it his being forsaken by the Son. The pain of the Father is not identical with the suffering of the Son, but it does correspond to that suffering.[14] Our liberation from the way in which we are shut off by sin, and our redemption from suffering, arise from the mercy of the whole Trinity: from the dying of the Son, the grief of the Father and the patience of the Spirit. For in this way the triune God enteres into the destiny of his world and accepts his creatures into the life of his inner love and shares his eternal life with them. God brings liberation to eternal life through his suffering, merciful love. The mercy is divine, not the power, the overwhelming power and the omnipotence, as patriarchalism says. This mercy endures all things and hopes all things, and in this sense is omnipotent.

The feminine element in the pain of God has often been seen in the form of the Pietà:[15] the Mother of Sorrows with her dead Son on her lap. But is not the grief of Mary also the human reflection of the grief of the divine Father over the death of the Son and the beginning of Christian participation in him?

5. Lordship and freedom

As the doctrine of the Trinity supersedes theism and the theology of the cross supersedes the notion of the impassible God, we are led to a new understanding of human life with God and in God. God as Lord and human beings as servants cannot be the only images for this. In fellowship with the merciful, suffering triune God we have a deeper experience of freedom. Where God is believed in as 'Lord', freedom is experienced as the service of God: those who are servants of the Most High may indeed be totally dependent on God, but they are free in relation to all others. 'We must obey God rather than men.' When God is believed in as 'Father', then freedom is experienced as that of children of God: those who see themselves as daughters or sons of God are free and equal members of the family of God. They do not simply hear a Lord, but the Father also listens to them. Everything that belongs to the Father also belongs to the children. Ultimately a freedom is experienced in the Spirit which goes even beyond the relationship of being a son: friendship with God. The friends of God no longer live 'under' God but with God and in God. They share in the grief and the joy of God. They have become 'one' with God (John 17.21).[16] The revelation of the 'suffering God' allows people to understand their suffering in God and to participate in the 'suffering of God in the world'.[17] 'Life in God' begins with the recognition of the Crucified One and in discipleship, in which we take our cross upon ourselves and participate in the messianic suffering of God in the world. In this comforting recognition and this liberating praxis the old patriarchal conceptions of the 'Father of all' and the religious images of the 'Lord God' fall away.[18]

3

The Question of Theodicy
and the Pain of God

For me, the question of God is deeply bound up with the experience of suffering. On the one hand people who suffer call upon God and seek meaning in meaninglessness. Does God allow human suffering? On the other hand, faith in God makes suffering a conscious pain, a pain of an unbearable kind. Do human beings share in God's pain at their suffering? The first question is the metaphysical question of the justification of God in the face of suffering (theodicy). The second question is the mystical question of communion with God in suffering.

The concept of theodicy goes back to G.W.F. Leibniz. However, the philosophers of the Stoa had already given classic formulation to the question of theodicy: '*Si Deus – unde malum?*' – 'If there is a God, where did evil come from?' Their answer was that either God wants to prevent evil but cannot, in which case he is good but not omnipotent; or God can prevent evil, but does not want to, in which case he is omnipotent but not good. As long as God is understood as the omnipotent Lord of life and death and as the one who guides history (*concursus generalis*) and each individual human life (*concursus specialis*), the question of theodicy remains unanswerable. Kant saw it in general, not individual, terms and understood it to be the question of the 'defence of the supreme wisdom of the author of the world against the accusation which reason levels against that wisdom on the basis of what is contrary to purpose in the world'. In this statement he presupposed the physico-theological argument for the existence of God from the time of the Enlightenment, and demonstrated on rational grounds that any theodicy is doomed to failure because it goes beyond the limits of finite human reason, which lie in the transcendental limitations of the possibility of scientific experience.

We keep finding three solutions in the history of religions and philosophies: 1. The *dualistic* idea of a good and an evil principle which struggle with each other in the world. In this struggle human beings must take the side of the good principle. All good things come from God, and all evil and all wickedness come from God's adversary. This dualism flourished in Parseeism, in Manichaeism and in Jewish and Christian apocalyptic. 2. The *monistic* conception: only the good exists; evil does not. All being is good. Evil is a deficiency of being or an annihilation of being. It has no quality of being but is the negation of being. 3. The *dialectical* conception: evil serves the good in history in one way or another, for the good demonstrates its quality of being in the negation of the negative. This view appears in Jewish and Christian faith in history and is developed in the dialectical view of history in German Idealism.

In the biblical traditions, especially in the Psalms, in Job, Lamentations and in the passion narratives of the Synoptic Gospels, the question of theodicy is not posed theoretically, from a contemplation of the course of the world, but existentially, from the historical experience of belief in God. If God is just, why must the pious suffer and why do things go well with the godless? If God is faithful, why is his people Israel delivered over to the violence of the Gentile nations? If God is 'the Father', why has he 'abandoned' (Mark 15.34) his beloved Son Jesus Christ, who dies on a Roman cross, and 'given him up' (Rom.8.3)? We find answers on various levels in the biblical writings.

1. There is an evil which human beings have to attribute to themselves. Doing evil carries its own punishment within itself in the form of evil consequences. This complex of action and consequence is itself part of the divine justice. God is responsible for the evil consequences, but not for the evil actions of human beings. The 'wrath of God' is not manifested in particular heavenly punishments but in the fact that sinners are 'given up' to the way that they themselves have chosen, to their temporal and eternal destruction (Rom.1.18ff.). Anyone who forsakes God is forsaken by God. This view can be found predominantly in the historical books of the Old Testament, in Matthew and Paul.

2. But there is also a suffering which is experienced not by the unrighteous but by the righteous. The sequence of action and consequence cannot be applied to the suffering of the righteous. As the book of Job shows, trust in God can be established only in a sustained complaint against God. God's action is unfathomable, and human beings are left with a persistent accusation or a silent humility (Rom.9.20).

3. Finally, there is a suffering which is endured not only by human beings but also by God himself in company with them. Through his covenant with Israel, God makes his name and his spirit dwell in his people. If Israel is smitten, God is smitten too. If Israel is persecuted, then God himself takes part in this through his 'indwelling' (Shekinah) and goes into captivity with Israel. The God of the covenant is also the companion of his people in suffering. So Israel is redeemed when the God who suffers with it redeems himself and glorifies himself through the liberation of the people. This rabbinic and kabbalistic notion of the God who shares in suffering has its parallel in the Christian idea that the passion of God is manifested in the story of the passion of Jesus Christ. The pain of the love of

27

God is manifested to all suffering and lost men and women on the cross of Christ. Expressed in terms of trinitarian theology, this means that the Father follows the Son whom he loves to the cross, in order to bring his eternal fellowship to all those who are lost. The 'giving up' of the Son by the Father (Rom.8.32) also means that 'God was in Christ reconciling the world to himself' (II Cor. 5.19). Christ is the merciful, compassionate servant of God who dies 'for many'. His suffering is divine suffering, i.e. suffering in solidarity and redemptive suffering.

The church fathers Irenaeus and Augustine attempted to solve the problem of theodicy by means of the philosophy of Middle Platonism. Evil does not exist and is an absence of the good. Because God created things good, he is not the cause of evil. Moral evil is a human act and thus sin. Physical evil is allowed by God as a means of education towards the good and the purification of souls. Even metaphyiscal evil – the devil – must ultimately serve the plans of God.

The Reformers rejected such justifications of God before a human forum, because for them the justification of human beings before God's forum was more important. In justifying by grace sinners who have no rights, God shows them righteousness as his creative, justifying and restorative righteousness. It is *justitia justificans,* not *justitia distributiva.* God shows himself to be the righteous One by justifying the sinner. Forgiveness is the divine answer to sin, and healing is the divine answer to sickness. Therefore resurrection will be the divine answer to death. The doctrine of justification was the Reformation answer to the question of theodicy. It originally took the form of reciprocal justification (*justificatio Dei activa et passiva*): God justifies sinners, and believers justify God by endorsing his judgment.

Only in the time of the old Protestant orthodoxy and the Enlightenment were the questions of evil and suffering again put in the context of the general governance of the world, i.e. in that of 'natural theology'. The following answers were then given. God allows evil without approving of it. God directs evil in such a way that it must benefit believers. God sets limits to evil and will completely overcome it at the end of the world in his kingdom of glory. It is understandable that on this basis the Lutheran philosopher Leibniz could formulate his optimistic conception of this world as 'the best of all possible worlds'. He also taught that God allows moral evil for the sake of human free will and uses physical evil as a punishment to educate and purify human beings. This pious trust in the gracious providence of God and this optimistic Enlightenment view of the world collapsed in the experience of the Lisbon earthquake of 1755. Ten thousand people died in a night. What theological significance could this natural catastrophe have? Is the God who allows such things a gracious God? Is he not rather a cruel monster? Is this world his good, orderly creation, or is it a godforsaken chaos?

With the Lisbon earthquake in the eighteenth century confidence in God as a gracious governor of the world and in the harmony of the world collapsed.

'God is dead' became the eloquent symbol of a far-reaching theological collapse and for European protest atheism. In the unspeakable crime and unutterable suffering of the Holocaust in Auschwitz, in the twentieth century human self-confidence also collapsed. Since Hiroshima in 1945, humankind has entered upon its end-time, i.e. that time in which the nuclear end of the human race is possible at any moment. 'The death of humankind' is the telling symbol of a momentous humanistic collapse and of European nihilism. Auschwitz and Hiroshima are the end of any theodicy and any anthropodicy. How can we still speak confidently of God after Auschwitz? How can we still speak self-confidently of human beings after Hiroshima?

Three important points have emerged from Jewish and Christian discussion of theology after Auschwitz:

1. The question of the justification of God by a just world cannot be answered in a history of injustice and violence, but it cannot ever be given up either, since it is identical with the very question of God itself. To ask about God means to cry out for justice, so that, as Horkheimer put it, 'the murderer shall not finally triumph over his victims'. The question of God lives on in the hunger for justice.

2. There can be no theology 'after Auschwitz' which does not take up the theology *in* Auschwitz, i.e. the prayers and cries of the victims. God was present where the Shema of Israel and the Lord's Prayer were prayed. As a companion in suffering God gave comfort where humanly there was nothing to hope for in that hell. The inexpressible sufferings in Auschwitz were also the sufferings of God himself.

3. The question of God which arises out of suffering cannot and may not be given any theoretical, metaphysical answer. Like Job, each innocent sufferer indignantly rejects any religious explanations of why he or she must suffer. But there is the mystical answer that God is bound to us in grief. Our true suffering is also his suffering, our sorrow is also his sorrow, our pains are also the pains of his love. Only a God in whose perfect being there is room for pain can comfort us and gain our respect. In our pain we would have to despise an impassible and indifferent being. But the living God is also the God who has mercy:

And when human hearts are breaking
under sorrow's iron rod,
then we find that self-same aching
deep within the heart of God.[1]

When Catherine of Siena once cried out, 'My God, where were you when my heart was in darkness and the shadow of death?', she heard the answer: 'My daughter, did you not feel it? I was in your heart.'

Those who cry out in grief to God, consciously or unconsciously join in the dying cry of Jesus Christ, 'My God, why have you forsaken me?' Those who recognize this, immediately feel that God is not that unfathomable Other in heaven, but is in a very personal sense the human God who cries with them, and the sympathetic Spirit who cries in them and will go on crying for them when they themselves are silenced. It is the comfort of the crucified Christ that he brings the love of God and the fellowship of the eternal Spirit into the abysses of our suffering and our hells of evil, so that we do not go under in pain but change suffering to life, whether here or there.

Bibliography

G.W.F.von Leibniz, *Essais de Theodicée sur la bonté de Dieu, la liberté de l'Homme et l'origine du mal,* 1710

I.Kant, *Über das Misslingen aller philosophischen Versuche in der Theodizee, Werke,* ed.W.Weischedel, Frankfurt 1964, 105-24

A.Heschel, *The Prophets,* Harper and Row 1955

J.Hick, *Evil and the God of Love,* Macmillan and Harper and Row 1966

E.Wiesel, *Night,* Penguin Books 1981

P.Kuhn, *Die Selbsterniedrigung Gottes in der Theologie der Rabbinen,* Munich 1968

J.Moltmann, *The Crucified God*

B.Albrecht, *Gott und das Leid der Menschen,* Munich 1976

D.Sölle, *Suffering,* Darton, Longman and Todd 1976

4

'I Believe in Jesus Christ, the Only Son of God'

Brotherly Talk of Christ

1. Critical questions

The classical Christian creeds call Jesus the 'Son of God' and add *unigenitum:* he is the only-begotten Son of God.[1] This confession of Christ often meets with misunderstanding and contradiction, and that is nothing new. I shall mention three objections and go into them.

1. Was this Son of God, who came from heaven, walked upon the earth and ascended into heaven, a real man, or a heavenly being who was only clothed in 'our flesh and blood'? What has this Son of God, 'God of God, light of light, very God of very God, begotten, not made, being of one substance with the Father', as the Niceno-Constantinopolitan creed celebrates him, to do with the Jewish Jesus of Nazareth? Did that Jesus of Nazareth see himself in this light? Is not this metaphysical light so alien to him that one can no longer recognize him in his radiance, which is why the creeds say nothing about his life and activity? Understood in metaphysical terms, Jesus' divine Sonship means his eternal divine nature. It is said to have been that element in his life which formed his person. So his human nature had no personality. How can one then identify this eternal God-man with the historical personality of Jesus of Nazareth? Modern Protestant theology has thought through these questions for two hundred years in a serious concern for the truth. Did it succeed in bringing the metaphysical divine Sonship and the historical Jesus under one heading? Did not the dilemma remain, that one had to talk either dogmatically of a God-man who came from heaven or historically of the man of God who was born in Nazareth? What is meant by the divine Sonship of Jesus: the Logos of God made flesh or the man filled with the Spirit?

2. Even if the question of the humanity of Jesus is not suppressed by the confession that he is Son of God, it points in a direction which raises new objections. Is not the Son of God a male? Does this not force women into the

31

background, though according to the first creation story they are equally and together with men 'in the image of God'? So was the 'incarnation' of God celebrated by the Nicene Creed just a matter of God becoming male? How can a woman who is becoming aware of herself find access to a male redeemer without becoming a male in spirit and subjecting herself to masculine patterns of thought? It is not just the modern feminist objections to the divine Sonship of Jesus understood in male terms which make this Sonship questionable; the thousand-year-old masculine arguments against the ordination of women have led to this misunderstanding, not to say this heresy, that God became male. Because God has revealed himself in his 'Son' and because Jesus was a man and not a woman, it is argued, God can be represented only by male priests and not by female priests. That has generally been the interpretation of the divine Sonship of Jesus by the Roman Catholic church and the Orthodox church and it continues to be so today. But was this masculinism and this exclusion of women meant when both Martha (John 11.27) and Peter (Mark 8.29) called Jesus the 'Son of the living God'?

3. Last but not least, there is yet another serious objection to the divine Sonship of Jesus, though it is one of which people are least aware in the modern world. Those who take belief in Christ and discipleship of Christ seriously have been fond of calling it the 'religion of the Son'. For them the Son, not the Father, stands in the centre. Communities which feel committed to a thoroughgoing faith in Christ have therefore been fond of calling themselves 'brotherhoods' and communities of 'brethren' and have developed both brotherly and sisterly forms of life. In brotherliness, in sisterliness, and most recently in brotherliness and sisterliness together, they find an inner fellowship of the Spirit with Jesus, their 'firstborn brother'. They find equality and freedom in a brotherly covenant with the Son of God. The practice of children of God addressing one another as 'brother' and 'sister' goes back to the New Testament and the original experience of Christ. But with these forms of expression ties between contemporaries are given priority over ties going back through the generations, for these are voluntary communities and not natural ones. The natural community of parents and children fades into the background in the face of the voluntary community of equal and free brothers and sisters. But in voluntary community with the Son of God do I become the 'brother' of my grandfather? Does my daughter become my 'sister' through baptism?

So the brotherliness of the 'religion of the Son' has gained a following in the same way as the patriarchalism of the 'religion of the Father'. The Christian brotherhoods founded Philadelphia in the USA in order to liberate themselves from the paternalistic power of tradition in the 'old world'. In the 'new world' all men and women are said to be born free and equal. The humanism of the freemasons broke through the class structure of the old feudal society, and the bourgeois 'Hymn to Joy' proclaimed that 'All men shall become brothers . . . '

32

The democratic forms of the state in the modern world are based on the principles of the French Revolution: 'Freedom, equality, brotherhood'. If we take it literally that 'All men shall become brothers', then women, mothers, fathers and children are included. Women can be included by association in a voluntary 'sisterhood', but not parents and children. That means no less than that the one-sided Christian qualification of voluntary brotherliness and sisterliness annuls the 'contract between the generations'. And this in particular is the current danger in modern society. If Jesus of Nazareth is the paradigm for being a child of God, then are his renunciation of his family and his childlessness normative for his community?

2. Jesus in the spirit of being a child of God

If we follow the narratives of Jesus' story according to the Gospels, we first come upon the gift of the Spirit to Jesus. 'God anointed Jesus of Nazareth with Holy Spirit and power' is the way in which Acts 10.38 sums it up. The reference is to the baptism of Jesus by John in the Jordan, which is said to have led to Jesus having an incomparable experience of the Spirit. The Holy Spirit descended upon him in the form of a dove and 'rested' upon him; i.e. the Spirit of God found its *shekinah*, its permanent dwelling in him. This is an 'anointing' like that of the kings and prophets of Israel, but 'beyond measure' (John 3.34). According to the messianic promise of the prophet Isaiah (61.1ff.), the messiah on whom the 'Spirit rests' will bring justice, mercy and the knowledge of God not only to Israel but also to the nations. The experience of the divine mercy and the experience of the Spirit of God essentially go together.

As Jesus has this experience of the Spirit the heavens open: he approaches God in the relationship of the messianic child, and God approaches him in the relationship of the intimate Abba, the loving Father. This child-Abba relationship can also be termed the Son-Father relationship, but it makes clear that at its heart it is not about Jesus' maleness, but his quality as a child; not about God's Fatherhood, but his inexpressible nearness. The mutual relationship between the messianic child Jesus and Abba, his loving Father, is from the start seen as exclusive: Jesus always speaks of 'my Father' and consequently understands himself as the Father's only child. 'No one knows the Son except the Father, and no one knows the Father except the Son and anyone to whom the Son chooses to reveal him' (Matt.11.27).

According to this story Jesus's divine Sonship is to be understood in pneumatological terms: in the Spirit of God the Son knows the Father and the Father the Son. Therefore it also comes about through the Spirit of God that believers are taken up into Jesus' relationship with God and like him cry 'Abba, beloved Father' (Rom.8.15). This original Spirit christology is the basis for the trinitarian understanding of the Sonship of Jesus and the Fatherhood of God. However, because it begins with the baptism of Jesus in the thirtieth year of his life, this christology has sometimes been turned into an adoptionist christology, for which Jesus after John the Baptist was the first man filled with the Spirit, the first among many brothers and sisters who are like him. In the Spirit Jesus is the child of God, as are all believers who call God 'Father' and know that they are his 'children'. This adoptionist Spirit christology has then been set against the Logos christology of the prologue of John and the two-natures christology which later developed from it.[2] Jesus is not God incarnate but the Spirit-filled man of God: is that a compelling alternative, or a back-projection of the liberal Protestantism of the modern world? I do not believe that this is in fact a real alternative.

1. The Spirit christology of the Synoptic Gospels also stresses the uniqueness of the relationship between Jesus and God over against the relationship of believers to God. Being a child of God is experienced in faith as grace. It presupposes Jesus' status as child of God, not as a paradigm, but as the source of this grace. Through his mercy Jesus opens up to others God's relationship with himself and takes men and women into his relationship with God. If one calls being a child of God by grace the gracious 'adoption' of strangers as children or the godless as loved by God, then Jesus' status as a child of God which is the foundation and origin of this cannot just be the result of an adoption. So Jesus' relationship has always been seen as an exclusive and special one. But can one say that it is a generative relationship with God as opposed to an adoptive one, or an essential relationship with God as opposed to a historically contingent one?

2. The relationship between Jesus and God opened up by the Spirit of God and experienced in the Spirit of God is a mutual one: it embraces Jesus' relationship to Abba, the loving Father, and God's relationship to Jesus, the beloved child. In this mutuality, Jesus' relationship to God logically precedes God's relationship to Jesus, since it constitutes it. It is made permanent by the Spirit of God 'resting' on Jesus and abiding in him. It follows that this relationship of Jesus to God is as divine as God himself, that it does not just come into being at the temporal moment of Jesus' baptism, but is 'from all eternity'. The Synoptic tradition certainly begins with the Spirit baptism of Jesus, but then it goes back to the Spirit birth of Jesus in order to say that Jesus does not just come 'with the Spirit', but also from the beginning derives 'from the Spirit'. Apparently no one saw any conflict in the different datings of the gift of the Spirit to Jesus, whether at baptism or from his mother's womb or even from his conception, presumably because this was not thought of in modern terms, in a linear-temporal way, but eternally in the depth-dimension of time. The 'today I have begotten you' refers to a *kairos* which only human beings experience in time: for God this is his 'eternal present'. The same goes for the saying on the cross, 'Today you will be with me in paradise' (Luke 23.43): this 'today' cannot relate to Good Friday, because no one claims that Jesus went 'to Paradise' on that day. On the contrary, he is said to have descended into hell.

So this 'today', too, means God's eternal present. Therefore to go on to argue from the Spirit birth of Jesus to his eternal pre-existence in the Spirit with the Father of which the Johannine prologue speaks does not seem to have been any problem. If Jesus' experience of the Spirit – at whatever point in time – is understood as an experience of God, and his experience of God also as God's experience, then there is an eternal transcendence in its contingent immanence. One discovers as it were continually deeper levels of this experience of the Spirit. God's relationship to Jesus as his beloved messianic child underlies Jesus's Abba relationship to God. This relationship of God to Jesus is as divine as God himself. It is foreseen from eternity. In the election of the Son, in his sending, in the surrendering of him, in his resurrection and exaltation, what is expressed is not a temporal but an eternal counsel of God: not an arbitrary action of the Father but an essential one.

Through his Abba relationship to God Jesus grows into the relationship of Son of God. By living out his relationship with God he grows into the role which was intended for him from eternity and makes it his own. His story is told as the story of his 'messianic secret'. Even for him, his divine secret is evidently deciphered only in his passion, his death and his resurrection. Therefore according to the earliest Christian witnesses, the knowledge that Jesus is the Son of God is essentially dependent on the Easter experiences of the risen Christ. If we distinguish between Jesus' relationship to God and God's relationship to Jesus, then his eternal divine Sonship and his historical experience of God cannot be contrasted.

3. Not least, we must look at the content of Jesus' message about God. His insight into the essential mercy of God is evidently bound up with his 'Abba' knowledge of God. The kingdom of God which he proclaims to the poor and the nearness of which he shows to the sick by healing them and to the excluded by accepting them is no 'royal rule', as the term *basileia* used for it might suggest. It is 1. the rule of Jesus' 'Abba' God and is no 'Lord'-ship but the lifegiving world of the divine mercy. Through his mercy on the forsaken, the sick and the dying, Jesus reveals the righteousness of God. According to Isa.11.4 the Messiah is to spread righteousness universally by showing mercy to the little ones and raising up those who are bowed down (cf. also Isa.61.1ff.; Luke 4.18ff.). If we draw conclusions from Jesus's behaviour towards the poor, the sick and the outcast not only about the God whom he reveals in this way but also about his own origin in God, then the love which he experienced in the Spirit of Abba, his beloved Father, and which he reciprocated in his living and dying, will have had the form of life-giving mercy. According to Matt.11.27 it is the mutual 'knowledge', i.e. the mutual love, which 'the Son' 'reveals' by calling the weary and heavy-laden to him to give them refreshment (Matt.11.28). That suggests that the Son has proceeded from the merciful 'bosom' of the Father and that this creative mercy of the Father overflows through the Son to

bring lost creatures together and to give new birth to dying creatures. The idea that the Son is born from the womb of the Father in eternity does not seem so strange if this overflowing divine mercy is recognized in the life of Jesus.

3. The only-begotten Son – the firstborn brother

It makes sense to distinguish two dimensions in the divine Sonship of Jesus: his relationship to God and his conduct towards men and women. This distinction is best recognized by talking of the 'only-begotten Son of God' (*monogenes*) and the 'firstborn among many brothers' (*prototokos*).

The 'only-begotten Son' is the one, eternally beloved Son of the Father, God's own Son. Of him alone is it said that the Father sends him into the world, that he gives him up to the passion on the cross 'for all of us', that he raises him from the dead and exalts him to be Lord of his kingdom, until the Son hands the kingdom over to the Father, so that God may be all in all. However one understands the unity of the Son with the Father, the expression 'the only-begotten Son' is bound up with the category of exclusiveness. It expresses what concerns Jesus alone, the one for the many.

By contrast, the 'firstborn among many brothers' refers to what ties Jesus to the many and what the many have in common with him. What the 'only-begotten Son' does and suffers is unique; what the firstborn does and suffers he does for the first time, but it will be repeated a hundred times by his followers and through them. The category of inclusiveness is bound up with the 'firstborn brother'. It expresses what Jesus experiences with his followers and what his followers experience in fellowship with him.

If the stress is solely on the 'only-begotten Son', then the predicate, that Jesus is the Son of God, raises Jesus above human beings to God and divinizes him in an illegitimate way. If the stress is only on the 'firstborn brother', then Jesus is made the first Christian among many others, and the special and unique character of his life and death is lost. Only if both dimensions in Jesus' divine Sonship are distinguished is there neither an apotheosis of Jesus nor a Jesus-humanism.

Does not what the dogmatic doctrine of the two natures designated the 'divinity of Christ' in truth mean that Jesus is the 'only-begotten Son' of the Father in his exclusiveness? Does not what it called the 'true humanity of Christ' in reality mean that Jesus is the 'firstborn among many brothers'? For the doctrine is not about two metaphysically different 'natures' in the person of Jesus Christ, but about two relationships which can be distinguished: his exclusive relationship with the Father through his origin and his inclusive relationship with his followers through fellowship. His relationship with God is the relationship of the beloved Son to *his* Father. His relationship to the world is his fundamental significance for the community of his own (Rom.8.29) and for all creatures (Col.1.15.) There can be no inclusive brotherhood of Christ without his exclusive Sonship, but his exclusive Sonship can never be separated from his open brotherhood with all human beings and all creatures. It is its condition and source.

What is meant by 'firstborn'? The way in which it is frequently associated with the term *eikon,* image, indicates that the firstborn Son of the Father is at the same time the prototype for brothers and sisters who in faith become 'conformed' with him, are brought into fellowship with the Father and with him become heirs of the coming kingdom. But what is also meant, as the connection with the idea of 'conformity' indicates, is that believers are drawn into the mission and passion of the Son. They take part in his messianic mission to liberate the poor, justify sinners and heal the sick. So they also take part in the apocalyptic 'suffering of Christ', suffering for Christ's sake, suffering for the sake of the kingdom of God, and suffering of the least of his brothers and sisters. The more what Dietrich Bonhoeffer called participation in the 'suffering of God in the world' shapes the lives of Christians, the more confident they become of their future conformity with the transfigured body of Christ in the glory of God (Phil.3.21). The 'Son of God' who was crucified exclusively 'for us', and before us raised from the dead, is also the 'brother' who is in solidarity with us. The 'Son of God' and the 'human brother' are two unique dimensions of the whole being of Jesus Christ.

4. The eternal Son

The developed doctrine of the Trinity concentrated above all on clarifying the concept of the 'only-begotten Son' in order to bring out the uniqueness of Jesus Christ over against other human beings and the depth of his communion with God. This came about through the metaphysical definition of the divine nature of Christ and its trinitarian differentiation from God the Father and the Holy Spirit. The original Spirit christology, according to which the unity and distinction of the Son and the Father is constituted in and through the Holy Spirit, gave way to the trinitarian differentiation of the one common divine nature: *una substantia - tres personae.* On this presupposition and in this paradigm of thought three definitions were made which were important for the christology of the Son.

1. The Son is the one Son of the Father, begotten and born in eternity. The generative metaphors are meant to convey that he is of one substance with the Father and has everything in common with the Father except the properties of his person. Therefore he is born from God and not created by God. The generative metaphors make the name 'Son' an exclusively theological, i.e. trinitarian concept. The world is God's creation, not his Son. Human beings are made in the image of God, not born as his children. World history is not the process of the self-realization of God but his merciful and hopeful preservation of creation. Thus the Godhead of the Son Jesus Christ is distinguished from the

37

world and its history. So it is not stressed in such a way as to lead to the apotheosis of the Son. Quite the opposite: the purpose is to be able to say that in communion with the Son Jesus Christ, full communion with God is opened up to men and women. In communion with the only-begotten Son of God, human beings become children of God, born again from the eternal Spirit of God, and in this way taken up into the eternal life of the triune God. In communion with the only-begotten Son the disordered cosmos is reconciled, created anew and transfigured. The trinitarian statements about the eternal conception and birth of the Son from the Father are the foundation of a soteriology which embraces both humankind and the cosmic world. But in both spheres it is necessary to formulate the transition from the exclusive definition of the only-begotten Son of the eternal Father to the firstborn of human beings and all creatures.

2. The Father who begets and gives birth shares everything with the beloved Son, but not his Fatherhood. Otherwise the Son would become a second Father and the personal mutual relationship of love would lose its meaning. The eternal Father and the Son are one in divine being. They are distinct yet one in the divine love which differentiates them and unites them. They are personally distinct from each other, but not different in substance. The Son is not the Father's self but, as his eternal counterpart, the Father's *alter ego*. That is also true, on the other hand, of the eternal Father. Only if one can think of their unity and their otherness together does one do justice to the relationship of Jesus to God: the Son of God and God the Father are one, yet not one. It is love which constitutes the personal otherness and the oneness in otherness. Therefore in the relation-ship between the eternal Father and the eternal Son a further distinction must be made between the evocative love of the Father and the responsive love of the Son. There is a 'bond of love', the *vinculum amoris,* as Augustine called it, which binds the two. It is a mutual love which binds them. However, the love of the Father and the love of the Son are not the same. They correspond to each other in the concordance of calling forth and responding. The generative metaphors which are used convey that, through the analogies between fatherly-motherly love and the love of a child. This difference between the characters of the Father and the Son is important for understanding the origins of the Holy Spirit. If one says with the Western church that the Spirit proceeds 'from the Father and from the Son', then one is predicating the same thing of the Son as of the Father and not distinguishing between the significance of the Father for the Spirit and the significance of the Son for him. The 'and' which duplicates the origin of the Spirit does away with the distinctions between the Father and the Son in respect of the Spirit. A theology which can no longer make distinc-tions is not good theology.

3. The begetting/birth of the Son comes from the eternal being of the Father and therefore is itself to be called eternal. No state in the Godhead is conceivable

in which there was no Trinity. If we were to think away the Trinity, no divine substance would be left. The Trinity is the Godhead and the Godhead is the Trinity. At any rate, that is the presupposition on which Christian theology stands or falls. Therefore the Son belongs just as much as the Father to the eternal constitution of the triune God. In Christian terms, no Godhead of the eternal Father can be conceived of without the Son. The simple theism of the one unknowable, unnameable and always transcendent God is impossible for Christianity. *Deus semper major*, 'God always greater', can certainly be a meaningful statement in comparisons between the creature and its Creator, but in connection with the God of Jesus Christ and the doctrine of the Trinity it has a disruptive effect. The simple religious patriarchalism of the heavenly Father-God is also impossible in Christianity because it destroys Jesus' relationship to God and the Christian 'religion of the Son'. The doctrine of the Trinity directs all ideas of God to Jesus. It does not really divinize Christ, but christifies God. God is believed in for the sake of Jesus, and is called to be Father for the sake of the Son who became our brother. 'Anyone who sees me sees the Father' (John 14.9) also applies to the view from which theological concepts begin and to which they should lead.

4. Last of all we turn to the question 'Why only Christ, why only through the Son?' Can one give a reason why it was not 'some member of the Trinity' but only the Son who became man? What divine motivation could there be for the incarnation of the eternal Son of the Father? This question may sound speculative, but it is not, since it does not allow of any random or arbitrary answers. If we begin from the difference between the love of the Father and the love of the Son, we discover a tendency for the begetting-childbearing love of the Father to predominate over the responsive love of the Son. There is as it were a potential surplus in evocative love over against responsive love. Therefore the evocative love of the Father seems to be open to further responses which correspond to the response of the Son, are in accord with his answering love, and thus fulfil the joy of the Father. In the creation of a large number of creatures in heaven and on earth, the love of the Father for the Son which begets and gives birth in eternity takes the form of creative love. It calls creatures into life for the sake of the Son and his responsive love, creatures who are created in the image of the Son and respond to the Creator's love in communion with the Son. If through the Son the Father goes beyond the Son into a wealth of creatures by virtue of his evocative love, then the only-begotten Son of the Father takes the form of the firstborn of creation (Col.1.15) and becomes its prototype and paradigm. That would mean that the whole of creation is called into life from the love of the Father to the Son through the Spirit. That is an inexhaustibly rich declaration of love by the Father to the Son. It would further mean that all creatures are destined to join in the responsive love and praise offered by the Son (Phil.2.11). The whole creation is a song of praise to the Creator (Hippolytus), about the

inexhaustible source of eternal life. Of course these are images and metaphors for joy at the new creation of all things, which is not yet (or only seldom) attainable in the pain of the old creation. But as answers to the experience of God in the community of Christ they are the beginnings of the new life.

5. The firstborn brother

The dimension of the brotherhood of Christ has not been developed adequately in comparison to that of his Sonship. The significance of Christ for other men and women was expressed in the creeds with honorific titles and in theological tradition with concepts relating to his rule: prophet, priest and king. The Reformers, especially Calvin, also spoke of the fellowship with Christ into which believers are brought increasingly deeply through the experiences of justification and sanctification, calling and rebirth. So Protestant orthodoxy added the 'mystical union' to the 'order of salvation' in order to express that this fellowship with Christ leads to mystical union with Christ: 'I live, yet not I, but Christ lives in me' (Gal.2.20). Liberal Protestantism and Catholic modernism replaced this with Christ as prototype and norm, understood in ethical terms. Christ is the perfect and therefore model human being, and moral discipleship leads to having a common will with him.

However, the ethical and mystical elements can be combined without forcing them if one begins from the 'firstborn among many brothers' of Rom.8.29 and sees fellowship with Christ as being 'conformity' to the 'image' of the Son. The firstborn of the many brothers and sisters is more than a prototype or criterion for them. For them he is the exemplary human being. The idea of such an example was already an essential part of Luther's christology.[3] It results, not in an *imitatio Christi* through which men and women attempt to be like Christ, but in a *conformitas Christi* through which men and women are conformed to Christ. They are conformed to the Christ who was tempted, anxious and cried out to God, not through their own attempts at imitation but through experiences of trial, anxiety and sorrow. As our brother, Christ experienced and suffered our distress, so that in our distresses we should experience his brotherhood.[4] That is not the sacramental 'Christ for us', nor is it the ethical 'Christ before us', but the brotherly 'Christ with us'. In this respect Christ experienced and suffered what millions experienced and suffered before him and after him. In this respect his passion is part of and participation in the passion story of his people and the history of the suffering of all humankind. In this respect his cross on Golgotha stands as just one of the millions of crosses in the history of injustice and violence, so that we can recognize the divine solidarity in him. Christ became the forsaken among the forsaken, the tempted among the tempted, the sufferer of injustice among the tortured, the dying one among the dying, in order to be with them as their brother. So those who recognize him and believe in him are also conformed to him through their experiences of life and suffering. Christ,

40

our brother in our distress, makes us his brothers and his sisters in his distress. It is 'the suffering of God in the world' that we share with Christ.[5]

In contrast to the idea of 'Christ the Lord', the idea of 'Christ the brother' expresses a social mutuality of deep fellowship rather than obedience and subordination. In contrast to the idea of 'Christ the prototype', it expresses the experience of fellowship in living and dying. The brotherhood of Christ also reaches out beyond the circle of believers and those who follow him, to include the most insignificant: the hungry, the prisoners, the poor and the sick.

The brotherhood of Christ also has what is nowadays called solidarity. Solidarity is a basic value of both Catholic social teaching and socialism. To be in solidarity means to suffer with one another and to bear one another's burdens. 'Suffering shared is suffering halved', says the proverb. But that does not just mean that the sum of suffering is divided so that we all bear part of it. It also means that no one is left alone in suffering, for the solitude of suffering is its real pain. Solidarity means not only sharing and helping, but first and last support – including support in suffering which cannot be overcome, in anguish and in mourning. Furthermore, solidarity means living in fellowship, not only with those who are like us but also with the others. It is living in that fellowship which comes into being through recognizing others in their otherness. Living in fellowship then means working together as comrades and resisting the isolation imposed on men and women by the competitive struggle. Finally, living in solidarity means fighting together against the oppression and the splintering which makes oppression possible. Solidarity is the power of the powerless and the power of the people. What we call the brotherhood of Christ and the love of neighbour is now being understood in a completely new way through experiences of solidarity in suffering, in life and in struggle. Certainly Christians should not appropriate any values which they themselves have not created. But they must understand their own values anew in the light of present experiences.

From an early stage the Christian community understood itself as a 'fellowship of brothers'. The experience of being equally and together children of God was the basis of this brotherhood. Because in Christianity from the beginning both women and men were baptized, and the baptism of women was never put in question, it was held that women and men were equally and together children of God, so that talk of fellowship is meaningful only as a fellowship of 'brothers and sisters' (even if the sisters were still being overlooked in Thesis III of the 1934 Barmen Theological Declaration or were included in the brotherhood). Even if patriarchalism established itself in the hierarchy of bishops, patriarchs and popes, there were always egalitarian opposition movements in Christianity claiming the brotherhood and sisterhood of all believers. However, they were either domesticated in the patriarchal hierarchy by the male and female orders or excluded as schismatic communities. In practice, the hierarchy did away with what had been given to all in common by one baptism, and replaced equality with inequality, agreement between free agents with the obedience of subjects, and the covenant with the power of tradition. In the established churches 'brotherhood' is usually at the same level and among the same class: brotherhood of bishops, of brothers-in-office, or those who have been led to the same mind in a revival.

The French Revolution called for freedom and equality on the basis of common brotherhood. Already according to the Declaration of Independence by the colony of Virginia in 1776, all human beings are 'free and equal', not because they are 'brothers' but because they have been 'created' in that way. No one knows from precisely what tradition *fraternité* came to be the third principle in the Revolution. The origins presumably lie both in Freemasonry and in the Christian orders and communities. Whereas in the Christian church shared, equal brotherhood and sisterhood was grounded in the fact that those who had received baptism were children of God and in the religious community was seen *sub specie aeternitas,* in the French Revolution it was made the basis of common and equal human rights. What consequences did this way of describing men and women have for communal life?

1. Both 'brotherhood' and 'sisterhood' stress the community of all those in a generation. If 'all men' become 'brothers', then 'all men' includes everyone living at the same time in the various areas of the earth. The link between the generations, between parents and children, is suppressed or even broken by this conspiracy of brothers and sisters. The connection between the generations included all those living in same area at different times. Those from the past influence those in the present through traditions. Those in the future influence them through hopes. The cult of ancestors, respect for the aged and observance of traditions governs this community over time, as does the prospect of children and of handing on the heritage. In the Indian tribes of North America important decisions were made in the presence of the ancestors and took seven future generations into account. The establishment of modern society on the cross-connection of brotherhood and sisterhood led to an unprecedented break in tradition, which sociologists have often noted. A society which is no longer based on its origins is not necessarily orientated on the future, as is often asserted. The society of free and equal 'brothers and sisters' is by definition as little interested in its children as in its parents. It is a society which is aware only of its own present. As such it threatens to become a society which lives at the expense of both its parents and its children.

2. In the Christian fraternities, communities of brethren, brethren of the common life, brotherhoods and so on, there were also parents and children, and often enough life was ordered in a patriarchal way. Free and equal brotherhood was experienced before God in the Spirit, lived out in the community of believers and practised in love. The 'communion of saints' embraced the living

and the dead across time in the eternal presence of God. This recognition does not necessarily do away with the differences between the generations, but it can also be the basis for it. However, if this community of brothers is lived out in a present which is understood only chronologically, and if these brothers live celibate lives, then the connection between the generations is broken. Brotherhood understood in exclusive terms is the final stage of the sequence of human generations that is present at any time and therefore no less than the apocalyptic end of the human race, the presence of which is experienced in any particular age. In a celibate brotherhood the human race becomes infertile and renounces its future.

If this situation is transferred from the religious community to modern society, and in modern society only the 'brothers and sisters' are taken seriously in their human dignity, and not the mothers and fathers, sons and daughters, then modern society will become the apocalypse of the human race. Modern competitive society favours competitive people aged between twenty-five and forty-five. Modern careers favour those who have no generation problems, either with their parents or with their children, e.g. women who have no children and men with no family responsibilities. Those who are always available and always ready for work get promoted. The best careers in modern society are thus tailored to be hostile to the family and forgetful of the generations.

Important as brotherhood and sisterhood in solidarity are in the fight for more freedom and better equality among men and women, brotherhood alone and nothing but sisterhood can become fatal for the human race.

5

Justice for Victims and Perpetrators

1. Is the justification of sinners abstract or concrete?

The Reformation doctrine of justification is grounded in the Pauline doctrine of justification.[1] Its presupposition is the universality of sin: 'For there is no distinction, since all have sinned and fall short of the glory of God' (Rom.3.23). Here 'all' means Jews and Gentiles (Greeks), as Paul explains in Romans 2 and 3. The 'glory' is the divine *doxa* which was originally associated with the image of God in human beings. Like Paul, the Reformers were convinced that through and since original sin 'the godlessness and unrighteousness of human beings' have come upon the world and have provoked God's wrath, i.e. the wounding of his love for his creatures. The gospel which saves and justifies is therefore addressed universally to all sinners and calls them to faith, since they 'are now justified by his grace as a gift, through the redemption that is in Christ Jesus' (Rom.3.30).

The presupposition of the doctrine of the righteousness of God which makes righteous, in Paul and the Reformers, is the *de facto* universality of sin, and its goal is the intended universality of salvation: 'For just as one man's trespass led to condemnation for all, so one man's act of righteousness leads to justification and life for all' (Rom.5.18). It has its christological foundation in a christology of an atoning sacrifice which regards both the death and the resurrection of Christ as representative for all men and women, 'who was handed over to death for our trespasses and was raised for our justification' (Rom.4.25).[2]

The Synoptic Gospels speak of 'sinners' in concrete and social terms. They are 'the sinners and tax collectors' who do not observe the law of God and who live in unrighteousness. They are those without rights, the poor and the home-less, who cannot observe the law and thus stand outside the law, without rights. As the Synoptic parables show, the situations which Jesus keeps tackling are those of human conflict: the healthy against the sick, the rich against the poor, men against women, Pharisees against tax collectors, the good against the wicked, the perpetrators against the victims.[3] In these conflicts one group is always dependent on the other. It is the rich who make the poor poor, and the healthy who handicap the handicapped; the good stigmatize the weak as sinners. Usually it is 'possessions' to which the 'haves' cling, and they exclude the 'have nots' from them.[4] 'Possessions' can be money, health and power, can be righteousness and being good, can be maleness. The issue is always one of power. Wherever such gifts of life are 'taken in possession', inexorable struggles develop over the distribution of work, possessions and opportunities in life. In these struggles what one has is always 'good' and what the other has is always 'evil'. There is only the either-or of the friend-enemy relationship. The devil is let loose in them, and their end is death.

The concrete history of human sin begins with the fratricide of Cain (Gen.4) and the spread of corruption on earth through 'violence' (Gen.6). The eating of the forbidden fruit in the garden of Eden (Gen.3) belongs in the realm of saga and myth, which are an attempt to provide a metaphysical interpretation of physical history. The myth of paradise and the Fall never played the fundamental role in Judaism that it did in Christianity. Judaism did not derive any doctrine of original sin from it. It is important for Christians to see the real history of injustice and violence as sin, in order to find from the Spirit of God the power to do what is right and to find peace.

The weakness of the universal concept of sin in the doctrine of justification in Paul and the Reformers lies in the fact that universal collective guilt makes us blind to specific guilt, indeed can be used as an excuse for accepting specific guilt. The universality of sin leads into the night in which all cats are grey, and even the use of mass means of destruction is no longer anything special. The misuse of the Christian doctrine of sin to justify sin and to adapt to a 'fallen world' can be recognized in many church declarations. If a collective incurs guilt through a crime committed jointly or a joint neglect in offering help, then there is concrete collective guilt. But some people hide their individual guilt in a universal guilt and excuse themselves by saying, 'We have all become more or less guilty.' Others mystify specific guilt so that it becomes generalized 'tragic complications' to which they have succumbed. Such excuses come to grief on those who have resisted, and on the innocent victims of violence. They compel us to make specific investigations into what we have neglected and to confess specifically where we have incurred guilt. Those who indulge in generalizations and abstractions here accuse themselves by excusing themselves. The Protestant pessimism about sin which is also presented as what Reinhold Niebuhr called 'Christian realism' is completely unjustified. Rather, according to Paul, the faith which justifies leads to an optimism of grace, for 'where sin increased, grace abounded even more' (Rom.5.20).

On the other hand, the doctrine of the universality of human sin can also lead to an insight into a solidarity which goes beyond all boundaries because it is boundless. As Dostoievsky put it, 'All are guilty of all and for all things.' In that case the specific criminals are simply the 'unfortunates' among us who must have our compassion since each and every one of us is capable of the same crime. In that case one ceases to accuse 'the others' and oneself takes responsibility for them.[5]

The Pauline and Synoptic interpretation of sin and the forgiveness of sins must not be contrasted. Nor may we play off the universal interpretation of justification against the particular or the metaphysical interpretation against the political. They must be understood as providing a basis for each other and confirming each other: because God has mercy on all sinners, he gives rights to those who have no rights and leads the unrighteous to repent. If there is a divine liberation from the universal power of sin through the dedication of the creative Spirit to righteousness, then liberations from economic injustice, from political oppression and from cultural alienation and personal discouragement are legitimated.[6] If there is an eternal life which will drive death from God's whole creation, then everything is justified that already serves life and resists death here and now. The Reformation doctrine of justification and the present-day theology of the liberation of the oppressed need not be opposites, but can provide mutual correction and enrichment. However, this theoretical statement presupposes a revision of Reformation history. Thomas Müntzer must be recognized as a fellow warrior with Luther in the Reformation, and Luther's erroneous judgments in the German Peasants' War must be revised. The true Reformation doctrine of justification is the theology of the liberation of those without rights *and* of the unjust. A one-sided restriction to the perpetrators and forgiveness of their active sins has made Protestantism blind to the suffering of the victims and their passive sins and to God's judging and saving 'option for the poor'.[7]

2. God's righteousness executes justice for the victims

It is amazing that Protestant theology has failed to note the analogy between God's righteousness which 'justifies' and God's justice which 'executes justice'.[8] This is presumably because of its sharp demarcation between the New Testament and the Old, since as for Paul the justification of the sinner becomes the revelation of God's righteousness in the world, so in the Old Testament, executing justice for those who have no rights is the embodiment of divine mercy and thus of God's righteousness. And the righteousness which executes justice is not a distributive justice (*justitia distributiva*) but a creative justice (*justitia justificans*).

'The one who executes justice for the oppressed' (Ps.146.7; 103.6) is the God who 'executes justice for the fatherless and the widow' (Deut.10.18; Ps.82.3; Isa.1.17). It is expected that the messiah 'will judge the poor with righteousness and decide with equity for the meek of the earth' (Isa.11.4). Because God makes his Spirit rest on his messiah, the messiah will 'bring forth justice to the nations' (Isa.42.1), and when 'the Spirit is poured out from on high, then . . . justice will dwell in the wilderness and righteousness abide in the fruitful field. And the

46

effect of righteousness will be peace' (Isa.32.15ff.). That means that the God who created heaven and earth is on the side of those who have to suffer oppression becuse they cannot defend themselves. Their right is their divine cause. On the other hand it means that God puts the weak and the vulnerable under his divine protection. Anyone who violates them violates him. 'All these things my hand has made, and so all these things are mine, says the Lord. But this is the one to whom I will look, the one that is humble and contrite in spirit' (Isa.66.2). One can call God's partisan support of his most vulnerable creatures 'God's preferential option for the poor',[9] provided that it is made clear that 'the poor' are the victims of violence and that God's empathy with the most insignificant is bound up with this divine 'option', so that what happens to them is done to him. According to Matthew 25, the Son of Man who is judge of the world identifies himself with them to such a degree that what happens to them 'is done to him'. God himself is the right of those who have no rights, just as he is the power of the powerless. God himself is the victim of the violent. God himself suffers the injustice that is done to them. And God will judge in accord with what he has experienced in the poor and in vulnerable creatures. God executes justice for those who have been deprived of their rights and have no rights, through his solidarity with them.

This impression becomes even stronger if we go on to look at the figure of the 'suffering servant of God' in Isa.53. 'Surely he has borne our sickness and carried our pains' (53.4) means that in the sick and those in pain the Messiah himself is the one who is sick and in pain. He himself bears the suffering of the world. He himself is the victim of violence. On the basis of this deep solidarity he is then said to be a representative: 'Upon him was the chastisement that made us whole, and with his wounds we are healed' (53.5). As the one who bears the suffering of the world, he also bears the sins of the world which cause that suffering. By 'bearing' and enduring sins he does atonement for the victims of violence; he makes the violent repent and so restores them.

The picture of the suffering servant of God from Isa.53 shaped the Christian passion stories and became the foundation for the original christology. With this image, in Jesus' way to death on the cross we again discover a christology of solidarity: the messianic Son of God unconditionally assumes the conditions of our vulnerable and mortal existence and becomes a human being like us. He goes the way of non-violent passion. He bears and endures injustice and violence, betrayal and denial, being forsaken by God and human beings, and dies on the Roman cross. These 'sufferings of Christ' are also the sufferings of the poor and vulnerable, of the people (*ochlos*) and of weaker creatures. Those who suffer violence rediscover their fate in the fate of Jesus. They can discover themselves in him and him in themselves.[10] The Christ who bears suffering, is tortured and murdered, is on the side of the victims, not the perpetrators. He himself becomes the victim among those who are sacrificed. The forsaken Christ is the most assailed of all who are assailed and who despair of God. He is the divine martyr among the millions of unknown martyrs in the history of the suffering of Israel, humankind and nature. In this respect the 'sufferings of Christ' are not exclusively the sufferings of Jesus but the sufferings of the poor and weak, which he shares in solidarity in his own body and his own soul (Heb.2.16-18; 11.26; 13.13). Therefore the 'sufferings of Christ' are open for future sufferers, both those who suffer with Christ (Col.1.24) and those with whom Christ will suffer, for the suffering of martyrs for the sake of his name and his kingdom, and for the coming apocalyptic suffering which will come upon all vulnerable creatures.

Luther put forward this christology of solidarity in his early period, in the form of a christology of conformity. Christ is the firstborn among many brothers and sisters.[11] For them he is the exemplary person and the prototype to which they are to be conformed through their experiences and their sufferings (Rom.8.29). As our brother, Christ experienced and suffered our distress so that we might experience his brotherhood in our distress. Christ – the brother – is the 'Christ with us': the tormented among those who are tormented, the one who suffers injustice among the victims of violence, the forsaken among the forsaken. But the brother in our distress also makes us brothers and sisters in his distress. 'Only the suffering God can help,' wrote Dietrich Bonhoeffer in his Gestapo cell.[12] In fact a God who cannot suffer, and suffer with us, could not even understand us. Therefore Christians stand 'by God in his suffering', as Bonhoeffer wrote in a poem.[13] In contrast to the idea of 'Christ the Lord', the idea of 'Christ the brother' expresses deep fellowship and mutuality in this communion with Christ.

Does this suffering of Christ in solidarity with the victims of the history of human violence have any significance for the victims? If he were just one more victim, then his suffering would have no particular significance. But if God himself is *in* Christ (II Cor.5.19), then Christ brings eternal communion with God and God's life-giving righteousness through his passion into the passion story of this world and identifies God with the victims of violence. Conversely, we also have here the identification of the victims with God, so that they are put under divine protection and, though lacking human rights, have rights with God. Not least these 'damned of the earth' become subjects in God's judgment on the world: 'What you have done to the least of these, you have done to me.'

3. God's justifying righteousness for the perpetrators

Violence by human beings against human beings and by human beings against weaker creatures is sin and a crime against life. There are always two sides to violence: on the one side are those who do violence, and on the other their victims. On the one side the master asserts himself; on the other the slave is humiliated. On the one side the exploiters win, on the other the exploited lose.

Violence destroys life on both sides, but in different ways: on the one side through evil and on the other through suffering. Those who do violence become inhuman and unjust; their victims are dehumanized and lose their rights. Because violence has these two sides, the way to freedom and justice must begin from both sides: the liberation of the oppressed from the suffering of oppression calls for the liberation of the oppressors from the injustice of oppression. Otherwise there is no liberation and no justice which makes peace. For the goal can only be an open community of human beings, and of human beings with other creatures, which is free of anxiety, from which violence has disappeared, and into which justice has been introduced. The liberation of the oppressed and the securing of rights for those who have no rights are self-evident in many situations, at any rate for the victims of violence. The liberation of the perpetrators of violence from their injustice is not self-evident in most cases, at any rate not for the violent who gain from their injustice. They do not see the sufferings which they cause their victims. They are blinded. They give many reasons to justify their injustice. They are self-righteous because basically they know that they are doing wrong and are unjust, and because they also know that injustice done cannot be undone. How can the unjust be justified?

Injustice has happened. No better future can ever 'make good' the suffering of the past. But how can one live with a guilt-laden past? According to the ancient legal conceptions of all nations, atonement is needed if infringements of justice are to be made good. This needs to take place in three dimensions: those of the victims, of the perpetrators, and lastly of the community in which victims and perpetrators live together. Guilt without the experience of atonement leads to the repression of guilt, to compensation for injustice and the compulsion to repeat the unjust action. The guilty cannot live without forgiveness of their guilt. But there is no forgiveness of guilt without atonement, just as there can be no reconciliation without the restoration of justice. What is atonement? Who can make atonement? These questions are vitally necessary for the perpetrators and those who have to exist in the long shadows of the perpetrators. We need to approach the answer carefully, so as not to get it wrong. As Germans we do this in awareness of Auschwitz. When we ask about 'atonement' we are asking about a power which liberates the perpetrators and their descendants from self-hatred and enables them to live in justice.[14]

Guilt, whether individual or collective, is a burden on the perpetrators and destroys their self-respect. The consequences are justifications of the self or destructions of the self. They give rise to the 'scapegoat syndrome'. A 'guilty' person is sought on whom one can unload one's own failure and who then has to be 'guilty of everything'. As one cannot live with guilt over injustice and violence because it is intolerable, and cannot get rid of it either by repression or transference, then one has 'ruined one's life' – as people used to say. Even if no punishment follows, it is impossible to find the strength to affirm a life which has so denied itself.[15]

Is atonement a human possibility? In the religions of many peoples it is imagined that the gods are made angry by human injustice and acts of violence. They have to be offered sacrifices to reconcile them. Behind this lies the idea of the universal harmony of the world which is destroyed by human injustice and can only be healed by a corresponding sacrifice. So evil has to be recompensed with evil. That has nothing to do with vengeance, but with the restoration of the world order.

According to the rituals and theology of Israel, God's love for his people is violated by injustice and the breach of the covenant in his people.[16] Violence against God's covenant-partners, against God's image in others, and against God's creatures is always also a violation of God himself. God's anger is God's love violated. This wrath of God is experienced by finding the face of God hidden, in one's own godforsakeness and the disappearance of the divine power of the Spirit in human beings. But if God's love is none other than God's love violated, then God must bear and sustain the pain of his love. God suffers injustice and violence as a violation of his love because and in so far as he maintains his love for the unjust and those who do violence. So his love must overcome his wrath by rising above the pain which is added to it. That takes place in his 'bearing' the sins of his people. This divine 'bearing' of sins is expressed:

1. In the cultic ritual of the atoning sacrifice which God himself makes to reconcile his people with him. The sins of the people are transferred to the 'scapegoat' who 'carries' them 'away' into the wilderness.

2. In the prophetic vision of the suffering servant of God, who 'bears' the sins of the people in his representative suffering.

3. In the theological understanding of the divine mercy, by which sinners are made righteous.

In each case, it is God himself who atones for the sins of his people. God gives himself as a ransom for Israel. There is no liberation from guilt without atonement! But only one who is not himself a sinner can atone. Atonement is not a human possibility, but only a divine one. It is realized by God, who transforms human guilt into divine suffering by 'bearing' human sin.[17] The God who himself suffers the godforsakenness of sinners is the God who atones. Therefore it is right to pray, 'You who bear the sins of the world, have mercy on us'. The divine mercy presupposes the bearing and enduring of human sin. Through the divine mercy, a life which has gone wrong and is ruined is reborn from death to sin for new life in righteousness. As long as the world exists, God bears not only the history of its suffering but also the history of human injustice. He bears it as the victim among the victims. Human beings are responsible and therefore cannot be represented by human beings. Each person is alone with his

50

or her guilt. Only God can represent us and bear us with our guilt. Modern insights into the dignity and personality of human beings make the old ideas of atonement and satisfaction, penance and ransom, obsolete. I can pay my debts, but I will not be able to change my status as a debtor. Guilt and sin affect men and women in their being and not just in their having. Even if we have 'burdened' ourselves with sins, we confess 'God, be gracious to me a sinner' (Luke 18.13). The sins which I 'have' can be forgiven me. The sinner who I am must be 'accepted' and reborn if I am to live. So I shall try to translate the theology of atonement from objectifying, legalistic terms into human and personal concepts.

In christological understanding, the drama played out in the violent arrest, torture and crucifixion of Jesus by the Romans is very different from what these outward human/inhuman circumstances suggest. The suffering and death of the Son brings about atonement for the sins of men and women and reconciliation of the world through God. The first Jewish-Christian community already understood the death of Christ as an atoning sacrifice, and in faith in the gospel which brings justification experienced the great liberation from the power of sin and the pressures to sin. On the basis of the representative atoning death of Christ they broke with this world of injustice, violence and death and dedicated themselves to the service of life (Rom.6.12-14, 19-23). In the symbol of baptism they felt that they had been reborn with Christ to eternal life. How is the death of Christ on the cross to be understood as atonement? It can be understood as atonement for the sins of the world only if we see God *in* Christ. So in this context Paul always keeps stressing that Christ is the Son of God.[18] But the consequence of that is that Christ's suffering is divine suffering and that his death is the death endured by God as the representative of all sinners who have fallen victim to death. Therefore it is wrong to assume that through his representative suffering, Christ has reconciled God's wrath over human sin, or that like a sadist God has crucified, or has had crucified, his own Son. The crucified Christ has nothing to do with a God of vengeance or a divine punitive judge. Such notions are completely contrary to 'the Father of Jesus Christ'. 'The cross is atonement *because* God is the Father.'[19] The Christ who atones is the revelation of the God who has mercy. Atonement which reconciles the hostile, sinful world is the form of suffering taken by the love of God for this world. The love of God wounded by human injustice and violence becomes the love of God which endures pain, and the 'wrath of God' becomes divine mercy.

What did Christ suffer on the cross that can be called 'atonement'? Not pains of body and soul. These he shares with the many who have been crucified and murdered in the history of the world. What he suffers are his particular pains over God: his experience of praying unheard in Gethsemane and being abandoned by God on the cross. Because the one who had experienced the nearness of God as 'Abba' in such an incomparable way that he knew himself to be the

51

messianic child, the Son of God, experiences being forsaken by God, he experiences the pain of divine love for sinners and accepts it. The suffering of Christ on the cross is human sin transformed into the atoning suffering of God. Therefore nothing can limit Christ's experience of being forsaken on the cross. As the young Luther stressed so emphatically in his theology of the cross, it is the experience of *hell*.[20] Paul, too, took this view of the godforsakenness of Christ on the cross: 'For our sake he made him to be sin who knew no sin' (II Cor.5.21). Christ became 'curse for us' (Gal.3.13). The Son of God, abandoned, cursed and damned, hangs on the cross. He hangs there 'for us' that we might have peace. Through his wounds we are healed. There is more here than Christ's solidarity with the 'damned of this earth'. There is the divine atonement for sin, for injustice and violence on earth. In this divine atonement the pain of God is made manifest. In the pain of God, God's faithfulness to his creatures is manifested as his indestructible love which overcomes a world in conflict. God reconciles this world in conflict by the way in which he suffers contradiction, not by contradicting the contradiction, i.e. through judgment. He turns the pain of his love into atonement for sinners.[21] So God becomes the God of sinners. He does not want their death, but turns to them so that they turn back to him.

If we understand sin and atonement in this way in personal and relational terms, then we are parting company with the inadequate images of the sacrificial theories: ransom, atoning sacrifice, satisfaction, and so on. It is not the case that our objectified sins (in the plural) have to be made good by objective acts of atonement. We ourselves have to be justifed as sinners because of the way in which we contradict life, and have to be restored to life. That happens through the atoning love of God. In the long run, Abelard was right, not Anselm. For God's representative action is manifest in the representative action of Christ.[22] In Christ's suffering and death for us it becomes certain that 'God is for us', as Paul says in the hymn in Rom.8.31-39 which celebrates the certainty of faith: 'God is here . . . Christ is here . . . nothing can separate us from the love of God which is in Jesus Christ our Lord.'

The mystery of God's atoning action as representative of the world is disclosed only when we see the event of the cross as an event of God and interpret it in trinitarian terms. A concept of God introduced from outside, whether it is the *Deus impassibilis* or the God of retribution, makes it impossible to recognize in Christ the 'love' of God which is 'for us'. But the power of the divine representation is the power of eternal love with which the Father, Son and Holy Spirit are there for one another. For the love with which the Father so loved the world that through his Son and in his suffering and death he takes upon himself atonement for the sins of the world is that very love which the triune God is in eternity. 'God so *loved* the world that he gave his only-begotten Son' (John 3.16) presupposes that 'God *is* love' (I John 4.16). Eternal love directs itself only to other objects. In the Trinity, the divine persons are there for one another in their mutual otherness, and accord with one another. On the cross of Christ this love is there for others, the sinners, those in conflict, enemies. The mutual surrender to one another in the Trinity is manifest in the surrender of Christ to a world which is hostile to God, an action which takes up all who believe in him into the eternal life of the divine love. So how does atonement come to those who do perpetrate injustice and violence? It comes from the mercy of the Father through the godforsakenness which the Son endures as a representative in the unburdening power of the Holy Spirit. A single movement of love arises out of the pain of the Father, is manifest in the suffering of the Son and is experienced in the Spirit of life. So God becomes the God of the godless. His justice justifies the unjust.

According to the traditions of the Western church, the atonement which liberates from sin is grounded exclusively in the death of Christ and not in his resurrection. His resurrection is always understood only as divine authentication or as the identification of God with Christ. As I have already indicated, that does not correspond with Paul's christology, according to which Christ has died for us, and indeed much more (*pollo mallon*) is risen for us (Rom.5.10). He 'represents us' not just as the one who died for us, but much more as the one who rose again and has been exalted to God (to the right hand of God). In our life, too, in order to live with the past it is not enough just to atone for past guilt, important though that is. Something new must be created so that 'the old has passed away' (II Cor.5.17) and one need no longer think about it. That is what is meant by the 'resurrection of Christ from the dead': the beginning of the new creation of the world: 'And God will wipe away all tears from their eyes and death will be no more . . . ' The beginning of the new creation of all things in righteousness begins with the dead. Therefore this new beginning is called the 'resurrection of the dead', as Ezekiel 37 foresees it on the field of corpses that makes up the history of Israel. Is that God's answer to the dead of Auschwitz, the recollection of which burdens our souls? That is why the Orthodox Church has proclaimed forgiveness at the Easter festival and celebrated Easter as the great feast of atonement.

The day of resurrection.
Let us become light at this feast.
Let us embrace one another.
Let us speak to those who hate us:
For the sake of the resurrection
let us forgive ourselves everything.
And so let us cry out together:
Christ is risen from the dead.
He is truly risen.[23]

4. The righteousness of God which brings justice to situations and structures

In the world of injustice there are not just victims on one side and perpetrators on the other. Between them there are also political circumstances and economic structures which make the ones victims and the others perpetrators. 'Sin' is not only what some do and others endure. There are also 'heretical structures', as Visser 't Hooft called the apartheid laws of the racist Boer state, and there are also 'structural sins' in dictatorships with their secret police and informers. A world economic order has come into being which makes the poor poorer and the rich richer, and which must therefore be regarded as a supra-personal 'power of sin', because one cannot really escape it either as a victim or as one who benefits from it.[24] I have called such systems of injustice 'vicious circles', because unless one tries to stop them at the beginning they develop a certain autonomy through which the whole system destroys itself: first the weaker and more vulnerable creatures die, and then even the strong will perish. First the children of the poor die, and then the rich will also die. 'First the forest dies, then people die.'[25] There are tendencies and regularities in the macro-project of modern society which will result in the ecological death of humankind and most other living beings through a progressive destruction of the environment – the atmosphere as well as the earth. There is no mistaking it: the deserts are growing, the forests are contracting, the greenhouse effect is increasing and the hole in the ozone layer keeps getting bigger.[26] We human beings are perpetrators and victims of such vicious circles and these spirals of death. For the moment the strong and the rich may foist the costs off on the weak and the poor, but in the end they themselves will become victims. The phenomena are well known and sufficiently clear. Here we have the concepts of structural sin and the righteousness of God which creates peace.

1. Structures are made by human beings. Persistent acts of violence lead to a violent society. Unhindered exploitation gives rise to dependent colonies, and thoughtless building developments produce the ecological crisis. Sin in the form of human acts of violence gives rise to a state of violence. People get used to things being like that. The first sin is committed freely, the second out of habit and the third out of inner compulsion, i.e. out of a lack of freedom. It's like dependence on drugs. What comes into being is what Augustine aptly described as *non posse non peccare*, not being able not to sin. That is not true only on a personal level. It leads to syndromes on the social and structural levels which in turn dominate people and put them under pressure. The products of evil overwhelm men and women and begin to dominate and to destroy them. 'Structural sin' is sin which has become autonomous, sin no longer as a human action but as a quasi-objective compulsive power over people. It is sin in the form of idolatry, fetishism, the deification of transitory things. Those who exist

in these structures become accomplices of sin, even if they want only good. Think of all the personal good that was done under the system of Nazi dictatorship – and it all served evil, to prolong the war and annihilate the Jews.

Structures are made by human beings: that is only a half-truth. Human beings are also made by structures. That is the other half. Human beings are not only producers but also products of their conditions. It is worth noting that this is not true of all structures: whereas unjust and evil structures compel people to evil because those who do not adapt to them are threatened with torture and death, just structures and good conditions do not automatically make people good. Here, rather, it depends on human beings themselves whether or not they use their freedom for what is good and right. That is also the difference between dictatorship and democracy. There is a dictatorship of evil, but there cannot be a dictatorship of good. One can reduce the mass causes of human unhappiness, and perhaps also remove many of them, but one cannot make people happy, because there is not one and the same happiness for all, nor can there be, whereas there can be one and the same unhappiness for all.[27]

2. In describing the relationship between politics and the kingdom of God, Karl Barth said that the world needs a parable, and can itself be a parable, of the kingdom of God and his righteousness.[28] The political world is not the kingdom of God, but it can correspond to the righteousness of God or can conflict with it. If we call institutionalized injustice structural sin, then we experience the righteousness of God as a contradicition to 'this world'. The crisis of Third World debt today is not a matter of indifference for the kingdom of God. The righteousnes of God dwells with the victims of this crisis and cries out for justice for those who have no rights. The Christ in solidarity is in solidarity with the least of the brothers and sisters. The righteousness of God puts in the wrong those who perpetrate and benefit from this crisis and liberates them for faith to repent through the atoning suffering of Christ. Those who recognize their righteousness in the suffering and death of Christ begin to die to this unjust world. They are as it were dead to the demands and rewards of the oppressive system. They no longer recognize the laws of structural violence. Those who have found their righteousness in the Christ crucified 'for us' break with the world of injustice. They are justified in Christ, and no longer through their race, class, sex or possessions. What those who follow Christ then do is a 'racial scandal' by the criteria of racism and a 'betrayal of class' by the criteria of capitalism. They take sides with the victims and break with the perpetrators. Those who do that often enough become 'strangers in their own people'. To show solidarity with the victims they give up loyalty to their own class and their own people. They then quickly find themselves in a social no man's land. One can also manoeuvre oneself outside society and lose all possibilities of influence. Unrealistic radicalism is often only an adolescent rejection of life. A concrete step towards a better righteousness is more important than the purity

of a good disposition. But personal integrity certainly remains the most important intrinsic criterion for resistance and assimilation.

3. What does the righteousness of God mean in respect of 'structural sins'? Jews and Christians will begin from their experience of God if they want to say what righteousness is. As I have shown in 2. and 3., God's righteousness is experienced as righteousness which is creative, executes justice and justifies. God is righteous because he executes justice for men and women without rights and puts the unjust right. He executes justice for those who suffer violence and he saves through his righteousness. Through this righteousness God creates that shared peace which at the same time means true life: Shalom.

6

'The Fellowship of the Holy Spirit'

On Trinitarian Pneumatology

1. The fellowship of the Holy Spirit

'The grace of our Lord Jesus Christ and the love of God the Father and the fellowship of the Holy Spirit be with us all.' So runs an old and widely used blessing in the Christian church. I am taking it up to enquire into the 'fellowship of the Holy Spirit'. Does the divine Spirit enter into a 'fellowship' with us human beings? Does he take us into the 'fellowship', the communion, of the Father and the Son? Why is there no mention in connection with the Holy Spirit of divine 'domination' and human 'subjection', but emphatically of 'fellowship'?

'Fellowship', we can say spontaneously on hearing the word, does not violate but liberate. 'Fellowship' does not subject but allows others to be themselves. 'Fellowship' means openness to one another, sharing with one another and respect for one another. It is the reciprocal communication of all that one has and is. What does that mean for the Holy Spirit in his life-giving fellowship with us and for us in the trinitarian fellowship of the Holy Spirit with the Father and the Son?

If we are to open ourselves to the experience of the fellowship of the Holy Spirit, we must recognize and overcome certain reductions and constraints in traditional pneumatology. I shall be discussing only problems in the Western church and within that primarily problems in Protestantism, but I believe that there are also problems for all of Christianity here.

Generally speaking, the issue is the relationshp between the Trinity and the kingdom of God, *trinitas* and *monarchia,* which has remained obscure from the beginning of Christian theology.[1] The rule of God can only be exercised by a single subject. There can only be an attitude of subjection to the rule of the one God. Therefore even the Son must be subordinated to the one God, and the Spirit must be subordinated to the Son. But the triune God is intrinsically a unique fellowship in which the Spirit 'together with the Father and the Son is worshipped and glorified', as the Nicene Creed puts it. One who is worshipped 'together with' cannot be subordinated to the other. He is of equal, eternal dignity and equal, divine quality. Through most theological controversies in the ancient church runs the conflict between the world-view of monarchical theism and trinitarian community faith. The Arians were not concerned to depose the Son but to exalt the monarchy of the one God, and so they subordinated the Son. The Pneumatomachoi were not concerned to depose the Spirit but to preserve the unique monarchy of the one God, and so they subordinated the Spirit to the Son and the Son to the Father.

According to the decisions of the councils of the early church, too, in the tradition of the Western church we constantly find a monarchical, i.e. subordinationist, pneumatology and not a trinitarian pneumatology: God rules through Christ, and the effect of his rule is the Spirit. In the world monarchy of the one God, the Spirit is none other than the working of his rule, the subjective side of his objective revelation and the inward fruit of his outward word and sacrament.

If this view becomes the only view of God and his revelation, it gives rise to those constraints and reductions in pneumatology about which, rightly, complaints have constantly been made. There is a need to overcome this monarchical pneumatology in trinitarian pneumatology.

Given the history of its influence in the West, the insertion of the *filioque* into the Nicene Creed is certainly not to be underestimated.[2] However, it should not be overestimated either. The *filioque* is not responsible for all the mistakes of the church and theology in the West, just as its omission is not responsible for all the virtues in the East. However, the *filioque* brought about a decisive shift made in the understanding of the Holy Spirit: the Holy Spirit was subordinated to the Father and the Son. What the Holy Spirit is, was determined not only by the Father but also by the Son. Through this order the relationship between the Son and the Spirit was made one-sided. It could no longer be understood reciprocally: if the Spirit also proceeds from the Son, the Son cannot also proceed from the Spirit. If through the *filioque* the original relationships of the Trinity are fixed to the order Father-Son-Spirit, then their relationships in salvation history must be understood accordingly: the Spirit proceeds from the invisible Father and from the incarnate Son. But the incarnate Son is present in the apostolic church through word and sacrament. Thus the Holy Spirit can only be that which according to apostolic tradition is brought about through the word and sacrament of the church of Christ. In practice that means that the ministry comes first and only then the Spirit; scripture comes first and only then faith. This sequence leads to a deep mistrust of the direct working of the Holy Spirit, the inspirations, feelings, visions and dreams of the Spirit. One can claim 'that the *filioque* subordinates the Holy Spirit to Christ, that it tends to "depersonalize"

58

the Holy Spirit, and that this tendency can also encourage a subordination of the Spirit to the church, as a result of which the church rigidifies in an authoritarian institutionalism'.[3]

Of course that need not necessarily be the case, but there is such a tendency. So in the West there were controversies between the 'official church' and the 'Spirit church' in the Middle Ages; between theology tied to scripture and the theology of the free spirit at the time of the Reformation; and between faith in the Word and heresy in modern times. One can avoid these false alternatives if one 'recognizes the mutual relationship and the mutual interaction of the Son and the Holy Spirit' in the original relationships of the Trinity.[4] But that means seeing the Holy Spirit in a fellowship with the Father and the Son and not as subordinated to them. If the *filioque* is dropped, and we begin with the simple issuing of the Spirit from the Father in pneumatology, the mutual relationship of the Son and the Spirit becomes conceivable, and the fellowship of the Spirit 'with the Father and the Son' is immediately obvious.

How is the trinitarian fellowship of the Holy Spirit to be understood? There are several possible ways of defining the unity of the triune God. Tertullian began from the unity of the one, homogeneous, divine being: *una substantia - tres personae*. The priority which he gave to the one divine being over the threeness of the divine persons was for a long time taken for granted in the tradition of the Western church. When the metaphysic of subjectivity replaced the metaphysic of substance at the beginning of modern times in Europe, God was no longer thought of just as the supreme substance, but at the same time also as the absolute subject (by Fichte and Hegel). The unity of the triune God then no longer lies just in the homogeneity of the divine substance, but also in the identity of the one, divine subject. From this there follows the formula of the modern doctrine of the Trinity: one divine subject – three different modes of being. This formula, too, gives priority to the unity of God over the threeness of the divine persons.

We go a step further when we say that the unity of the triune God does not just consist in the one, homogeneous, divine substance nor just in the identical divine subject but above all in the unique fellowship, communion, of the three persons. The persons of the Trinity together possess the divine being and the divine rule. Therefore their trinitarian unity, their unity of substance and their unity of subject, comes first. The English expression 'triunity' really denotes 'three persons – one fellowship' in a remarkable unity. Here we are putting the trinitarian concept of the unity of God before the metaphysical concept of unity. In their relationships to one another, the divine persons Father, Son and Holy Spirit exist at the same time for each other and in each other in such an intimate way that through themselves they form their complete, trinitarian unity. The old ideas of *circumincessio* and *perichoresis* describe this unique unity in which the three persons live by virtue of their mutual relationships. If we call this unity of triunity 'fellowship' or 'communion' (*koinonia*), then we are expressing what binds the Holy Spirit 'to the Father and the Son'. By that we mean a fellowship of a special and incomparable kind, such as is sought only by human beings in their fellowship with one another, guessed at only in their love for one another, and experienced only from afar in moments of mystical union.

However, the unity of the triune God really becomes manifest in that event of which the Son says: 'That they may all be *one*, as you, Father, are *in me* and I *in you*, that they may also be one *in us*' (John 17.21). The fellowship of the triune God is so open and inviting that it is depicted in the fellowship of the Holy Spirit which human beings experience with one another – 'as you, Father, are in me and I in you' – and takes this true human felllowship into itself and gives it a share in itself: 'that they may also be *in us*'. True human fellowship is to correspond to the triune God and be his image on earth. True human fellowship will participate in the inner life of the triune God. 'The fellowship of the Holy Spirit' brings human beings into a fellowship which corresponds to the trinitarian being of God and participates in that being. No matter how monarchical or subordinationist the terms in which pneumatology is defined, this trinitarian pneumatology is its origin and its goal. I want now to describe the 'fellowship of the Holy Spirit' at three central points of Christian doctrine – anthropology, ecclesiology and the doctrine of scripture - and to end with some thoughts on the unity of the monarchical, eucharistic and doxological concept of the Trinity.

2. Trinitarian anthropology: the social image of God

In its history, Christian theology has taken up two different analogies to understand the mystery of human beings in fellowship with God: the analogy of the soul which controls the body and the analogy of the total communion between man and woman – in other words the individual and the social analogy. Since Augustine, the former has led to the development of the psychological doctrine of the Trinity in the West, and the latter has led to the development of a social doctrine of the Trinity in the East.

Gregory of Nazianzen found the analogy and the image of the triune God on earth in the original nuclear family of Adam, Eve and Seth. What corresponds to the triune God is not the human individual *per se*, but this primal cell of the human community. These three persons, too, are of one flesh and blood and form one family. The triune God can be recognized again in the original human community of husband, wife and child.[5]

Augustine struggled with this social analogy and rejected it.[6] If it were correct, he argued, then the husband would only be in the image of God from the point at which he found a wife and had a child by her. But when scripture speaks of the image of God, it is speaking of individual persons. There is as yet no mention of Seth in the creation story. For Augustine it is Paul who tilts the

60

balance, by calling the husband the 'image and honour of God' and the wife only the 'honour of the husband' in I Cor.11.7. From this Augustine concludes that while the wife is the image of God in so far as she shares human nature with her husband, by herself she is not an image of God in so far as according to the Yahwistic creation story she is created as the man's 'helpmeet'. Only the husband is in the image of God. Therefore Augustine claims: 1. that the image of God is a quality of the soul and as such is independent of gender; 2. that the wife can be regarded as the image of God only under her head, her husband.

Michael Schmaus regarded this as a 'profound and deeply spiritual solution' of the problem.[7] But it must be called 'spirit'-less in the literal sense because it is a solution without the 'fellowship of the Holy Spirit'. Certainly the image of the original nuclear family of Adam, Eve and Seth is open to misunderstanding and is attested only in the Priestly Writing, which does not know of any Fall. Nor can the family state be normative for the view that human beings are in the image of God. Nevertheless, this does not lead to individualism, since the anthropological triangle determines the existence of all human beings. Any human being is a husband or wife and the child of parents. 'Husband' and 'wife' are terms to denote the indissoluble sociality of human beings, and 'parents' and 'children' terms to denote the sequence of human generations which is equally indissoluble. The one is human community in space and the other human community in time. If the whole, real human being is destined to be in the image of God, then that is also the destiny of the society in which human beings are whole and real; the community of the sexes and the community of the generations.

However, Augustine reduced the image of God to the human soul: the soul which dominates the body corresponds to the God who dominates the world. The soul is the best part in the human being, since it is elevated above the body: it gives life to the body and controls it, and uses it as its instrument: *anima formans corporis*. The soul has an influence on the body, but the body does not have an influence on the soul. The soul is the side of human nature which is related to God. 'Nothing is more powerful than that creature which is called the rational spirit,' declared Augustine. 'If you are in the Spirit, you are in the centre: if you look downwards, there is the body, and if you look upwards, there is God.'[8] Only the soul which controls the body is the image of God. The body which is subject to it displays only traces of God (*vestigia Dei*). Because the soul is the subject in each individual, all individuals are themselves the image of God on earth. This is the content of Augustine's so-called 'psychological doctrine of the Trinity': through spirit – knowledge – love the human subject corresponds to the divine subject. The analogy of the image of God does not relate to the inner being of God but to God's external relationship to the world. As God acts towards the world as ruler, so the soul acts towards the body. As God possesses the world, so human beings possess themselves. The relationships within the Trinity cannot be depicted, since externally the Trinity always acts in an undivided way and as a unity.[9] As a generalization one can say that in the West, monarchical theism in the concept of God led to individualism in anthropology.[10] Because it was not the Trinity but the rule of God which was made the object of the image of God in human beings, the individual human being rather than the community of human persons took on divine dignity.

Here the critical question in anthropology is: if the human body is not part of the image of God, how can the body become the 'temple of the Holy Spirit', as Paul says in I Cor.6? Here I am taking up a discussion from the time of the Reformation.[11] Andreas Osiander answered the question by saying that the body is also part of the image of God, because the whole human being (*totus homo*) was made to be in the image of God. Jean Calvin at first answered the question in the negative: the image of God has a spiritual nature, since God is Spirit. Therefore only the soul is the 'seat' of the image of God. The image shapes the soul. The soul is a mirror of God. The body is not part of the image of God. Here Calvin was only repeating the tradition of Augustine and the Middle Ages. But then, following the biblical tradition, he distinguished between the image of God in creation and in redemption: human beings are *created* to be the image of the 'invisible God', but they are *redeemed* in the image of the 'incarnate God'. In fellowship with Christ, believers become the image of Christ, the incarnate Word, and their bodies become the 'temple of the Holy Spirit' (I Cor.6.13ff.). Therefore in the process of redemption and consummation believers become the image of God *tam in corpore quam in anima* (both in body and in soul).[12]

In the 'fellowship of the Holy Spirit' the whole person, body, soul and spirit, becomes the clear image of God on earth. Human beings are drawn physically into the redeeming and transfiguring fellowship of God. They praise and glorify God in their bodies. There can no longer be any question of a degradation and subjection of the mortal body by an immortal soul among those who await the 'resurrection of the body' and 'the new earth' in the future world. Here already body and soul form a communion under the guidance of the life-giving Spirit.

But if human beings are the image of God on earth in their corporeality, then they are also the image of God in the sexual differentiation of masculinity and femininity. If according to the account of creation in the Priestly Writing God created his image on earth 'male and female', then this original difference and community of man and woman is already to be understood in terms of the image of God. It is not the sexless soul or the solitary individual which is thought worthy to correspond to God and participate in God's eternal being but the human fellowship of persons. Here we necessarily return to the idea of the social image of God which is found in the Greek church fathers.

Even Augustine himself could not completely avoid the social analogy. Certainly he reduced the image of God to the soul of each individual, but he did not abstract this completely from corporeality; he reduced the image of God in the wife to the rule of the husband, who is to be her 'head'.[13] Augustine followed the Pauline *kephale* theology, according to which the man is the head of the wife, as Christ is the head of the husband and God is the head of Christ (I Cor.11.3f.). This theological hierarchy, God – Christ – man, is not yet a developed trinitarian theology, judged by the conceptuality of the early church.

If we understand the whole person, husband, wife and child, as the image of God, then we understand true human community as the image of the triune God, not just as the image of his rule but also as the image of his inner being. In the 'fellowship of the Holy Spirit', human fellowship corresponds to the unique, incomparable fellowship of the Father, the Son and the Holy Spirit.[14]

3. Trinitarian ecclesiology: the community of brothers and sisters

In the West, theological ecclesiologies traditionally have their focal point in the grounding of the authority of ministry in the church. The way in which they are grounded in the fellowship of the people of God falls well behind this. The gathered community is often seen only as an effect of the ministry: it owes its existence and its unity only to the ministry of the Word and sacrament. This view leads to an underestimation of the charisms of the Holy Spirit which were poured out on the whole community. It also led to the reduction of the 'charismatic community' to the charisma of the one ministry.[15] According to the experience of the New Testament, however, the community of Christ is itself already the charismatic community (I Cor.12; Rom.12.3ff.; Eph.4.7). The church has a charismatic structure. Often enough, the theological grounding of the authority of the ministry ignored the existence of the community. Here I shall refer only to the doctrine of the monarchical episcopate which Ignatius of Antioch developed and which led to the onesidednesses in the concept of the church that I have mentioned. The principle of the monarchical episcopate was 'one bishop, one community'. The argument behind it went, 'one God, one Christ, one bishop, one community'. The bishop represents Christ to the community, just as Christ represents God. That certainly guarantees the unity of the community, but it also ties the Spirit to the ministry, so that an intrinsically charismatic community can hardly develop because the community remains passive: it is a recipient of the actions of the church's ministry. The salvation-historical derivations of church authority along the line 'God, Christ, Peter, Pope, bishops, priest' also led to an underestimation of the intrinsically charaismatic community and thus to a failure to recognize the 'fellowship of the Holy Spirit' which is 'with us all'.

The charismatic community does not find its unity first in the monarchical episcopate or in the universal episcopate of the Pope, but already in the fellowship of the Son with the Father in which the Holy Spirit is included, as John 17.20f. suggests.[16] The unity of the community is in truth the trinitarian fellowship of God himself, of which it is a reflection and in which it participates.

This fellowship with the Trinity and in the Trinity is held out to the community of the disciples because it is grounded in the prayer of Jesus, which the community is certain is heard by the Father. The community is the 'lived out' Trinity. In the community, that mutual love is practised which corresponds to the eternal love of the Trinity. The groundings of the church's ministry in the rule of God which I have mentioned cannot exist apart from this grounding of the community in the triune God himself. The pneumatology of the monarchical episcopate must therefore be taken up into the trinitarian pneumatology of the whole community of God if the reductions and constraints in the understanding of the Holy Spirit which I mentioned at the beginning are to be overcome. Sobornost is the church – the one, entire church.

In the fellowship of the Holy Spirit there comes into being a fellowship of men and women without superiors or inferiors, a fellowship of men and women freed through love. If we are to understand this fellowship better than has been the case previously it may be helpful to take up again an old idea from pneumatology, which has often been suppressed and on many occasions forgotten: the idea of the Motherhood of the Holy Spirit.

When Count Zinzendorf founded the first American community of brothers and sisters in Pennsylvania in 1741, at the same time he preached the recognition of the Motherly office of the Holy Spirit: 'That the Father of our Lord Jesus Christ is our true Father and the Spirit of Jesus Christ is our true Mother; because the Son of the living God, his one, only-begotten Son, is our true Brother . . . The Father must love us and cannot do otherwise, the Mother must guide us through the world and cannot do otherwise, and the Son, our Brother, must love the soul as his own soul, the body as his own body, because we are flesh of his flesh and bone of his bone, and he cannot do otherwise.'[17] Certainly the doctrine of the Motherly office of the Spirit can lead to unjustified speculations about the Trinity as a 'divine family' with Father, Mother and Child. But what is meant is first and foremost the Motherhood of God, which has equal rights with his Fatherhood; this justifies the full and independent integration of femininity into the dignity of the image of God and leads to a community of brothers and sisters, not just of 'brothers'.

Zinzendorf was stimulated to this recognition by the homilies of Makarios, which had recently been retranslated in his time by none other than Gottfried Arnold. Of course Makarios's famous *Fifty Homilies* also deeply influenced the mysticism of the Orthodox churches. Historically, they were probably not by the Egyptian desert father Makarios, but by the Syrian leader of the Messalians, Symeon of Mesopotamia.[18] Symeon the new theologian was influenced by him. Historical research indicates that the historical Makarios is to be understood in terms of the theology of the Syrian and Jewish-Christian communities. Hebrew and Syriac make it easy to call the Holy Spirit 'the heavenly Mother', since *ruach* and *ruho* are feminine. And in the Gospel to the Hebrews, too, we find:

'Even so did my Mother, the Holy Spirit, take me by one of my hairs and carry me away to the great mountain Tabor.'[19] But Makarios/Symeon also has two important theological arguments for the motherly office of the Holy Spirit: 1. He quotes John 14.26 with Isa.66.13: the Holy Spirit is the Paraclete, the promised Comforter, who will 'comfort you as one is comforted by one's mother'. 2. Only those who are 'born again' can see the kingdom of God. Men and women are born again from the Spirit (John 3.3-6). So believers are 'children of the Spirit'. The Spirit is their 'mother'.[20]

So the designation of the Holy Spirit as Mother is of Syrian origin. In contrast to Basil, for whom the Spirit proceeds from the Father, and Augustine, for whom the Spirit represents the bond of love between the Father and the Son, the Syrian and later also the Ethiopian church fathers introduced into the discussion the image of the femininity and the Motherly office of the Spirit and the image of the 'family'.[21] This idea helps to overcome patriarchalism in the image of God and the domination of men in the church. It serves to justify a liberated community in which women and men are brothers and sisters, as Paul envisaged it in Gal.3.28f., on the basis of the same baptism and the same eschatological inheritance in the kingdom of God.

The personality of the Holy Spirit can be grasped more precisely with the image of the Mother than with other images. The unique fellowship of the Trinity can be understood better with the image of the Mother than with any other ideas of the Spirit. Moreover the symbol of the dove for the Holy Spirit is also feminine and points in the same direction. In its feminine and motherly characteristics 'the fellowship of the Holy Spirit' has a healing, liberating and sensitizing effect.

4. A trinitarian doctrine of scripture: the fulfilment of scripture in the Spirit

The Protestant church understands itself to be the church of the Holy Spirit. It is a *creatura verbi*. Protestant theology recognizes Holy Scripture as the *norma normans*, the normative norm: it is 'scriptural' theology. More than any other Christian church, the Protestant church has stressed the scriptural principle and subjected everything to the criticism of Holy Scripture. But in this tradition reductions and one-sidednesses in pneumatology have arisen which could be overcome without giving up the scriptural principle, rightly understood.

The post-Reformation, old Protestant doctrine of the verbal inspiration of scripture down to the Massoretic punctuation of the Old Testament texts led to Protestant biblicism and evangelical fundamentalism: Holy Scripture is given by the Spirit and thus has become the revelation of God in the Holy Spirit. There is no revelation of the Holy Spirit outside scripture or beyond it. Holy Scripture is the 'perfect', 'exhaustive', 'clear', 'inerrant' revelation of God. So it has normative authority in all things to do with God.[22]

What pneumatology is to be found in this old Protestant doctrine of scripture? God reveals himself through his eternal Word. This eternal Word has become flesh in Jesus Christ. It was attested in writing in the Holy Scriptures of the Old and New Testaments. So there is no longer any difference between the Word of God and its written form because scripture according to God's will contains this Word of God completely and fully. The power of God through which Holy Scripture came into being is the Holy Spirit. Therefore his influence is called verbal inspiration. Word and sacrament are to be used in the church 'in accordance with scripture' (Augsburg Confession VII).

Here we find the following order of legitimation: God – Word of God – Holy Scripture. As far as God's Word is concerned we can follow Karl Barth in making a further distinction between the eternal Word of God, the Word of God incarnate, the Word of God made scripture and the Word of God proclaimed through the church.[23] The Holy Spirit is mentioned in the inspiration of holy scripture. If one wanted to grasp his activity further, one could say that as he becomes active in the incarnation of the Word in Mary, so he becomes active in the written expression of the Word in holy scripture, and therefore also in the reception of the Word in human hearts. Nevertheless there is an irrefutable impression that this pneumatology is a subordinationist pneumatology: the Holy Spirit is none other than the effectiveness of the Word of God. The monarchical orientation is unmistakable: God rules through his Word. His holy scripture has normative authority. It calls for an attitude of unconditional recognition and obedience. So God rules through Christ by virtue of the Holy Spirit.

In order to elevate this monarchical pneumatology into a more comprehensive trinitarian pneumatology and to preserve its truth there, we need first to supplement it with eucharistic pneumatology. Holy Scripture is not just testimony to the Word of God but at the same time also testimony to the human answer. It is not just testimony to the history of God with human beings, but also testimony to the history of human beings with God. To the Word corresponds the answer, to the promise hope, to the gospel faith, to the word of judgment the complaint, to God's silence human despair, and to the divine charis the human eucharist. The parallel exegesis of scripture as the testimony of human beings encountered by faith, i.e. existentialist interpretation, need not conflict with the exegesis of scripture as the revelation of God.

What human beings experience in their history with the Word of God we call the workings of the Holy Spirit. By the inspiration of the Spirit they respond to the divine Word and introduce their whole experience of life into their thanksgiving, just as they introduce their whole experience of suffering into their lamentation. In this broader sense holy scripture is also the testimony of human responses, and in it and with it at the same time also the revelation of the sighs and thanksgivings of the Spirit of God. Scripture itself is not only commandment but also prayer; not only proclamation but also narrative; not only recollection but also a vision full of hope. Through scripture not only does God speak to human beings but human beings also speak to God.

With regard to revelation, one can regard Holy Scripture literally as final proclamation, in so far as it attests the one through whom God has spoken to us 'last of all': the Son, whom he has made Lord of the world (Heb.1.2). With regard to the eucharist, however, scripture is open to the unlimited wealth of the Holy Spirit and the experiences of his powers which are still to come, and which 'will be poured out on all flesh'. With regard to revelation, the divine revelation is concentrated on the final Christ, the only-begotten Son. But with regard to the eucharist the response of praise extends to the whole creation, to earth and heaven (Phil.2.10f.). So we may understand scripture as being closed christologically but open pneumatologically to the future of the kingdom of glory. That is no contradiction. However, this difference in points of reference is concealed by the doctrine of the verbal inspiration of scripture in so far as it gives the impression that inspiration is complete with the closing of the canon. But in truth the inspiration of scripture is also the inverbation of the Spirit. This is focussed on the indwelling of the Spirit in the community and in the heart, which is in turn focussed on the innovation of heaven and earth, if the Holy Spirit is in other respects the power of the new creation.

If we take the two perspectives together, it becomes clear that holy scripture may not be isolated from the future which is specific to it because it is promised by it. If Christ is called 'the centre of scripture' by the Reformers, then the kingdom of God must be called 'the future of scripture'. Scripture points beyond itself to the history of the coming kingdom of God. This history is the history of the Spirit, which brings together God's people for the coming kingdom, communicates the powers of healing, and preserves and establishes creation for the day of glory. Holy scripture is no self-contained system of a heavenly doctrine, but promise open to its own fulfilment. It is God's promise made scripture and a pledge of God's future. The 'scriptural' foundation 'It is written' applies in history, but it applies until the dawn of that future in which everyone sees that 'It has happened'. In this eschatological respect holy scripture is history, namely historical testimony to a history which points beyond itself. Holy scripture is a history in which the future of the kingdom of glory has already become event and has dawned. So holy scripture is initially fulfilled in the experience of the Holy Spirit and completely fulfilled in the realm of the glory to come. The goal of the history of Christ which is attested in it (*finis historiae Christi*) is 1. justification in faith; 2. sanctification in the rule of Christ; and 3. glorification in the kingdom of God.[24]

So we can supplement the subordinationist pneumatology of the old Protestant doctrine of scripture with eucharistic pneumatology and incorporate both into trinitarian pneumatology. We then get a doctrine of scripture which describes the function of scripture in the comprehensive history of the Trinity without giving up the normative and the critical sense of the evangelical scriptural principle. Through scripture and Spirit the triune God leads his creation to his kingdom and glorifies himself in it. The gift of scripture, its 'patience and its comfort' (Rom.15.4), are part of the 'fellowship of the Holy Spirit': the best part of it. If I might put it that way, in the 'fellowship of the Holy Spirit' the relationship of obedience becomes a relationship of friendship towards the biblical writers and communities.

5. Trinitarian doxology: The fellowship of the Spirit 'with the Father and the Son'

We know of two forms of trinitarian doctrine from the theological tradition: monarchical and eucharistic.[25] In conclusion I want to attempt to elevate both orders of the Trinity which arise out of the knowledge of salvation history into the trinitarian doxology of the eternal God.

The monarchical form of the Trinity is manifest from all the works of God: the Father creates *through* the Son *in* the power of the Holy Spirit. The Father sends the Son and the Spirit. The Father redeems through the surrender of the Son by virtue of the Holy Spirit. In this respect all activities proceed from the Father. They are mediated through the Son and effective in the Spirit. The Spirit brings to fulfilment the action of the Father and the Son. Here the distinctive activity of the Spirit consists in the fact that the Spirit does nothing on his own, but realizes the work of the Father and the Son.[26] All that God brings about takes place in the Holy Spirit. All divine action is therefore to be understood to have a pneumatological focus. However, here the personality of the Spirit can hardly be recognized: if he is nothing other than the effect of the divine activity and the goal of divine action, then the Spirit could just as well be thought of as a power. Nor does the Holy Spirit have any activity here which is not that of the Father and the Son: the Spirit proceeds from the Father and is sent by the Son into the world. He receives his existence from the Father and his mission from the Son and gives nothing to the Father and the Son from his side. The Western church, and Protestant theology in particular, have often enough made this form of the Trinity a single form: all activity proceeds from God in the light of creation, revelation, mission and sanctification. The church takes part in this activity by being obedient to its mission. It then has it were the revealing, sending God behind it and the world as its mission field before it.

The eucharistic form of the Trinity is the direct reversal of the monarchical form of the Trinity which I have just described. In the sighing of lamentation, in thanksgiving, in the praise and glorification of the Father, all activity proceeds from the Holy Spirit. The Holy Spirit glorifies the Son, and through the Son and together with him the Father, until the goal of creation and of all the works of God has been reached, and the praise of God fills heaven and earth and brings it bliss. So in the 'fellowship of the Holy Spirit' we not only experience the works of God, but also begin to realize their goal through thanksgiving. In the power of the Spirit we recognize the Father in the image of the Son, call through the Son to the Father, and praise the Father for the sake of the Son. In the eucharistic form of the Trinity, activity proceeds from the Spirit and through the Son and with him to the Father. The Father receves the praise of a creation renewed in the Spirit. Here the Holy Spirit is not only the creator of this praise but also unites the whole of creation through the Son with the Father. If we think theologically in this movement of the eucharist, then we have as it were God before us and the world in us and around us. In that case we are not only representing God before the world but the world before God, and are giving thanks and praise representatively for the whole creation.

Both forms of the Trinity belong to the history of salvation. Both show the Trinity from a particular perspective and in an order aimed at a particular goal: Father - Son - Spirit and Spirit - Son - Father. In the monarchical form of the Trinity the Spirit appears subordinated to the Father and the Son: he is their activity. In the eucharistic form of the Trinity the Spirit appears similarly subordinated to the Son and the Father: he glorifies them.

Both forms of the Trinity are elevated and transcended by the trinitarian doxology which the Nicene creed indicates with the statement, 'Who with the Father and the Son together is worshipped and glorified.' Worship and glorification certainly stem from the experience of salvation and the expression of thanksgiving, but they go beyond them. In worship and glorification the triune God is loved and praised for his own sake.

With the trinitarian doxology, the beatific vision, seeing God face to face, begins. Therefore the trinitarian doxology looks beyond the history of salvation into the eternal being of the Trinity itself. And in this eternal being of the Trinity the Spirit no longer appears in its temporal order, *after* or *under* the Son and the Father, but in its eternal fellowship *with* the Father and the Son.

In its monarchical form the Trinity opens itself up for creation and its salvation. In its eucharistic form the Trinity takes up the redeemed creation into its glory. In the trinitarian doxology the Trinity appears in its eternal perfection. In this doxology of God for God's sake, all trinitarian pneumatology finds its fulfilment.

7

'Come Holy Spirit –
Renew the Whole of Creation'

1. The cry from the depths

The theme of the Seventh Assembly of the World Council of Churches is a prayer. It is a cry from the despair of death and a breath of the Spirit from this threatened creation, which is hungry for life.

At the beginning of every experience of divine salvation there is a cry from the creaturely depths. There is the cry of the tormented people of Israel in Egypt (Exodus 3.7). There is the dying cry of the forsaken Christ on the Roman cross (Mark 15.34). And God hears the cry from the depth of distress: he leads his people out of slavery into the freedom of the promised land; he leads his Christ out of death to the life of the future world. The sighing of the creatures who want to live and yet must die rises up to God today from our ravaged earth: 'The whole creation has been groaning together in travail with us until now' (Romans 8.22). It suffers under the power of time, is dying from the violence of death and cries out for the presence of the eternal God in which it can live and abide.

Today an expectation is rising up from our ravaged earthly world. It is the cry for the liberating and life-giving power of God. In this cry the threatened creation is already open to the coming of the Spirit of God. Mourning and expectation lie together upon the whole unredeemed earth. So in this sighing and crying for the saving Spirit of God we can also already trace the coming of this Spirit which when we fall silent 'intercedes for us with sighs which cannot be uttered' (Romans 8.26). The prayer 'Come Holy Spirit' expresses the dying cry of dying creatures and in the breath of the Spirit calls for freedom and life.

What is the distress from which the creation cries to its Creator? It is twofold. It is the distress of the inexorable and progressive destruction of nature by human beings, and it is the distress of the destructibility of nature itself which makes possible this human aggression against it. Today nature is increasingly being subjected to the domination and exploitation of human civilization. But that is possible only because earthly creatures, plants, animals and human beings are subject to transitoriness, the power of time and the violence of death. The

70

liberation of non-human nature from the rule of human violence is one side, and the liberation of nature and human beings from the violent rule of time and death is the other side of their outcry from the depths for life.

The facts and trends of the present 'ecological crisis' are so well-known and generally felt so painfully that they need no more than a mention.[1]

The extension of existing technological civilization is irreversibly destroying more and more species of plants and animals each year. It is poisoning the air and soil, and turning the fertile earth into wildernesses. These forms of the destruction of nature, which are following one another with increasing rapidity, derive primarily from the industrial states.

At the same time the human population is increasing. After an equilibrium which lasted for a thousand years, in the last sixty years it has quadrupled and at the beginning of the next millennium will have reached the figure of 10 billion. The need of human beings for food and energy is rising as rapidly as resources are declining. The increase in population is coming primarily from Third World countries.

Injustice and violence have split human beings into a First World and a Third World and have led to devastating human and environmental catastrophes in the Third World. Humankind has got caught up in a vicious circle in which exploitation leads to debt and debt leads to the squandering of the natural foundations of the life of peoples. The spread of human civilization has already reached the limits of the cosmic conditions for life on earth and is beginning to disturb their equilibrium, as is shown by the 'greenhouse effect', which will steadily alter the climatic zones on earth over the next century. Life on this earth will become increasingly difficult. First of all the weakest members of the community of creation, the plants and animals, will die, and then human beings – first the children, the poor and the sick.

Because we can no longer recover the poisons which are rising into the atmosphere and seeping into the ground, and cannot assess the damage they are causing, we do not even know whether human life on this earth still has a future or even a present, which is unavoidably becoming past. Because we cannot control the population explosion, and many peoples evidently do not even want to control it, for the majority of those in the Third World life will become increasingly hard and increasingly short. This is the real distress of living beings on earth which makes us human beings cry together with, and as representatives of, all other living beings to the God who creates life and loves life. It is a mortal distress which has long made those weaker living beings on earth, together with us human beings and as our representatives, cry out to the God of life. There is a fellowship of creation, but today it has become a fellowship of suffering in which victims and perpretrators share and from which there is no escape.

Now this human destruction of nature would not happen were not non-human nature itself fragile and destructible. Human beings would not destroy them-

71

selves were they incapable of such destruction and were they themselves not mortal. Evidently the earthly creation is no longer in the sound state it was at the beginning, of which the Creator could say, 'See, it is all very good', but has succumbed to the powers of destruction. Evidently the present creation is not yet in the state of perfection in which it can remain eternally. Evidently the earthly creation has come under the power of time and the violence of death. So Paul called it a 'creation in bondage' (Rom.8.21). What we now empirically call nature is no longer the paradise of the original creation nor yet the new eternal creation. At present a sorrow lies upon the earthly creation. A longing for abiding and happy life torments it. At present we live in a winter of creation and are waiting for the spring of its new creation. We expect from such a 'renewal of the whole creation' not only the overcoming of that destruction which we human beings have caused to nature and to ourselves, but also a transformation of the present conditions of this earthly creation, the destructibility of nature and the destructive capacity of human beings. The whole creation must be reborn from the power of time and the violence of death to its eternal life. We human beings must be born again if we are to unlearn how to do evil and are no longer to know death. All that lives, including us human beings, longs for such a 'rebirth of the cosmos' (Matt.19.28).

Why do all mortal creatures cry out, and why do all victims of violence call to the 'Holy Spirit'? According to the messianic traditions of Judaism and Christianity, God has created all things through his wisdom in the power of his Spirit. Through his Spirit the Creator is present in each of his creatures. By virtue of his Spirit he forms the community of creation. In his Spirit they come to life, and without his Spirit they die (Ps.104). His eternal Spirit is the motive force in all things. In all that lives, life is dominated by suffering and anxiety about death. Therefore all that lives cries to the Spirit of God in which alone it can live and need not die. What is there and cannot abide, longs for the eternal being of God in which it can abide. Whatever feels forsaken and destroyed cries out for the Holy Spirit as children cry out for their mothers, in order to be safe. So the Holy Spirit is also called 'the Lord who frees' and 'the Mother who brings to life': *dominum et vivificantem,* as the Nicene Creed has it. If we are waiting with the earthly creation for the coming of the Holy Spirit, then we are waiting for both liberation from injustice and violence, and liberation from time and death.

2. Creation in the Spirit of God

According to Christian understanding creation is a trinitarian process: God the Father creates through the Son in the power of the Holy Spirit. All things are therefore created 'by God', formed 'through God' and exist 'in God'.[2] 'See in the creation of this being the Father as the origin who underlies it, the Son as the one who creates, and the Spirit as the one who completes, so that the serving spirits have their beginning in the will of the Father, are brought into being

72

through the activity of the Son, and are completed through the existence of the Spirit.' So already wrote Basil the Great.[3] For a long time the tradition of the Western church stressed only the first aspect, in order to distinguish God the Creator from the world as his creation and to stress his transcendence. In so doing it robbed nature of its divine mystery and surrendered it to desacralization through secularization. The important thing today is to rediscover the immanence of the Creator in his creation in order to draw all creation into reverence for the Creator. The best help towards doing that is the christological concept of creation by the Word of God and the pneumatological understanding of creation in the Spirit of God.

According to Proverbs 8.22-31 God created the world through his daughter, Wisdom:

> The Lord created me at the beginning of his work,
> the first of his acts of old.
> Ages ago I was set up,
> at the first before the beginning of the earth . . .
> And I was beside him, like a master workman;
> and I was daily his delight,
> rejoicing before him always,
> rejoicing in his inhabited world
> and delighting in the children of men.

According to the wisdom literature this creative wisdom can also be called the Word of God or the Spirit of God.[4] But what is meant is always the presence of God, immanent in the world, in all things. If all things are created by a God, then their multiplicity is preceded by an immanent unity. Through wisdom is formed the fellowship of creatures which exist with one another and for one another.

On the basis of the resurrection experiences, Christian theology saw in Christ both the Wisdom and the Word of God, through which the world was created. It recognized in Christ the cosmic wisdom through which all things exist, as Colossians shows. Christ is the divine mystery of the world. Anyone who honours Christ, also honours all created things in him and him in all created things.

> I am the light which is over all.
> I am the all; the all came forth from me
> and the all has returned to me.

> Lift up the stone and there you will find me.
> Cleave the wood and I am there.[5]

Where the Word of God is, there is also the Spirit of God. According to Gen.1.2, creation through the Word is preceded by the vibrant energy of the Spirit of God. God creates all things through his words, which name, distinguish and pass judgment. Therefore all things are individually different, 'each according to its kind'. But God always speaks in the breath of his Spirit, which brings to life. Word and Spirit complement each other in the fellowship of creation: the Word specifies and differentiates, the Spirit binds together and forms accord. Just as in human speech words are different, but are communicated in the same breath, so in a transferred sense one can say that God speaks through individual creatures and 'God breathes through all creation'.[6] The totality of creation which I here call the 'fellowship of creation' is supported by the breath of the Spirit of God.

Through Word and Spirit the Creator communicates himself to his creation and enters into it, as Wisdom 12.1 says:

> O Lord who loves the living,
> your immortal spirit is in all things.

So creation is not just to be called 'a work of his hands'. It is also the indirect mediating presence of God. All things are created in order that the 'common home' of all creatures shall become the 'house of God', in which God can live eternally with his creatures and his creatures can live eternally with him. That is expressed biblically with the image of the temple of God:

> The Most High does not dwell in temples made with hands; as the prophet says, 'Heaven is my throne, and earth my footstool. What house will you build for me, says the Lord, or what is the place of my rest?' (Acts 7.48f., citing Isa.66.1f.).

The vision in Rev.21.1-4 of the new creation of all things contains along with the image of the heavenly Jerusalem the idea that in the end the whole world will become the temple into which the glory of God can enter and rest. From the original creation onwards, the Spirit of God is present everywhere, and sustains, nurtures and gives life to all things in heaven and on earth. His power and his wisdom is at work in all things and shares existence, life and movement with them.[7] According to prophetic and apocalyptic hopes, the new creation of all things will then make heaven and earth God's dwelling, in which God finds his eternal sabbath rest, and as his guests God's creatures will partake in his eternal life and his eternal joy.

From this view of the Spirit of God in all things and the preparation of all things to be the dwelling place of God there follows a cosmic worship of God and a worship of God in all things. What believers do in churches is representatively applied to the whole cosmos. Solomon's temple was already built to the dimensions of the cosmos as they were then understood, so that it could represent the macrocosm in microcosm and correspond to it. The presence of the Word and Spirit of God in the church of Christ is the foreshadowing and the beginning of the presence of the Word and Spirit of God in the new creation of all things. By its foundation and nature the church is orientated on the cosmos. It was dangerous modern reductionism to limit the church to the human world. But if the world is orientated on the cosmos, then the 'ecological crisis' of the earthly creation is also its own crisis, since through this destruction of the earth there is a destruction of the 'flesh of her flesh and bone of her bone'. When the weaker creatures die, the whole community of creation suffers. If the church understands itself as a representative of creation, then in the church this suffering of the weaker creatures becomes a conscious pain, and it has to cry out this pain in public protest. What suffers is no longer our 'human environment' but the creation which is destined to be 'God's environment'. Any intervention in creation which cannot be made good is sacrilege. Its consequence is that the perpetrators excommunicate themselves. The nihilistic destruction of nature is atheism put into practice.[8]

3. The preservation of creation through the Holy Spirit

All creatures are dependent on the presence of the Spirit of God: 'When you take away their breath, they die and return to the dust. When you send forth your Spirit they are created, and you renew the face of the earth' (Ps.104.29f.). According to Christian understanding, the earth was created *ex nihilo*. It follows from this that it is constantly threatened by nothingness and can only exist and live through the presence of the divine Spirit. The Creator must constantly fortify his creation and preserve it from annihilation. The tradition expresses that by saying either that God sustains what he has created or that at every moment the Creator repeats his original Yes to his creation. The former is the idea of the preservation of the world (*conservatio mundi*) and the latter is the idea of continual creation (*creatio continua*).[9] Both ideas, however, are one-sidedly related to the original creation and do not yet suggest the new creation of all things. The original creation and its preservation serve a goal. It is the consummation of creation in the realm of divine glory.[10] All that is created longs to participate in the divine glory. What has been created is preserved for that. That is the goal of the continuation of creation. The 'creation in the beginning' (Gen.1.1) suggests this goal and the longing of all suffering creatures waits for this coming (Rom.8.19ff.). Anyone who wants to speak of the present activity of God in the world must have this goal in mind: God preserves his creatures for their consummation. His preservation of creation is itself already a preparation for their consummation. Every act which preserves creation from destruction is an act of hope for its future. When we say that 'God's grace is new every morning' (Lam.3.23), we recognize in each sunrise a prelude to the new creation: 'Behold, I make all things new' (Rev.21.5).

How does God preserve his creation? He preserves its spirit of life despite

75

human sin and cosmic disorder. He preserves it through his patience, since through his toleration of what conflicts with life he creates time for his creatures to live. His long-suffering gives room to his creatures. The preserver of creation is omnipotent to the degree that he 'hopes all things and endures all things' (I Cor.13.7). In this way God loves his creatures and lures them to return from death to life and to come home to his eternal kingdom. If we look on the miracle of creation as a communication of the creative love of God, than we shall discover this love's inexhaustible power of suffering in the miracle of the preservation of creation. Both express the hope of God for the future of his creation. The history of the suffering of creation is also the history of the suffering of God. The history of the repentance of God's creatures as they turn towards life is also a history of God's joy in his creatures. For through his immanent Spirit he takes part in the fate of his creatures. In the sighing and groaning of suffering creatures, the Spirit of God itself sighs and groans and calls for redemption. The God who suffers with his creatures through his indwelling Spirit is the firm hope of the creatures. This makes it certain that the creator loves his creatures and has not forsaken them.

The Pauline talk of 'creation in bondage' (Rom.8) and the stress on the reconciliation of all things through Christ (Col.1) presupposes that the present reality is no longer the original creation nor yet the new creation. It has come under the power of time and the violence of death and is exposed to destruction. No matter how one explains this incomplete state of creation between origin and consummation, the only important thing is the community of suffering between human beings and other earthly creatures. Here the fellowship of creation is the fellowship of suffering. Nature is not saved if it is made part of the human world, nor are human beings redeemed if they return to nature. There is redemption in this unredeemed world only in a shared hope for the reconciliation and new creation of all things.[11]

The new creation of all things is like the spring, when all that lives becomes green and fertile again, and the ice under which the streams of life are hidden begins to break. Many Christian Christmas and Easter hymns depict the new creation as the final, eternal spring of creation.

For the present ecological discussion this means that we discover independent nature in the human environment and the sighing creation of God in independent nature. The usual term 'environment' is anthropocentric. It denotes nature only in so far as it is related to human beings. The environment is nature in so far as it is appropriated and controlled by human beings. If we look on the whole of nature only as our own 'environment', then our aim is none other than the total dissolution of the independence of nature. The desacralization of nature is followed by its degradation, so that it becomes the human environment. In this context 'environment' is an explicitly aggressive term. It may be that nature is reacting to it in an unfriendly way and beginning counter-evolutions.

76

It is therefore vitally necessary to rediscover nature behind our own 'environment', as a subject with rights of its own. The 1982 UN World Charter for Nature rightly says that 'Every form of life is unique, warranting respect regardless of its worth for man.'[12] Human culture must be 'environmentally friendly', but the human environment must also be nature-friendly and take into account the laws and rhythms of nature and the natural environments of other living beings – plants, trees and animals. Only if nature's own rights are respected can one discover the inner side of nature, turned towards God, which we call creation. 'Nature' is the present, immanent side of creation; creation is the transcendent side of nature. That means that every natural being contains an immanent transcendence, and transcendence is immanent in every natural being. To call the reality in which and with which we live 'creation' is the strongest expression of resistance against the transformation of nature into the human environment and against its destruction. This resistance arises out of the hope for the liberation of creation from its present natural state to the eternal spring of the new world. It is resistance not only to the ecological self-destruction of humankind which is annihilating the foundations of its own life, but also to the fetters of its fragility and its sorrow.

4. The new creation of all things through the Spirit of God

The final new creation of all things goes far beyond the daily preservation of creation. It is the overcoming not only of destruction but of destructibility, not only of death through human violence but also of creaturely mortality. The fundamental conditions of present creation will be changed. Creation will be liberated from the power of time for the presence of eternity and from the power of death for eternal life. The creation which is everywhere threatened by chaos and annihilation will become completely safe in the eternal love of God.

Christ proclaimed this new creation of all things when he brought the kingdom of God to the poor, God's salvation to the sick and God's justice to sinners. For Christian hope, this new creation of all things begins with the resurrection of Christ from the dead and the overcoming of the power of death by his resurrection.

In Christian understanding, the day of Christ's resurrection is the first day of the new creation. Therefore it begins with the new creation of light. That is the 'knowledge of the glory of God in the face of Jesus Christ' (II Cor.4.6). According to what the witnesses tell us, the 'Easter appearances' took place in the cosmic light of the first day of the new creation. Therefore at a very early stage the Christians called the day of resurrection the 'eighth day', i.e. the first day of the new creation. They understood the resurrection in cosmic and not just in historical dimensions, as the beginning of the new world in which all tears will be wiped away and death will be no more.

So the Orthodox Easter liturgy says:

Now all is filled with light
– heaven, earth and the kingdom of the dead.
The whole creation celebrates
the resurrection of Christ
in which it is grounded.

Paul Gerhardt's Protestant Easter hymn conveys the same message:

The sun, the earth, all creation,
all that formerly was troubled,
now rejoices on this day
when the prince of this world was laid low.

It is not by chance that the Christian Easter festival coincides with the spring festival: spring in nature was understood as the symbol of the eternal spring of the new creation of all things. Nor is it by chance that Christian Pentecost coincides with the beginning of summer: the greening and blossoming of nature was seen as a symbol of the eternal enlivening of the whole of creation in the breath of the divine Spirit. With the resurrection of Christ from the dead and the annihilation of death which takes place through him, the eschatological process of the new creation of all transitory and mortal things begins. Anyone who cries out for the 'Creator Spirit' from the mortal distress of the earthly creation expects the resurrection of the body and the resurrection of nature along with the resurrection of Christ.

With the rebirth of Christ from death to eternal life we also expect the rebirth of the whole cosmos. Nothing that God has created is lost. Everything returns in transfigured form. So from the Spirit of the new creation of all things we expect the overcoming of human violence and cosmic chaos. In addition, we expect the overcoming of the power of time and the violence of death. Finally, we expect eternal comfort in the wiping of tears from our eyes. We expect eternal joy in the dance of fellowship with all creatures and with the triune God.

We use many images in an attempt to picture for ourselves this new creation of all things for which we long. They are all strong in denying the negative aspects under which we suffer: 'There shall be no mourning nor crying nor pain any more', for 'God will wipe every tear from their eyes and death will be no more' (Rev.21.4). However, they are weak on the positive side, because in this damaged life we cannot yet have any experience of that. Yet we could not form any concepts of the negative without anticipations of the positive. We suffer because we love; we fear dying because we want to live; we want to abide and not pass away. From the positive experinces of life, love, abiding we form conceptions of hope for the new creation of all things. So we speak of the 'kingdom of God' which will drive away the powers of chaos and death. We speak of the 'eternal life' which overcomes death. We hope for the 'divine righteousness' which will drive injustice and violence from the earth. We attempt to hope for the resurrection of dead creatures and their rebirth to eternal life. Otherwise we would despair over the mass deaths which take place around us every day. From hope for eternal life is born new love for this vulnerable and mortal life. This love does not give up. If we had to give up hope for even one creature, then Christ would not have risen for us. Love grounded in hope is the strongest medicine against the spread of the sickness of resignation. Modern cynicism which can tolerate the death of so many creatures is a covenant with death. But we Christians are what Christoph Blumhardt called 'protest people against death'. So we cry from the depths of mortal distress to the Spirit of God. So we call to the Spirit which sustains all creation and wait for the Spirit of the new creation of all things. Our cry from the depths is a sign of life – a sign of God's life.

8

The Inviting Unity of the Triune God

The more you reflect on the mystery of the Trinity, the less you seem to understand it definitively. What had been settled becomes an open question, and what you understood proves elusive again. You keep beginning again from the beginning. Therefore the doctrine of the Trinity remains incomplete. For those theologians who are preoccupied with it, indeed caught up in it, it is an ongoing process of learning. But for that reason the doctrine of the Trinity also remains indispensable: you cannot get rid of it, even if you turn to other theological themes, for example 'political theology'.[1] For theologians, a doctrine of the Trinity is the supreme but certainly also the most humbling task that is posed to them.

I begin with these remarks, which I also apply to myself, because in this short chapter I cannot cover either the whole of the doctrine of the Trinity or even its incalculable consequences for the understanding of human beings, history and the cosmos. But in connection with my book on *The Trinity and the Kingdom of God* I shall limit myself here to a few remarks which are meant to help with critical points in contemporary discussion. I shall concentrate these remarks on questions about the grounding of the Trinity in the history of salvation and the trinitarian determination of the unity of the Trinity.

1. The starting point for the development of the Christian doctrine of the Trinity

Since antiquity, like the Christian doctrine of God generally, the Christian doctrine of the Trinity has had two sides: one philosophical and biblical, the other speculative and salvation-historical. We can also see these two sides as two elements in the one, hermeneutical process. Even then, however, the question remains from which side one must start, and which side should be the subject and which the predicate.

With the help of the natural light of reason, by the cosmological proofs for the existence of God, Thomas Aquinas demonstrated that there is one God and that God is one. He took up the Christian tradition in order to know and understand this God as the Father, the Son and the Holy Spirit. According to his method, knowledge of the existence and unity of God precedes the revelatory knowledge of the triune God and also governs it; it is as it were the universal framework for the particular salvation- historical picture. Conversely, however, the salvation-historical image of the Trinity makes it necessary to see the universal framework as already being itself divided in a threefold way.

When Tertullian coined the formula *una substantia - tres personae* he derived knowledge of the three persons from salvation history and introduced them into the concept of the one, eternal divine substance, so that this was then to be thought of as existing in three persons or hypostases. The three great Cappadocian fathers proceeded in precisely the same way. Augustine and Thomas also developed a trinitarian ontology of supreme being from the knowledge of the Trinity in salvation history.[2] They already thought of God, to use Hegel's terminology, not only as supreme substance but at the same time also as absolute subject, stating that God is the subject who knows himself and wills himself in eternity, and then saw the 'Father' in the divine subject of understanding and will, the 'Son' in the word which proceeds from his understanding, and the 'Holy Spirit' in the love which proceeds from his understanding and his will. If there was an image of this one divine subject, it followed for them that this could only be in each individual human soul governing the body.

Insight into the threefold nature of the supreme being gained in this way derives from salvation history. Through this insight the knowledge from salvation history becomes eternal. However, if we understand the unfolding of the Christian doctrine of the Trinity like this we are already on the wrong track: the knowledge of the triune God is governed by revelation and salvation history, and the knowledge of the Godhead of this triune God is to be described in terms of philosophy, i.e. of cosmology, world history and ontology. In epistemological questions about the Christian Trinity no way leads from above downwards which has not begun below. There is no way from the universal to the particular which does not begin in the particular. This is shown clearly, in my view, by the speculative doctrines of the Trinity in German Idealism which attempt to think of God in terms of the modern 'metaphysics of subjectivity', as Martin Heidegger has called them.

Now if God is to be understood in terms of his concept as the absolute subject, he must also be capable of distinguishing himself from himself, differentiating himself in himself, and identifying himself with himself.[3] The process of reflection and love make up the process within the Trinity in the immediate divine life.

If we take this starting point for the presentation of a modern doctrine of the Trinity, as has been done most recently by Karl Barth and Karl Rahner, we can still give reasons why the historical revelation of the absolute divine subject

81

must be his 'self-revelation', why human salvation must lie in the 'self-communication' of the absolute divine subject, and why this self-revelation or self-communication must have the inner self-differentiation of the divine subject as the transcendental condition of its possibility.[4] But it is impossible to deduce that this 'self-revelation' and this 'self-communication' took place specifically in Jesus of Nazareth, crucified under Pontius Pilate, according to that 'little bundle of reports from the time of the Roman empire', as Barth called the New Testament. For that very reason it is also difficult to apply the concepts derived from the metaphysics of the absolute subject to the salvation history attested in the Bible. Neither Barth's formula of the 'one personal God in three modes of being' nor Rahner's thesis of the one divine 'subject in three distinct modes of subsistence' does justice to the history which is played out between Jesus the Son, 'Abba' his Father, and the Spirit. The personal encounter of the Father who loves the Son, the Son who prays to the Father, and the Spirit who confesses and glorifies the Father and the Son, which is so impressively attested in the New Testament, is not covered by those formulae in modern doctrines of the Trinity which are arrived at deductively.[5]

From this I conclude that the starting point for the Christian doctrine of the Trinity must be the salvation history attested in the Bible: the history of the Father, the Son and the Spirit. I further conclude that the method of the Christian doctrine of the Trinity must correspond to the method of the Old Testament knowledge of God: there we always have 'Yahweh is God' and 'Yahweh has become king'. The starting point is the historical and particular revelation of Yahweh which is experienced in a concrete way, but the end is the universal recognition that Yahweh is God and none beside him. The name reveals the subject and the subject determines the predicate. That means that the Christian doctrine of the Trinity proceeds from the concrete and particular history of the Father, Son and Spirit attested in the Bible and leads to the universal revelation of its unity and Godhead.

'Natural revelation is not that from which we come but the light towards which we go.'[6] The light of nature has always also been understood in Christian tradition as the radiance and aura of the light of glory.

From a biblical perspective it is not the Trinity but the unity of God that is the main problem. It is not possible to presuppose the unity of the Father, the Son and the Spirit and derive it from other sources of knowledge. The question of their unity derives from the specific history of the sending, surrender and resurrection of the Son and from the specific history of the sending, indwelling and making alive of the Holy Spirit which is bound up with it. So the answer will be a trinitarian one; it cannot be pre-trinitarian and theistic. The answer will be eschatological; it cannot be speculative.

By 'salvation-historical' approach I mean the orientation of the Christian doctrine of the Trinity on the history of God with Israel, with Christ and with the church in the power of his Spirit, that is attested in the Bible. I call this approach 'salvation-historical' in order to open up the limits which are set with the term 'biblical'. The divine salvation history presupposes the divine history of creation and is directed towards the realm of divine glory.

So those who begin from this salvation history begin not only from the history of Christ but also from the history of the Spirit which is bound up with the history of Christ. They perceive the eschatological horizon of this salvation history which is denoted by the symbol 'kingdom of God' and which consists in the glorification of the Father. Those who embark on such a salvation-historical approach begin with the knowledge of Jesus, the 'beloved Son', with the faith in 'Abba', the 'Father of Jesus Christ', and with the experience of the Holy Spirit which renews people in faith. They begin, therefore, with the recognition of these three indivisible and different subjects and their one, unique collaboration in their history, and investigate the relationship and the unity of these subjects. So they perceive this salvation history as the history of the revelation of these subjects and recognize their history as the history of the living, changing and unitive relationships of the three subjects I have mentioned. Because their history is the history of their relationships in community, I call it the trinitarian history of the Father, the Son and the Spirit.[7] This trinitarian history becomes salvation history as poor, sinful and dying people are taken up into the history of the Son and the Spirit with the Father to find in it divine life, until finally the whole creation finds its eternal life in the kingdom of glory.

Through 'being conformed with the Son' (Rom.8.29) by virtue of calling, justification and sanctification, men and women receive 'Sonship' and are taken up into the relationship of Jesus with the Father. Through the gift of the Holy Spirit they become 'children' of God, and like the Son and with him pray, 'Abba, beloved Father' (Rom.8.14f.). So 'salvation' means being taken up by the trinitarian history into the eternal life of the Trinity. 'The embodiment of revelation and redemption is the opening up to human beings of the cycle of divine relationships and the involvement of the soul in God's ownmost stream of life.'[8]

To differentiate this salvation-historical approach more closely, we speak of it in christological, pneumatological and eschatological terms. It is this differentiation which first leads to the development of a comprehensive, biblically-based doctrine of the Trinity. The christological orientation is undisputed. It was only with the development of the early church's christology from the New Testament christology of the Son that the need arose to develop the doctrine of the Trinity in the concept of God, because otherwise the unity of Jesus the Son with the Father and the Father with the Son cannot be expressed. But the christological foundation of the doctrine of the Trinity was predominant in the West and led to constraints which were rightly criticized by the theologians of the Eastern church as 'christomonistic'. Christology will already presuppose a pneumatology if it seeks to do justice to the history of Jesus attested by the Synoptic Gospels and if it is to preserve the history of the tradition of earliest Christian christology.[9] Jesus the Son comes from the Father in the power of the Holy Spirit: conceived by the Spirit, baptized by the Spirit, led by the Spirit into the wilderness to be tempted, proclaiming the gospel to the poor in the Spirit, healing the sick, and lastly sacrificing himself through the Spirit. In this respect the history of Jesus is a history of the Spirit. So christology will begin biblically with a pneumatological christology. It is only with the resurrection and exaltation of Jesus that the relationship is reversed: the Son sends the Spirit and is himself present in the life-giving Spirit. In this respect pneumatology will be christological pneumatology. The Holy Spirit is the 'Spirit of the Son', and the cross of Christ is the criterion for discerning the spirits. The history of the Son and the history of the Spirit condition each other. Through this recognition the tendency towards (clerical) christomonism is also excluded, as is the enthusiastic tendency towards the free flourishing of spiritualistic or even spiritistic pneumatology.[10]

The historical interaction of Spirit and Christ, Christ and Spirit, brings salvation for the godless and godforsaken creation, because it takes it up into fellowship with the Father. At the same time this historical interaction takes place for the revelation and glorification of the Father. If lost creatures find their salvation in fellowship with God, then God also comes into his own in his creation; and where God comes into his own in his creation we speak of the kingdom and the glory of God. The history of Christ and the Spirit takes place 'to the glory of the Father' (Phil.2.11). This eschatological consummation of salvation history is described christologically by saying that the Son hands over the kingdom to the Father, 'that God may be all in all' (I Cor.15.28), and pneumatologically by saying that the new creation is happy in praise of the triune God (Rev.1.6). I have understood salvation history as trinitarian history. So we shall see its eschatological consummation in trinitarian doxology. What takes place in the trinitarian history finds its goal in the doxology of the Trinity.[11]

2. Trinitarian concepts for the trinitarian history of salvation

Because the Christian 'doctrine' of God derives from the 'history' of God which is experienced and narrated, its task consists in providing an introduction to this history and its danger in doing away with this history in the concept. If trinitarian salvation history is the starting point for the doctrine of the Trinity, then the doctrine of the Trinity must be related to this history in such a way that it accredits itself in this history and initiates into this history. The concepts used in it must be drawn from the trinitarian history between the Father, the Son and the Holy Spirit and remain applicable to them. That means, first, that the doctrine of the Trinity must begin from the three distinct subjects of this history.

Biblically, Father, Son and Spirit are in fact subjects with a will and

84

understanding, who speak with one another, turn to one another in love, and together are 'one'. Whereas by 'God' Paul and the Synoptic Gospels mean the Father and clearly subordinate the Son to him, in the Gospel of John we find a developed trinitarian language: 'I and the Father are one', says the Johannine Jesus. He distinguishes between 'I' and 'you' and points to the unity which consists not only in knowing and willing but also in mutual indwelling: 'I in the Father – the Father in me' (14.11; 17.21, etc.). So the Father and the Son cannot be understood as being two modes of being of a single divine subject. They are not 'one' but 'at one', i.e. united, as is expressed by the plurals 'we' and 'us'.

So the concept of God may not do away with the subjective differences between the persons, because otherwise it would do away with the history which takes place between the Father, the Son and the Spirit for the salvation of the world. If we were to take up the neo-scholastic thesis of 'the one nature, the one knowledge, the one consciousness in God' along the lines of Karl Rahner and Karl Barth[12] and say that 'the one God subsists in three different modes of subsistence' or 'exists in three modes of being', then trinitarian salvation history would lose its concrete agents, for it is not distinct modes of subsistence of a single subject which act with each other in Gethesemane, and on the cross on Golgotha we do not have one mode of being of the one 'personal God' crying out to another mode of being.

What the 'one God', who will be 'all in all', *is*, i.e. his being, is first made manifest by the history of the Father and the Son and the Spirit.

Therefore the complementarity of the trinitarian concepts of person, relation, *perichoresis* and illumination must be noted in the doctrine of the Trinity. In connection with the trinitarian history of salvation, the concepts of the traditional doctrine of the Trinity are to be understood in a complementary way: no concept may subsume another and be made a generic term including the other.

Person and relation are to be understood as being complementary, because personality and relationality come into being at the same time. Person and relation are equally original. That means that Abba, the Father of Jesus Christ, is the Father of *this* Son. His Fatherhood in respect of the Son constitutes his person. His person as Father is determined by this unique relationship to the Son (the only-begotten Son). One cannot either say that God in himself is Father and that he only 'manifests' himself as such in respect of the Son, as some Orthodox theologians are inclined to assume, or that his person is none other than this relationship, as is occasionally said in scholastic theology. What distinguishes the Father from a Fatherhood is the same as what distinguishes a concrete being from a mode of being. One can address a father (*pater*) but not a fatherhood (*paternitas*). So the person does not precede the relationship, nor does the relationship precede the person. Both come into being at the same time, and therefore neither reduction nor subsuming are allowed.

The divine persons exist not only in relationships to one another but also, as the Johannine formulations show, *in one another*: the Son *in* the Father, the Father *in* the Son, the Holy Spirit *in* the Father and the Son, and the Father and the Son *in* the Holy Spirit. This intimate indwelling and complete interpenetration of the persons in one another is expressed by the doctrine of the trinitarian *perichoresis*. It denotes that trinitarian unity which goes out beyond the doctrine of persons and their relations: by virtue of their eternal love, the divine persons exist so intimately with one another, for one another and in one another that they constitute themselves in their unique, incomparable and complete unity.[13] The trinitarian unity is not a secondary 'communion' of the divine persons, nor are these persons 'modes of being' or 'repetitions' of the one God. Their relations within the Trinity and the trinitarian *perichoresis* are complementary: the perichoretic unity does not do away with the distinct relations any more than these damage it. The perichoretic concept of trinitarian unity gets over the dangers of tritheism and modalism equally. For the doctrine of *perichoresis* combines the threeness and the oneness without reducing the threeness to the oneness or the oneness to the threeness. The perichoretic unity is to be thought of as being equally original for the divine persons and the divine relations. If the life within the Trinity is understood perichoretically, then the divine life is as little lived by one subject alone as is the trinitarian history of the Father, the Son and the Spirit. It is the perichoretic concept of unity which is the trinitarian concept of triunity.[14]

Not only unity but also uniqueness is to be found in this perichoretic unity of the divine persons. The divine persons come to illuminate one another with eternal glory in the eternal *perichoresis* through their indwelling: the Holy Spirit glorifies the Son, and glorifies the Father together with the Son. The Father glorifies himself in the Son and in the Spirit, and the Son glorifies the Father through the Spirit. They do not just live relationally for one another; they do not just exist perichoretically in one another; they also express themselves and depict themselves with one another in the eternal light. As a result the perichoretic unity becomes a unity reflected in glory. The perichoretic integration of the persons in relation is complementary to their manifested distinctions.

Last of all we have to reflect on the complementarity of the trinitarian and soteriological concept of the unity of the triune God. If we follow salvation history as it is attested and experienced, we must understand the unity of the Father, the Son and the Holy Spirit in trinitarian terms and may not understand it monadically. If the consummation of salvation lies in the reunion with the triune God of creatures who have been separated and torn apart in themselves, then we must understand this unity of the Father, the Son and the Spirit as an open, inviting, reuniting, integrating unity.

According to the testimony of the Bible, the unity of the Son Jesus with the Father is a unity of will in sending and obedience, in surrender and resurrection: it is a relational unity. In addition, it is a unity of the mutual indwelling of the

Father in the Son and the Son in the Father, and of the Spirit in the Father and the Son: so it is a perichoretic unity. Furthermore it is a unity in transfiguration through the Holy Spirit. It is a reflected and manifested unity. The unity of the divine nature of the triune God is constituted by the definitions of unity which I have cited and does not do away with these.

However, the perichoretic concept of the unity of the Father, the Son and the Holy Spirit would not correspond to salvation history were it not understood soteriologically as an integrating concept of unity.[15] If the misery of creation lies in sin as separation from God, then salvation consists in the gracious acceptance of the creature into communion with God. Salvation lies in this union. The union with God of what is separated is not just an external union. It takes place by the Son accepting human beings into his relationship with the Father and making them children, sons and daughters, of the Father. It takes place by the Holy Spirit accepting human beings into his relationship with the Son and the Father and letting them participate in his eternal love and his eternal song of praise.

Therefore, conversely, we discover in the love through which the Father gives up the Son (John 3.16) the eternal love which is God himself (I John 4.16).[16] The affirmation with which the Father loves the world is the same affirmation through which he is himself in eternity. The salvation of creation consists in being accepted into the cycle of divine relationships and the mutual indwellings of the Father, the Son and the Spirit. Their mutual indwelling includes men and women: 'Whoever abides in love, abides in God and God in him' (I John 4.16). The indwelling is also the mystery of the new creation, 'That God may be all in all' (I Cor.15.28).

In this respect, the perichoretic unity of the triune God is an inviting and uniting unity, and as such a unity which is open to human beings and the world. 'The relationship of the divine persons to one another is so wide that there is room for the whole world in it' (Adrienne von Speyr). So we may not understand the trinitarian concept of the unity of the triune God exclusively, but must understand it inclusively. This is what I mean by my expression the 'open Trinity',[17] which I have used as a contrast to the traditional figures of the circular or triangular Trinity. The Trinity is 'open' by virtue of its overflowing, gracious love. It is 'open' to its beloved creatures who are found and accepted.

3. The problem of universal concepts in the Trinity

Finally, a starting point for the doctrine of the Trinity in the trinitarian history of salvation raises critical questions about the use of generic terms in the traditional doctrine of the Trinity.[18]

The 'begetting' of the Son by the Father and the 'proceeding' of the Spirit from the Father are different. If they are both subsumed under the generic term *processio* and there is talk of 'two processions', the danger of such an abstraction immediately becomes evident. The concrete particularity of the Son in his relationship to the Father and of the Spirit in his relationship to the Father are overlooked. In that case the Spirit can all too easily be understood as a second Son or the Son as another Spirit. So at this point it is illegitimate to form some generic term for the 'begetting' of the Son by the Father and the 'proceeding' of the Spirit from the Father. It is necesary to remain specific and *narrate* the one after the other, since each is unique.

The 'proceeding' of the Spirit from the Father and the 'reception' of his relational form by the Father and the Son are different. This difference is obliterated by the *filioque* of the Western church. This formula all too easily gives the impression that the Holy Spirit has two origins of his existence, in the Father and in the Son. So we may not summarize here, as happens with the formula 'and from the Son', which leaves quite open what comes from the Father and what from the Son. We have to remain specific and can only narrate the relationship of the Father to the Holy Spirit and of the Son to the Holy Spirit, one after the other, since each is unique.

Orthodox theologians explained their justified repudiation of the non-dif-ferentiated *filioque* formula by the monarchy of the Father, but this in turn is undifferentiated. The uniqueness of the Father over against the Son and the Holy Spirit can certainly be stressed by the Aristotelian concept of cause (*aitia, arche*), introduced into the doctrine of the Trinity by the Cappadocians, which was not undisputed in the early church. But if the Father is said to be only the 'cause' of the Godhead of the Son and the Godhead of the Holy Spirit, then the specific difference between the 'begetting of the Son' and the 'proceeding' of the Holy Spirit is obliterated. The introduction of the concept of cause is certainly understandable as a safeguard against a non- differentiated doctrine of the *filioque*. But it harbours a similar danger.

Moreover it transfers the universal relationship of God to the world, his monarchy of the world, to God's inner-trinitarian life. However, one cannot drive out the dangerous 'filioquism' from the doctrine of the Trinity by a 'monopatrism' without getting into similar difficulties. For the concept of the Father as sole cause threatens to obliterate the specific relationships within the Trinity. Thus the concept of cause can be used only in a transferred sense. It is not a generic term for begetting and breathing.

The doctrine of the three hypostases or three persons of the Trinity – and of course the terminology of three subjects which I myself am using in this chapter – is dangerous, because it applies one and the same concept of person or subject to the Father, the Son and the Holy Spirit, and thus gives the impression that they are homogeneous and equal: hypostases, persons or subjects. The generic terms hypostasis, person and mode of being obliterate the specific differences between the Father, the Son and the Holy Spirit. These are different, not only in respect of their relations to one another, but also in respect of their personality, unless the person is to be understood in its relations and not apart from them. If we wanted to keep to concrete terms, we would have to use a distinct, individual and unique concept of person in each case for the Father, the Son and the Spirit. To denote them as divine 'persons' already carries with it an intrinsic tendency to modalism. For the generic term hypostasis or person stresses what they have in common and what is the same, not what is their own and distinct about them.

From this brief account of the dangers involved in the introduction of generic terms into the doctrine of the Trinity, we must draw the conclusion that no subsuming generic terms may be used in the doctrine of the Trinity. In the life of the immanent Trinity everything is unique. Only because everything is unique in the triune God himself can it be recognized as original and prototypical for others in the ways and works of God. In the doctrine of the immanent Trinity we may basically only narrate, and not subsume. We have to remain concrete, since, as history shows, heresies lurk in abstractions. By contrast, the foundation of orthodoxy lies in narrative differentiation. Understanding and narrating are reciprocally related and so lead to understanding. Here a distinction has to be made between historical contingency in trinitarian history, which makes the narration necessary, and the contingency of origin in the Trinity itself, which compels praise.

At the centre of Christian theology is the history which is the triune God in himself. Any narrative needs time. For the narration of the trinitarian history of God, people need to take their time, and for the wondering and inexhaustible praise of the triune God himself they need eternity.

'Concepts create idols, only wonder grasps anything,' remarked Gregory of Nyssa rightly.[19] For the doctrine of the Trinity that means that the significance of the formation of trinitarian concepts is to be seen in the way in which they depict wonder at God and offer an invitation to this wonder.

II

THE TRINITARIAN VIEW
OF HISTORY

1

Christian Hope – Messianic or Transcendent?

A Theological Conversation with
Joachim of Fiore and Thomas Aquinas

1. The conversation resumed

Thomas of Aquinas engaged in a critical discussion with the basic theses of Joachim of Fiore in *Summa Theologica* I-II q 106 ad 4.1.[1] It is regarded as *the* Catholic answer to the abbot of Calabria's spiritualistic interpretation of the church and messianic interpretation of history. It seemed to decide the dispute over the theology of the church and the theology of salvation history in the Middle Ages. 'St Thomas succeeded in refuting the prophetic construction of history in types put forward by Joachim of Fiore.'[2]

Nevertheless the visions of Joachim were at least as influential in European cultural history as the definitions of Thomas Aquinas. Down to the present day there has been a dispute between a messianic orientation of Christian hope and a transcendental determination of it. Is Christian hope orientated on its fulfilment in a historical future or is it a 'theological', 'supernatural' virtue along with faith and love? Is Christian hope a forward-looking historical power which overcomes the old and creates the new, because it seeks its historical fulfilment in the future? Or is the hope of Christians directed 'above' to the transcendent God in whom alone they find bliss and in whom alone the human heart can find rest, so that it depicts the special openness of human existence in grace to God and expresses this abidingly in its truth?

I am using as a basis the historical research into Joachim and Joachimitism and into early spiritualistic Franciscanism by H.Grundmann,[3] A.Dempf,[4] E.Buonaiuti,[5] E.Benz,[6] H.Mottu,[7] A.Crocco[8] and others.[9] But I shall go into the controversy of the time only in terms of systematic theology. I am taking Joachim and Thomas seriously as theological contemporaries in the one holy church and relativizing the intervening difference in time.

I owe the occasion for resuming the theological conversation first of all to Henri de Lubac, who in his great work *The Spiritual Posterity of Joachim of Fiore*[10] begins from my *Theology of Hope* (1964) and takes up a comment which I made in 1965 in a letter to Karl Barth: 'Nowadays, Joachim of Fiore is more topical than Augustine.' The passage literally goes like this: 'In recent times the doctrine of the Holy Spirit has come to have a wholly enthusiastic and chiliastic stamp. Joachim is more alive today than Augustine. Thus some depict direct knowledge as a transcending of faith and others depict faith as a transcending of the Christ event. Through an eschatology christologically grounded in the cross and resurrection of Jesus both, I think, might be taken up again into the history at whose eschaton God will be all in all, and they might be changed thereby.'[11] Because I still advocate this thesis today, I shall develop it in the following conversation.

The second occasion was provided by Hans Urs von Balthasar. In his challenging article 'On a Christian Theology of Hope',[12] he condemned any messianic interpretation of hope as 'Jewish', 'Old Testament' and thus pre-Christian and said that only a 'vertical', 'presential' hope, focussed on heaven and the beyond, was Christian. He relegated Moltmann and Bloch, Metz and Marx, the Frankfurt School and Freud to Judaism, discovered a Jewish spirit in all significant, modern, revolutionary and atheistic movements, and declared the father of all these supposed heresies, Joachim of Fiore, to be a 'born Jew'[13] (though as far as I can see there is no support for this in his biography). In Balthasar's view that was the great danger. Basically, however, he is only repeating Thomas's doctrinal decision against Joachim. So I must begin with this if I am to give him a proper answer.

The conditions for this theological conversation may be mentioned briefly. Joachim of Fiore was an exegete and a biblical theologian. He made his great discoveries through the *concordia* of the Old and New Testaments.[14] He developed his messianic hope for the future from the connection which he recognized between the history of promise in the Old Testament and that in the new.[15] By comparison, Thomas Aquinas was a scientific theologian. He developed theology as a scientifically grounded doctrine of the church on the basis of Aristotle's ethics and metaphysics. The *quaestio* which we shall be considering is an example of theological logic and dialectic. I shall take it as a basis for the conversation in full awareness that in so doing I am doing more justice to Thomas than to Joachim. However, in this conversation it is not the doctrine of the church or the experience of history which will be the judge, but the gospel as it is attested in Old and New Testaments.

2. The theses for the conversation

Thomas formulates the question under dispute like this: *utrumque lex nova sit duratura usque ad finem mundi* (Is the new law to last till the end of the world?). By the *lex nova* he understands the law of Christ which has replaced the law of Moses, i.e. the gospel as it is proclaimed authoritatively by the church in the power of the Spirit in word and sacrament. This *nova lex* determines the status of the history of God with men and women to the end of the world.[16] The new law is the foundation of the church. The church conveys, mediates and realizes the new law. So the question of the time and duration of the new law is bound up with the question of the time and duration of the church. Is the church a provisional phenomenon in time, or does it extend to the goal, to the end of the world, eternity?

1. *Joachim's thesis: It seems that the new law is not to last till the end of the world. For as Paul says (I Cor.13.10), When that which is perfect comes, that which is in part will be done away. But the new law is 'in part', for Paul says in the same place, We know in part, and we prophesy in part. Therefore the new law is to be done away, succeeded by a more perfect state.*

That is how Thomas sums up the view of his opponent. Taking Joachim's work as a whole, we can add by way of explanation: on the basis of exegesis Joachim recognized that the old law was 'sublated' (*evacuare*) by the gospel and had been superseded in God's history with humankind.[17] He also transferred this relationship between gospel and law to the relationship between the gospel of Christ and the future which Christ himself promised. When this future of Christ appears, then the *nova lex,* the gospel, will also be 'sublated'. But that presupposes that the gospel cannot itself already be the fulfilment and thus the abolition of the promise of the old law, but only its acceptance and confirmation, since for its part it is itself promise. The *concordia* of the Old and New Testaments becomes manifest with respect to the future of God promised by both together.[18] For Joachim, this future which brings fulfilment, and in so doing does away with all that is transitory in salvation history, is historical future, future to be experienced with the senses and to be calculated in time. It is in the coming kingdom of the Spirit and the coming kingdom of Christ that the promises of the old and new law will be fulfilled. However, these historical abolitions of the previous law and state of the history of God are at any rate not just temporal and thus transitory fulfilments, but eschatological and thus abiding fulfilments. With the fulfilment of historical promises in time, an age begins which can no longer be determined 'historically'. This is the beginning of the messianic age, and with it of the chiliastic age. This messianic expectation offers an insight into the provisionality of the church's *nova lex* in the present and its mediating function as a transition to something greater. Like the *nova lex*, so too the church points beyond itself into the future of the Spirit.

2. *Thomas's thesis: Reply: The state of the world may vary in two ways. Firstly, by way of a diversity of law. In this sense no further state will follow upon this present state of the new law. For the state of the new law succeeded the state of the old as a more perfect state following upon a less perfect one. Now no state of our present life can be more perfect than the state of the new law; for nothing can be closer to the last end than something which immediately leads into it. But this is what the new law does, as Paul says, 'Having confidence therefore, brethren, to enter the sanctuary by the blood of Jesus, by the new way which he opened for us, let us draw near him' (Heb.10.19f.). So there can be no more perfect state of our present life than the state of the new law; for the closer something is to the last end, the more perfect it is.*

Because Thomas is describing his own view in this thesis, elaborations and explanations are superfluous. Here I would draw attention only to the difference in modes of thought. Joachim is thinking historically within the framework of his typological exegesis of history: promises call forth hopes, and these hopes call for the fulfilment of the promises. But Thomas is thinking finalistically in the framework of his metaphysics of perfection: the imperfect points towards the perfect. What is closest to the end and leads directly to the end is the most perfect state. The end (*finis*) of all perfection is eternal bliss.[19] It lies in the beatific vision and is therefore transcendent. It cannot be fulfilled in time and history. The one, complete mediation of transcendent, eternal bliss is offered by the new law, the church: 'Nothing can be interposed between the things which lead directly to the final end and the final end itself . . . So too no other state is to be interposed as a middle end (*medius finis*) between any state of the church militant in the time from the death of Christ to the church triumphant, but only the immediate goal, eternal life.'[20] For Thomas, there is only one single transition *in* the history of God with human beings, that from Israel to the church. However, the transition from the church to the kingdom of God is a step from history into eternity. Therefore the *nova lex* lasts till the end of the world. The church leads directly into eternity. The church alone represents eternity in time. Because it is immediate to eternal bliss, it remains absolute and cannot be superseded until the end of the world.

3. *My thesis*: Joachim recognized quite rightly the irremovable 'forward'[21] character of the biblical promises, orientated on historical and eschatological fulfilment. The divine promise opens up the experience of history, because it leads to an expectation of its fulfilment in the reality of creaturely history. History is 'the element of the future'.[22] But Joachim translated the biblical eschatology into chronology, in order to be able to calculate the ages of salvation history by the sequence of the predestined generations. In so doing he turned the historical eschatology of the Bible into an eschatology of world history as a

whole.

By contrast, Thomas replaces the biblical history of promise with a finalistic metaphysics. He replaces the hope which seeks the fulfilment of the promise with the natural striving for happiness which according to Augustine can come to fulfilment only in God himself. The 'coming God', *ho erchomenos, deus adventurus*, is replaced by the 'unmoved Mover' who draws all creatures to him by virtue of *eros*. The eschatological promise of the 'new heaven and new earth' – 'Behold, I make all things new' (Rev.21.5) – is replaced by the *visio Dei beatifica in patria*, i.e., in heaven, the bliss of the pure spirits in the world beyond. 'In this way the whole of eschatology and the whole eschatological tension of the Christian promise is set off against the idea of a goal understood in transcendentalist terms.'[23] Thomas did not translate biblical language into any other language or mode of thought, but basically liquidated it. His 'theology of hope' is in truth not the theology of a biblical 'hope' but the anthropology of the natural desire (*appetitus naturalis*) of the inner self-transcendence of human beings which finds its answer in the metaphysical theology of the supreme good (*summum bonum*).[24]

If we want to do justice to the biblical history of promise and its eschatology, then we must avoid any translation of it into a chronology of world history. The chronological concept of time does not correspond to the biblical concept of time, which is conditioned by eschatology.[25] But even more we must avoid the replacement of biblical eschatology with finalistic metaphysics. I have suggested that we should not think of the future in either chronological or finalistic terms, but in terms of advent.[26] Future, *adventus, parousia*, means what comes to the present, not what develops from the present. In the promise, the promised future casts its aura forwards into the present and governs the present by virtue of the hope which it arouses. Hope is the perception of the presence of the future in the word which promises and the events which promise. Those who live in hope, live by the future which is announced and already anticipate it in the Spirit and its way of life.[27]

In relation to the question of Christian eschatology in dispute between Joachim and Thomas, that means recognizing the presence of the coming glory of God in the history of the messiah Jesus (II Cor.4.6). There can be no christology without eschatology and no eschatology without christology.[28]

In detail, that means seeing in the proclamation and the healings of the historical Jesus the promise and the hidden beginning of the messianic age, of the messianic sabbath; recognizing in his being given up to death on the cross the representative anticipation of God's judgment on all godless being; understanding his 'resurrection from the dead' as the beginning of the general 'resurrection of the dead'; and discovering in the rule of the risen Christ the historical beginning of that eschatological kingdom in which God will be all in all.

If we think about the future in terms of advent, then we discover the present as a making present, an arrival of this future. The power of the Holy Spirit is already present in a hidden way in the rule of Christ, since with his resurrection the 'firstfruits of the Spirit' are made present. In the power of the Spirit the parousia of Christ is present in a spiritual way. In and with the messianic kingdom of Christ, the kingdom of God will be made present. The eschatological future of history arrives in a series of particular presents (or states, as Joachim and Thomas call them) which have different contents: in the historical age determined by the promise; in the messianic age determined by the messiah; in the spiritual age determined by the Spirit of the new creation; in the chiliastic age determined by the kingdom of Christ; in the eschatological age determined by the judgment and kingdom of God; and finally by the eternal age of the new creation in the feast of glory.[29] The ages defined in this way overlap.[30] They are strata and transitions in the one eschatological movement of history. On each occasion, the age is defined anew by historical fulfilments. Without these new determinations of ages, fulfilments would be transitory and hopes would become hopeless.

For theology, it follows from this that there is no history of promise without the messianism of hope; no messianism without eschatology; no eschatology without chiliasm focussed on the messianic age and apocalyptic focussed on eternity. The modern abstraction of eschatology from these contexts has destroyed eschatology or turned it into an expression of the metaphysics of transcendence.

Does the church remain to the end of the world? I would turn this question round and first answer with the Second Vatican Council: 'Already the final age of the world is with us (cf. I Cor.10.11) and the renewal of the world is irrevocably under way; it is even now anticipated in a certain real way, for the Church on earth is endowed already with a sanctity that is real though imperfect. However, until there be realized new heavens and a new earth in which justice dwells (cf. II Peter 3.13), the pilgrim church, in its sacraments and institutions, which belong to this present age, carries the mark of this world which will pass, and she herself takes her place among the creatures which groan and travail yet and await the revelation of the sons of God (cf. Rom.8.19-22).'[31] The eschatological new creation of the world is first present in the church only in a churchly way, i.e. in a form conditioned by this age. It is made present in a spiritual way in the Spirit, who is mediated and promised by word and sacrament and church community. It is made present in the messianic kingdom of Christ in such a way that a new community of Jews and Christians comes into being of a kind that cannot arise in the church at the time of the hardening of Israel. It will finally take place in the eschatological present of God. To put it the other way round, the church remains until the end of the world; not, however, as church in its present form, but as the new creation of the world made present. What will be overcome is the historically provisional form of the eschatological presence of God; what abides is this presence itself.

3. 'We see here in a glass darkly'

Having presented the different theses, I now want to go on to discuss the most important arguments. Here once again I am following the presentation of them by Thomas, but I shall attempt as far as possible and where necessary to supplement his account of Joachim's position. I shall test the theological arguments against the biblical traditions that they quote and by their theological and practical consequences.

In the first argument there is a dispute as to whether I Cor.13.10 speaks of a coming time of consummation or of a coming consummation of time in eternity.

1. *Joachim's argument: It seems that the new law is not to last till the end of the world. For as Paul says, When that which is perfect comes, that which is in part will be done away (I Cor.13.10). But the new law is 'in part', for Paul says in the same place, We know in part, and we prophesy in part. Therefore the new law is to be done away, succeeded by a more perfect state.*

E.Benz mentions three concomitant arguments from Joachim's writings: 1. If 'up till now' the Jews do not know the saving truth of the gospel of Christ, then believers' knowledge of the truth is also itself still incomplete. 2. If in fact the truth itself were now already completely manifest, how can there still be so many heretics? However, there is perfect and direct knowledge of the truth when the Holy Spirit grasps human hearts. So in respect of the old law, the truth in the gospel is 'now already' manifest, but in respect of the coming of the Holy Spirit the perfect truth is 'not yet' manifest now. In the age and state of the Holy Spirit, the rule of the flesh will cease. Those grasped by the Spirit will no longer know the truth of the gospel in parable and in riddles but directly. They will no longer know it through the institutional mediation of the present church but through their own insight.[32]

2. *Thomas's argument: No state of our present life can be more perfect than the state of the new law; for nothing can be closer to the last end than something which immediately leads to it . . . for the closer something is to the last end, the more perfect it is.*

According to Thomas there is no mediation and no intermediary period between the teaching of the church here and heavenly perfection there. Since the time of the apostles the church already has the Holy Spirit. It is itself the 'age of the Spirit' and therefore does not wait for a coming age of the Spirit. Because 'the perfect' is the last and transcendent goal, in its way the church is already perfect, since it leads directly to this goal. The church possesses the perfection of the only way. So it is the only way to salvation. After it comes only the goal itself.

3. *Discussion*: If we first compare the two views with I Corinthians 13, it is

striking that neither of them has taken the 'coming' of the perfect seriously. The perfect does not *follow* the imperfect, as Joachim seems to think. Still less, however, is the perfect the goal of the imperfect or something to which the imperfect *leads*. 'When the perfect *comes,* that which is fragmentary will cease.' So it is caught up in an eschatological movement towards the historical present. In the face of this advent of the perfect, the present becomes manifest as a fragment.

What is meant by 'the perfect'? Joachim means the knowledge of the truth in the Spirit. Thomas means the final end of the heavenly vision of God face to face. But beyond question Paul means the parousia of Christ, his manifestation in glory. Then Christ will no longer be mediated through the human testimony of the gospel, but will be manifest directly in his own person. Then his own will know him as they are now already known by him, and will grasp and be perfect, as they are now already grasped by Christ (Phil.3.13). What Christ is now 'for them', they will then be 'with him'. Then faith will become sight, and hope for the redemption of the body and of the whole creation in waiting will be filled with the revelation of the freedom of the children of God (Rom.8.19ff.). The parousia of Christ 'is coming', and because it is expected as something that is 'coming', this expectation makes the church's representation of Christ in word, sacrament and church community a fragment, an anticipation and a representation of his future. In this future perspective the experience of the Holy Spirit, too, is just the experience of a 'pledge', a 'down-payment', a 'firstfruit'.

However, there are transitions here. In I Cor.13.12 Paul speaks not only of faith here and vision there, but also of knowledge 'now' and 'then'. This knowledge presupposes faith and is a step of hope towards vision. It is the *intellectus fidei*, a middle between believing and seeing, as Anselm said. It is that theological knowledge which is already possible here on the basis of faith and in the power of the Spirit. In it there is a fragmentary anticipation 'as in a glass darkly' of what the vision in the parousia will bring. So this fragmentary and anticipatory knowledge of God and of one's own self, of the meaning of an enigmatic history and an obscure nature, will 'cease' when the light of glory illuminates everything because it redeems all that sighs here in the pain of its own nothingness.

By contrast, 'faith, hope and love will abide, and the greatest of these is love' (I Cor.13.13). If here it is said that hope, too, abides, then must not hope be understood as an abiding virtue and not as a historical response of human beings to a divine promise which passes over into joy when the promise is fulfilled?

This exegesis overlooks the fact that Paul says 'But now abide . . . ' This is surely to be understood in a temporal sense, as is indicated by the contrast 'now – but then' in v.12.[33] On the other hand, the category of abiding is always meant eschatologically, as is demonstrated by the contrast to 'being done away' in v.8 and v.10. But in that case how are we to understand the abiding of faith and hope which still come to fulfilment? If we take the two together, we can say that in contrast to the other transitory gifts of the Spirit, faith, hope and love remain 'valid' until the parousia. Certainly faith will be replaced by sight (II Cor.5.7), and hope too is provisional until its fulfilment (Rom.8.24f.). However, the sight is itself already anticipated in a hidden way in faith, and the fulfilment is already anticipated in a hidden way in hope. Therefore faith and hope contain the elements of the recognition of God and anticipatory joy at its fulfilment, which also 'abide' in the kingdom of God.[34] In sight, faith is not just done away with, but also taken up and transcended. Hope does not just cease in fulfilment but is also consummated. The historical provisionality of believing and hoping and their eschatological finality are not opposites. Any transitory provisionality is excluded from their eschatological provisionality, and any premature absolutizing is ruled out.

4. The promise of the Spirit of truth

In the second argument there is a dispute as to whether the promise of the 'Spirit of truth' is referred by Christ in John 16.12 to a future time of the Spirit or to the time of the church founded by Christ and the apostles and its message.

1. *Joachim's argument: Moreover the Lord promised his disciples the knowledge of all truth at the coming of the Holy Spirit, the Paraclete (John 16). But the church does not yet know all truth in the state of the new covenant. Therefore we should look forward to another state, in which all truth will be revealed by the Holy Spirit.*

That is how Thomas renders Joachim's view. Again I shall supplement his account from the studies of E.Benz.[35] According to Joachim the knowledge of 'all truth' (*omnis veritas*) is evidently a spiritual, direct vision of the truth itself. Whereas here and now the truth is at the same time manifest and revealed in the sensory figures and images of the New Testament, it will be unveiled and known without metaphor in the Holy Spirit. Joachim relates this to the apocalyptic promise of the 'eternal gospel' (Rev.14.6). For him the 'eternal gospel' is the gospel without letters, figures and images. It is the gospel in the Spirit, which gives life. So the eternal gospel is the spiritual knowledge of the truth of the gospel of Christ without book, without flesh, without image, and the gospel of Christ is the gospel of Christ concealed in a parable. The later interpretation that this eternal gospel is Joachim's own typological and spiritualistic interpretation of the Bible, disseminated by Petrus Olivi, does not fit Joachim himself.

2. *Thomas's argument: According to Augustine* (in his book against Faustus – but it is not there but in his book on the heresies in connection with heresies 26 and 46), *Montanus and Priscilla maintained that the Lord's promise to give the Holy Spirit was fulfilled in them, not in the Apostles. The Manichees too held that it was fulfilled in Manichaeus, whom they called the Paraclete. For this reason neither of them accepted the Acts of the Apostles, where it is clearly*

shown that the Lord's promise was fulfilled in the Apostles. We learn there that the Lord repeated his promise to them, 'You shall be baptized with the Holy Spirit before many days' (Acts 1.5), and we read of this fulfilment in Acts 2. But these empty notions are refuted by the text of John (7.39), 'The Spirit had not yet been given, because Jesus was not yet glorified', from which we may learn that the Holy Spirit was given as soon as Christ was glorified in the resurrection and the ascension. And this is sufficient to expose the emptiness of anyone else who says that we should look forward to some new time of the Holy Spirit. Now the Holy Spirit taught the Apostles all truth in regard to what is necessary for salvation, that is, what is to be believed and what is to be done. But he did not teach them about everything else which was to happen in the future. This was not their business, as they were told, 'It is not for you to know the times or seasons which the Father has set on his own authority' (Acts 1.7).

3. *Discussion*: Thomas identifies Joachim's teaching with the heresy of Montanism, so as to subject it to a judgment on heresy from the early church. This comparison is correct only externally, in that Montanus, too, put the promise of the Paraclete from John 16 in the centre. But it is false in so far as Montanus saw himself as the incarnation of the promised Paraclete who was to fulfil Christianity in the Spirit. This idea does not appear in Joachim. He does not speak of an incarnation of the Holy Spirit but of a knowledge of the truth in the Spirit: 'a purely internal knowledge, a withdrawing of the veil from the letter, the flesh, the figure, which lie before the eye of the knower, and a filling with the knowledge of divine things as they are in themselves'.[36]

Joachim's idea of an inner, spiritual and immediate knowledge of the truth in the time and state of the Holy Spirit has Jewish models: the messianic world will be a world without likenesses, in which the likeness and that of which it is made need no longer be related, because here a form of being will emerge which no longer needs to be depicted.[37] This perspective is important for the understanding of the parables of Jesus: Jesus expressed the kingdom of God in parable and as parable. His gospel of the kingdom therefore points beyond itself to a presence of the kingdom which need no longer be communicated by parables and images, as Mark's theory of parables indicates: 'To you it is given to know the mystery of the kingdom of God, but to those outside everything happens through parables . . .' (Mark 4.11).

Did Joachim really deny the outpouring of the Spirit on the apostles and the apostolic church at Pentecost in order to expect an 'other time of the Holy Spirit', as Thomas claims? Can Thomas for his part limit the outpouring of the Spirit to the Pentecost event and the apostolic church? Again we must note in Joachim the cateogry of the future hidden in the present: he does not deny the gift of the Spirit to the apostles and the apostolic church, but expects that the Spirit will lead believers into all truth, so that they are brought from knowledge conveyed by the senses to a direct spiritual knowledge of the truth. 'Since according to

100

this exegesis all the past contains in itself a reference to and an anticipatory image of that which will be fully realized in the future, alongside the "spiritual understanding" which relates this promise of the outpouring of the Spirit to the coming world age of the Holy Spirit there is also the reference of this promise to Pentecost as the fulfilment of this promise at the beginning of the second world age.'[38]

Joachim's thought is more complex than Thomas's account suggests. I shall attempt to take it up and look at the elements of truth in it, so that we can assimilate it critically. If we omit the chronological extrapolations of time from Joachim's theology of history, there remains a twofold perspective on the outpouring and experience of the Holy Spirit: christological and eschatological. In christological terms – this is Joachim's 'second age of the world' – the Holy Spirit is poured out on the apostles at Pentecost. If the church remains in the apostolic tradition, it remains in the Holy Spirit. The Holy Spirit 'taught the apostles all truth of what is necessary for salvation, what one should believe and what one should do'. That means that the Holy Spirit glorifies Christ and teaches the *nova lex*. What he teaches and gives is wholly governed by Christ and his teaching. This christological perspective on the Holy Spirit must be supplemented by the eschatological perspective: the Holy Spirit does not just teach the *nova lex* but also creates in human beings the capacity to understand it and live with it. No one can call Christ Lord except in the Holy Spirit. In this respect the Holy Spirit, who creates knowledge and faith, hope and love in believers, is the goal of Christ's mission and the fulfilment of the teaching of the church. The gospel achieves its end in justifying faith; the word achieves its end in the Spirit, and the church achieves its end in the kingdom of God.

With the advent of faith the new creation in humankind begins. So where Christ is taken up in the Holy Spirit, the power of the new creation is already present. Where the outward word achieves its end in the inner certainty of the Holy Spirit, the eschatological knowledge of God begins in a spiritual way. That does not mean – even for Joachim, as his diagram of the Trinity in the *Liber figurarum* shows (p.105) – that there is a 'future of the Spirit without Christ', as H.de Lubac claims.[39] But it does mean that there can be no future of Christ without the Spirit. The 'firstfruit of the Holy Spirit' is the power of the new creation and is therefore to be understood in the light of eschatology. In the Holy Spirit the transition from the gospel of Christ to the parousia of Christ takes place historically. The personal transition from faith in the gospel on the basis of the authority of the church to one's own faith on the basis of personal insight, i.e. the transition from the *fides historica* to the *fides justificans*, as the Reformers put it, comes about in the power of the Holy Spirit. This power also includes the *testimonium Spiritus Sancti internum*, the inner testimony of the Holy Spirit, which was stressed by Reformed theology. And Joachim's 'spiritual understanding', too, is at home in this inner testimony of the Spirit.[40] Joachim's truth is the doctrine of eschatologically motivated historical transitions. Thomas Aquinas failed to recognize that when he ecclesiasticized the Spirit in his argument and declared that the church itself was part of the time and state of the Holy Spirit.

5. The historical doctrine of the Trinity

The third argument relates to the ideas of the historical Trinity and the trinitarian history of God.

1. *Joachim's argument: Moreover, just as the Father is other than the Son and the Son other than the Father, so the Holy Spirit is other than the Father and the Son. But there has been a state which fitted the person of the Father: this was the state of the old law, when men were concerned with the procreation of sons. Similarly there is another state fitting the person of the Son, and this is the state of the new law, in which clerics, concerned with wisdom (which is appropriate to the Son), take the first place. Therefore there wil be a third state of the Holy Spirit, in which spiritual men will take the first place.*

In Benz's view this statement reproduces Joachim's teaching most exactly.[41] Joachim developed this doctrine of the three stages in many individual pieces of exegesis and kept summarizing it, so that historically it has become the most influential of all his doctrines. But do we understand it rightly if we only look at the summary and leave the reasons behind it out of account? One can examine this summary in the diagram in the *Liber Figurarum*.[42]

2. *Thomas's argument: On the third point it is to be said that the old law did not belong only to the Father but also to the Son, for Christ was figured in the old law. So the Lord said, 'If you believed Moses, you would believe me, for he wrote about me' (John 5.46). Likewise the new law too does not belong only to Christ but also to the Holy Spirit: 'The law of the Spirit of life in Christ Jesus etc.' So we are not to look forward to some further law proper to the Holy Spirit.*

In these sentences Thomas attempts to demonstrate in Joachim's field, namely exegesis, the doctrine which had been predominant in the West since Augustine, according to which all the works of the Trinity *ad extra* are the undivided works of the whole Trinity and not of individual trinitarian persons: Christ already present in the history of the old law, the holy Spirit already at work in history of Christ. Against Joachim's historical theology of the three world ages Thomas sets his historical theology of the two world ages. They are governed by the old law and the new law respectively. In history there is only one meaningful transition, the transition from Israel to the church. The kingdom of God lies beyond history.

3. *Discussion:* To correct the account of Joachim's doctrine of three stages which has become customary since Thomas one can bring in the diagram I have already mentioned. From it we can recognize that Joachim saw not only Christ but also the Holy Spirit already at work in the first circle of the Father, just as

he also had the Father and the Son working together in the third circle of the Holy Spirit. The circles overlap in such a way that they cannot be separated and looked at independently of one another. In speaking, in his refutation, of Christ in the time of the old law and the Holy Spirit in the time of the new law, Thomas is not in fact contradicting Joachim but following him, apart from his expectation of a third state of the Holy Spirit.

Despite the accusation which has been repeated by theologians for centuries, we do not find in Joachim any dissolution of the Trinity into history nor any replacement of the doctrine of the Trinity by a historical doctrine of three kingdoms, but merely a historical evaluation of the trinitarian doctrine of appropriations. Regardless of the classical statement by Augustine, the theological tradition has always attributed the work of creation to the Father without excluding the Son and the Spirit, for the Father creates through the Son in the Spirit. Similarly, it has attributed the work of reconciliation to the incarnate Son and the work of redemption to the Holy Spirit, without excluding the involvement of the Father. Joachim simply transferred these three great appropriations to times and states in salvation history. What he develops in diachronical historical terms as a sequence of three ages of the world, he can also depict synchronously as the one working of the triune God.

Thomas did not follow this salvation-historical doctrine of appropriations because for him history is determined only by the opposition between old and new law, Israel and the church. For Thomas, what Joachim designates the kingdom of the Holy Spirit coincides with the kingdom of Christ, i.e. the rule of the new law. This has two far-reaching consequences: 1. In salvation history the new law takes the place of the old law, and the church the place of Israel. There is no future salvation for Israel other than the church. 2. The kingdom of God lies beyond history. Its effect on history is only by way of the church and the new law. This moving of the kingdom of God into the world beyond results in the doctrine of two kingdoms for history: nature and grace, law and gospel, necessity and freedom. These oppositions are not resolved in history.[43] If we compare Joachim's doctrine of three kingdoms with this we find that he in no way dissolves the other-worldly kingdom of glory in trinitarian history, but rather that these three historical times of Father, the Son and the Spirit are summed up and consummated in the kingdom of the glory of the triune God. Schematically the comparison looks like this:

Joachim:
Time of the Father - time of the Son - time of the Spirit: eternal consummation

Thomas:
Time of the old law - time of the new law: eternal consummation.

If there are no objections to the distinction between the old and the new law and to the appropriation of the old law to the Father and the new law to the Son, then there cannot be any objections to the distinction between the law of Christ and the law of the Spirit and the appropriation of the 'spiritual understanding' to the Holy Spirit. Just as Christ cannot be identified with the Father, although he is already at work in the old law, so the Spirit cannot be identified with Christ, although he is already at work in and with Christ. If one follows the content rather than the chronology of Joachim's scheme, it is also impossible to identify the third age of the Holy Spirit with the end of history and the kingdom of God. The time of the Holy Spirit is not the church nor the kingdom of God, but no more and no less than the transitional age between the kingdom of God and the church and between the church and the kingdom of God.

In terms of systematic theology, the relationship between the Trinity and the kingdom of God, and in it the relationship between Trinity and eschatology, has always remained an open problem. Eschatology is the foundation for the dynamic of history, repentance and a new start. Its watchword is 'the new'. But the Trinity seems to have the form of divine perfection and self-sufficiency. Its watchword is the present 'for ever and ever'. In Thomas the doctrine of the Trinity has neutralized and stilled the eschatological dynamic of the biblical history of promise. Anyone who thinks in a pattern of time and eternity is hardly interested in the progress of the ages. By contrast, Joachim was the first, but not the only one, to see Trinity and history together eschatologically in such a way that the history of the kingdom has a trinitarian determination and the Trinity is thought of in the realm of its own glory as the consummation of its own trinitarian history.

An interesting but previously little-noted parallel or even prelude to Joachim's trinitarian view of history appears in the christological Kabbala of converted Jews in Spain. Among other things, it goes back to the rabbinic notion of the three ages of world history: 'There are three ages: two thousand years of chaos; two thousand years of the law beginning with the revelation on mount Sinai; two thousand years of the messianic kingdom; and then finally the world which is only sabbath, rest in eternal life.' When the 'days of the Messiah' come, the 'days of the Torah' come to an end (cf. Sanhedrin 97a and Tamid VIII.4).

'In the Middle Ages, there were several attempts to use the theosophies cherished in the Jewish Kabbala to explain the divine triunity. The most significant impetus towards a Christian Kabbala came from Petrus Alphonsi (1062-c.1110), a convert from Judaism. In his *Dialogi,* in which he evaluates his prior Jewish-esoteric knowledge, he attempts to depict the mystery of the Trinity as an unfolding of the name YHWH.

The Trinity is subtle, inexpressible, difficult to explain. The prophets spoke about it only mysteriously and in a veiled way until Christ came, one of the three persons. He revealed the Trinity to believers in accordance with their powers of comprehension. However, if you want to penetrate further into this exalted sphere, then consider that name of God which has become manifest in its innermost mystery, that is the name YHWH. This name consists of three different consonants. It has four consonantal signs, but one consonant occurs twice. If you look closely, you will see that the one name is one and three. To the degree that it is one it relates to the threeness of the persons. But it is clear that if you join together the four consonantal signs which are three different consonants, namely Y and H and W, and connect the first with the second, the Y with the H, then a name emerges. A name also emerges if you combine the second consonant with the third, i.e. the H with the W. If you combine the third consonant with the fourth, the W with the H, then a third name emerges. If you then put them all together again in a row, then just one name appears. The following figure can depict this:

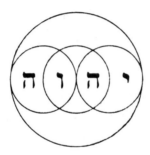

The diagram from the *Liber figurarum* which is mentioned in the text has been used as the cover illustration for the English edition.

105

Consider now, O Moses, what a mystery this is and how subtle and inexpressible this name is. Only a perceptive mind can have access to it. Intensive research is needed. In the book of Deuteronomy (4.39), Moses says: "You should know today and consider in your heart that the Lord is himself God: in heaven above and on earth below. And there is none other." Where there is "Lord" in Latin, in Hebrew there is YHWH. But where there is *Deus* in Latin, in Hebrew there is Elohim, a term which has a plural form. However, it is evident here that it relates to the one God, who is solemnly addressed with a word in the singular and a word in the plural, and so that no one should think that there are two Gods here, we find at this point: "And there is no other" (PL 157, 611).

Following Petrus Alphonsi and other Jews who had been converted to Christianity, a Christian Kabbala came into being which undertook to make use of Jewish esoteric theology in the service of speculations on the Trinity.'[44]

6. The gospel and the parousia of Christ

The last argument relates to Joachim's distinction between the gospel of Christ and the gospel of the kingdom and his eschatological expectation of the eternal gospel.

1. *Joachim's argument: Moreover the Lord says, 'This gospel of the kingdom will be preached throughout the earth, and then the consummation will come' (Matt.24.14). But the gospel of Christ has now been preached for a long time throughout the earth, yet the consummation has not come. Therefore the gospel of Christ is not the gospel of the kingdom, but another gospel of the Holy Spirit is still to come, as it were another law.*

By the 'kingdom of God' Joachim means the state of consummation and fulfilment of all promises of the Old and New Testaments. It is the kingdom of the glory of the triune God.[45] The gospel of the kingdom is its last revelation in history. So the gospel of the kingdom marks the beginning of the time of the Holy Spirit, the end-time, the last age before the end of history, the last mediation of the eternal kingdom in historical time.

2. *Thomas's argument: Since Christ began his preaching of the gospel by saying 'The kingdom of heaven is at hand' (Matt.3.2), it is absurd to say that the gospel of Christ is not the gospel of the kingdom. But the preaching of the gospel of Christ can be understood in two senses. Firstly, as regards the public proclamation of the news of Christ; and in this sense the gospel was preached throughout the earth even in the time of the Apostles, as Chrysostom says (in Homily 76 on Matthew a little after the beginning). Then the second part of the statement, 'And then the consummation will come', refers to the destruction of Jerusalem, in the literal sense of what was then being said. In a second sense, the preaching of the Gospel throughout the earth can be understood to refer to*

106

its full realization, when the church has been founded in each of the people on earth. In this sense, as Augustine says (in his letter to Hesychius in the middle), the gospel has not yet been preached throughout the earth, but once this has happened, there will come the consummation of the world.

3. *Discussion*: The problem which Joachim wanted to solve with his distinction between the gospel of Christ and the gospel of the kingdom is neither mentioned by Thomas nor solved in his manner: the problem of Israel.[46]

So for Joachim the church of Christ with the gospel of Christ is a historically provisional revelation because 'even now' all Israel is hardened. Because Joachim hopes for a future of salvation for Israel, he expects a future time of the Spirit and the eternal gospel which will convince not only heathen but also the Jews. For Thomas, however, the church with the new law has taken the place of Israel and its own law. With the spread of the gospel among all peoples no special position for Israel can be seen any longer. So no form of the gospel is to be expected in the future other than the new law of the church, which remains to the end. When the church is firmly established in all peoples – also among the Jews? – then the end will come.

But Joachim recognized the inadequacy of a church without Israel. 'For up to now only non-Jews glorify Christ. But that day will bring as it were the fulfilment of Jews and non-Jews.'[47] The heathen recognize Jesus as the Christ and perceive the truth of his gospel which brings salvation, from which the Jews 'up till now' have shut themselves off: 'Why do I say "up to now", where the people which is called heathen has received the true faith since then? Is it not because our knowledge is in part and our prophecy is in part . . .'[48] The fulfilment of what was promised in the time of Christ will take place in the third age of the Spirit. This fulfilment begins with the complete conversion of the Jews 'which the Holy Spirit will bring about on that sabbath, i.e. in that seventh age, i.e. in the time of the coming consummation, the beginning time of the state of the Spirit'.[49]

I take up this reference from Joachim, and with Paul go beyond it:

1. The church of the nations exists only because all Israel has refused to accept Jesus as the promised messiah. The time of the 'hardening' of Israel (by God) is the time of the mission to the nations by the gospel of Christ. The existence of the church of the nations and the rejection of the gospel of Christ by all Israel are indissolubly connected. However, this is the history of the gospel, which represents an eschatological mystery, not a gospel of history, as the 'theology of history' says.

2. The hope which Paul associates with the proclamation of the gospel of Christ among all nations is hope for the redemption of Israel through the parousia of Christ: 'For if their rejection means the reconciliation of the world, what will their acceptance mean but life from the dead?' (Rom.11.15). So for Paul the Jews are 'enemies of God, for your sake: but as regards election they

are beloved for the sake of their forefathers' (Rom.11.28).

3. What will the redemption of Israel look like? Israel will not be redeemed by the church's gospel of Christ, since this came about as a result of the repudiation of Israel, and has its salvation-historical destination among the nations and its own age in salvation history. But Israel will be redeemed through the appearing in glory of the messiah, whose name to Christians is 'Jesus'. Just as Paul himself was converted, so that the one who denied Christ became the apostle of the gospel of Christ to the nations (Gal.1.12,15f.), so will all Israel be redeemed by the universal appearance of Christ.

4. However, that means that it is not the church of the nations which can already be the future salvation of Israel, as Thomas Aquinas seems to think, but only the parousia and the kingdom of Jesus. But on the other hand that means that Israel cannot already be the future of the church of Christ; that will be the parousia and the kingdom of the messiah.

5. The recognition of the permanent election of Israel and the pain over the repudiation of the gospel of Christ by the Jews are the deepest reasons for the dissatisfaction of Christians with the church and for their eschatological hope for the coming kingdom of Christ. Without Israel the church is incomplete. Together with Israel the church hopes for the messianic kingdom which combines both. At the end of history is not the church triumphant or Israel triumphant, but only Christ triumphant, who is the hope of both.

7. Result

Do the parousia and the kingdom of Christ still fall in history, or do they lie beyond history? Is an 'earthly future' or a heavenly future meant? That is the question of the future of the kingdom which is symbolically called millenarian, of chiliasm.[50]

In most New Testament writings the eschatological expectation has chiliastic features. When Jesus says in Mark 14.25, at the institution of the eucharist, 'Truly, I say to you that I shall not drink henceforth of the fruit of the vine until the day when I drink it new in the kingdom of God', then he is expecting 'days' and 'wine' in the kingdom of God. So bread and wine in the Christian eucharist are focussed on the day and the wine in the kingdom of God. The eucharist cannot be understood as Jesus understood it without this realistic hope for this earthly future of the kingdom of God. And when in Rom.9-11 Paul speaks of the future salvation of Israel, he directs his gaze to Jerusalem: 'And so all Israel will be saved; as it is written, "The Deliverer will come from Zion, he will banish ungodliness from Jacob"' (Rom.11.26).

It was only with the establishment of the church in the Roman empire that chiliasm disappeared from eschatology. It did not disappear because of 'experiences of disappointment', as has been continually claimed since Albert Schweitzer and Rudolf Bultmann, but because of dreams of fulfilment. The imperial theologians in Constantine's empire declared this Christian empire to be a 'thousand-year kingdom'. Tyconius and Augustine, the church theologians in Rome, declared the church to be the thousand-year kingdom of Christ. Even Thomas Aquinas was in this sense a chiliast of the present state of the church.[51] So he could not recognize any special calling of Israel alongside the church, and for him the church lasted right to the end of the world and heavenly bliss.

However, for those who interpret their own present in chiliastic terms, whether in the Christian state or in the Christian church, there is nothing left but eschatological hope: the end of the world, judgment and the kingdom of God. By contrast, those who hope for the chiliasm of the messianic kingdom in the future must define their own present in church and society in messianic and historical terms. In its historical and messianic transitoriness the church of the nations then opens up and recognizes Israel as an independent companion on the way.

Chiliasm is the immanent side of eschatology. Eschatology is the transcendent side of chiliasm. So there may be no chiliasm without eschatology. That leads to the political chiliasm which has had such disastrous effects in European history. So too there may be no eschatology without chiliasm. That leads to the dissolution of the Christian hope in transcendent longing and has had no less disastrous effects in the church history of Europe.

Joachim and Thomas stand for the two sides of Christian hope, for the chiliastic and the eschatological side. I have resumed their conversation in order to liberate Christian hope from its speculative translation into a chronology of world history and its no less speculative replacement by supernatural virtue, and with the help of both to understand afresh that Christian hope is messianic hope against a horizon of eschatological expectation.

2

Being a Christian, Being Human and the Kingdom of God

(i) A Conversation with Karl Rahner

Honouring a theological teacher means taking up the conversation about the Word of God that he has stimulated and carrying it further. The focal point must not be the theologian in person, but rather the cause to which he devoted all his heart and soul and strength during his life. If that is done, the wisdom and goodness of his person also begin to shine forth. However, if one takes up the theological conversation about the Word of God, the limitations of human understanding also become evident by the greater mystery of God. Here we see 'as in a glass darkly'; our best thoughts are incomplete fragments of a totality which we have still to grasp and the ambiguous anticipation of a beauty which has not yet appeared. That does not put them to shame. That is their supreme worth. Even the great and almost perfect theological Summas and systems are fragments in respect of what they seek to understand and say. They begin to shine forth precisely where they begin to fall apart, at the point at which the calculation does not work out, where it becomes impossible for the system to be free of contradiction because it indicates something greater that is to come. Gregory of Nyssa once said, 'Concepts create idols. Only wonder grasps something.' In Rahner's writings this thoughtful wonder occurs at decisive points.

Many pupils learned this from Karl Rahner. Unlike some of those who completed theological systems, his strength lies precisely at the points where he has thought and said everything that could be thought and said on his presuppositions and then retreats and keeps silent and lets the matter emerge of its own accord. I find that not only an expression of theological humility before God but also a gesture of theological fellowship with those who were and are on the same track.

In this chapter I would like to resume a conversation with Karl Rahner which he began many years ago with his controversial theses on 'Anonymous Christians'.[1] If it proves successful I hope to take the matter further. For the theological foundation of his theses I am also using his article 'On the Theology of the Incarnation'.[2] I shall limit myself to these two writings, since I am not concerned to give a comprehensive account of Rahner's ideas, but simply to discuss them.

1. The Christian claim to universality, the particular existence of the church and the pluralistic reality of modern society

'Our topic with all its urgency cannot be avoided or dismissed as unimportant either by a theology of grace and of the Church which has a true understanding of itself, or by an honest pastoral theology which looks at our times dispassionately.'[3] Rahner is referring to the relationship between being a Christian and being human, but puts this in the context of the deeper aporia of the church, which in a pluralistic society and in the pluralism of the various cultures and religions of the world can put forward its universal claim of salvation only in a relative and particular way. The church's old claim to absoluteness in the Christian empire has gone. Article 4.1 of the basic law of the Federal Republic of Germany guarantees 'freedom of religion and ideological confession' for all and makes Christian faith a 'possible form of a religious interpretation of existence which stands alongside others, whether with the same right or even with greater promise'.[4] The old claim that religion is represented only through the Christian church also disappears, the more the church becomes one religion among many other world religions and discovers how difficult it is to get a foothold in the ancient cultures of Asia. Certainly the church is present in all peoples, but only as what is usually a marginal minority. Even in the West the church seems to be contracting into a 'little flock'.

Behind these contemporary problems of the church in the external and internal pluralism of societies and religion there is the even deeper, substantial problem of the church and Christianity generally. How can an absolute, the infinite, eternal God, be depicted by a relative, the finite, limited, human people of God? How can a universal, the kingdom of God and true humankind in it, be represented by a particular, being a Christian? The question is not whether the absolute can ever be depicted and represented by the relative and the universal by the particular, but how it can happen in such a way that the absolute remains absolute and the relative relative, the universal universal and the particular particular, and the representative identifications of the former are replaced by the latter.

This is not just an aporia for the Christian church; it was already one for Israel. How can a chosen people bear witness to that glory of God which will fill all lands without glorifying its own election? This is also the ideological dilemma of the two so-called 'world powers' today. How can the United States advocate 'freedom and human rights' for all without this degenerating into the

111

American ideology of the pre-eminence of the West? And how can the 'first state of workers and farmers' in the USSR advocate the socialism of an 'all-human society' without this being used as an ideology for Soviet imperialism? So the question which Rahner takes up is a problem with many layers, and not just a question within the church. If it should prove soluble, its solution has significance beyond the church and Christianity for the world human community which at present is coming into being and which we need if we are to survive.

2. The self-transcendence of human beings and the self-communication of God

Like any claim to universality, the universality of the Christian claim of salvation is grounded in an exclusive claim, namely that no other way leads to salvation. 'The Christian is convinced that in order to achieve salvation man must believe in God, and not merely in God but in Christ,' says Rahner, and immediately associates this eschatological claim with the ecclesiological claim of 'membership of the one true church', from which it follows that 'there really is no salvation outside the church, as the old theological formula has it'.[5] However, in contrast to the tradition of his church he speaks of 'the one true church' and does not explicitly call it 'the Roman Catholic church'. The 'one true church' is the community of the faithful constituted by the Holy Spirit. Of course this definition does not exclude the Roman Catholic church, but at the same time it is open to the Orthodox and the Protestant definitions of the church. As Rahner states, the decision about human salvation stands or falls with faith in Christ. The old maxim 'no salvation outside the church' (*extra ecclesiam nulla salus*) has to mean 'no salvation outside Christ' (*extra Christum nulla salus*), because it is included in this: at least, where Christ is and is believed, there too the church is and is believed to be the body of Christ.

Now this exclusivity of the Christian claim to salvation is contrasted with inclusive universality, for 'God wants everyone to be saved' (I Tim.2.4). So Rahner asks, 'Can the Christian believe even for a moment that the overwhelming mass of his brothers, not only those before the appearance of Christ . . . but also those of the present and of the future before us, are unquestionably and in principle excluded from the fulfilment of their lives and condemned to eternal meaninglessness?' Because Christians have to believe in God's universal will to salvation, they cannot believe this, but must believe, 'somehow all men must be capable of being members of the church'.[6] If this 'must be capable' is not meant hypothetically, but understood as a 'real and historically concrete possibility', it means that 'it must be possible to be not only an anonymous "theist", but also an anonymous Christian, and this . . . with a *certain* making visible and tangible of this anonymous relationship'.[7] That is the task which Rahner has set himself: 'But how is a relationship of this kind to be conceived?'

112

The theological context in which Rahner attempts to give the answer is the old scholastic scheme of 'nature and grace'. Let us first see what his answer looks like, and then ask whether this scheme is not too narrow to give an appropriate answer to the world situation which I described at the beginning, which is essentially different from that of the Middle Ages.

Just as grace 'presupposes' nature, so God's free communication of himself presupposes this creature which owes itself with its being and its possibilities of being to the omnipotence of God. But over and above this, this creature must 'be given the possibility of hearing and accepting as beyond itself the incalculable new turning of God towards it in his revelation'. In this respect Rahner calls the human being 'a being of unlimited openness for the limitless being of God'. For him 'openness' means on the one hand 'an indefinability come to consciousness of itself',[8] and on the other hand (divine) spirit, namely being directed towards 'the infinite mystery', the 'incomprehensible God'. This orientation becomes evident in knowledge of this God's 'superiority over the world and his personality' and is the foundation of the capacity 'to hear a new, possible word from his hidden God'. In the light of their presupposed nature and by virtue of the supernatural possibility bestowed on them, human beings are orientated on God. Rahner calls this tendency in human existence 'anonymous theism'. It is none other than the old Aristotelian Thomistic doctrine of the 'natural desire'. But whereas Thomas located this human desire in the intellect, according to Rahner it embraces the emotion of the whole person.

But does this tendency towards God include an orientation towards the God made man, towards Christ? Rahner answers in the affirmative, but excludes on the one hand the idea of an automatic subordination and on the other the conception of a purely fortuitous tie. Christ is 'the freest and in this sense . . . the most contingent fact of reality', but at the same time also 'the most decisive and important and moreover the fact which has the most obvious relevance to man'. Rahner makes the link by saying that from the divine perspective man is the being that comes about if God becomes man and shows himself in the region of the non-godly, expresses himself there and empties himself. From the human perspective man is the being who comes to himself when he surrenders himself to the incomprehensible mystery of God. In this respect the incarnation of God is 'the uniquely supreme case of the actualization of man's nature in general'.[9] The constitutive self-transcendence of man therefore comes in his achievement and his fulfilment in God's communication of himself. In the incarnation of God man finally comes to God. According to Rahner there are two views of one and the same event: the coming to being of human reality and the incarnation of God, God's giving away of himself to human beings and human self-surrender to the mystery of God. Therefore he can relate these two sides as 'internal and external', 'anonymous and explicit', and say 'that man in experiencing his transcendence . . . also already experiences the offer of grace', that 'the revelation of the word in Christ . . . is only the explicitation of what we already are by grace', and that thus 'the expressly Christian revelation becomes the explicit statement of the revelation of grace which man always experiences implicitly in the depths of his being'.[10]

The 'self-communication of God' offered to all human beings and fulfilled in Christ to the highest degree is 'the goal of creation generally'.[11] That means in an exclusive sense that human beings only come to fulfil their nature and perfect their being by being Christians. In an inclusive sense it means that to be a Christian is none other than to be a true human being. In a constantly amazing shift of thought known from mystical theology, Rahner concludes from this that those who come to their being and the perfection of their being are Christians whether they know it or not, for such a person 'also already accepts this revelation when he really accepts himself completely, for it already speaks *in* him'.[12] 'He takes upon himself in that Yes to himself the grace of the mystery which has radically approached us.' The revelation of God in Christ is on the one hand God's communication of himself and on the other side gives expression to and names what human beings have always already experienced in the depth of their being as their most authentic characteristics. From this there follows the twofold thesis: 1. human beings are anonymous Christians in their most authentic possibilities; Christians are human beings who are expressed in their true reality.

3. Open questions in the scheme of 'nature and grace'

First of all we shall keep to the scheme of 'nature and grace' which Rahner uses as the basis for his arguments and ask some critical questions:

1. Can Rahner's definition of the human being as 'indefinability come to itself', as 'self-transcendence' and 'unlimited openness to the boundless being of God', be universalized? From the perspective of those 'ancient cultures of Asia' this is not a definition of 'the human being' but a description of the European who has been moulded by Christianity. Just as Heidegger's existentialia did not represent basic conditions of human beings in themselves but conditions in the perspective of central Europeans of the 1920s, so too it is easy to recognize in Rahner's ontological anthropology a particular ideal of existence, one which has been moulded by European Christianity. The Augustinian 'restless heart' is regarded as a human state in accordance with creation, but in Augustine and in Christian culture after him it has always been determined by the biblical stories of the exodus of Abraham, the exodus of Israel and the wandering people of God in the Letter to the Hebrews. For human beings who live in the thousand-year-old religions of external and internal equilibrium (Taoism, Hinduism, Buddhism) this future-orientated restlessness which derives from the Abrahamic religions (Judaism, Christianity and Islam) is both alien and shocking. So they must understand the view that this restlessness is

part of human nature generally, everywhere and at all times as an attempt at Christian missionizing, and reject it as European alienation.

So is Rahner's universal definition of humankind also capable of receiving universal assent? As the definition of human indefinability shows, it contains the greatest possible freedom, because it embraces and goes beyond all conceivable definitions. Assent is to be obtained more in indefinite negatives than in a fixation on a positive. A greater fellowship comes about in silence before the infinite mystery than through talk which all too quickly provokes contradiction. Nevertheless, the problem in defining what is universal is not the objective truth itself, but the subjective right to apply this definition to all others. If there is a common humanity and if there is to be a human world community, who and what institutions have the right to lay down these conditions and enact these laws for it?

In this respect, in his article Rahner has clearly defined universal humanity in terms of Christianity, so that there can be 'anonymous Christianity' within universal humanity, for it was his intention to say this. For him, being human appears as a universal foil to the particularity of being Christian. But from that, conversely, does there not follow the universal claim of Christians to be the one, authentic interpretation of humanity? And from that does there not follow in turn the universal claim of the Christian church that it alone can define and interpret human nature correctly in the light of the revelation of salvation in Christ?

2. If on the other hand Rahner's definition of the Christian revelation is 'experienced as the explicitation of what we always already are by grace' and as an 'explicit statement of the revelation of grace which man always experiences implicitly in the depths of his being', is justice done to the underivably new and special element in the revelation of Christ? Certainly Rahner calls the fact of Christ, 'the freest and in this sense the most chance fact of reality', but in this context he is merely explicitating the degree to which it is the fact 'which is most clearly related to man'. The reference to human beings is termed the 'explicitation' of what is always already there in human beings, or rather what must be able to be in them. In this respect the revelation of Christ does not actually add anything new, but merely discloses, expresses and mentions by name what is already there or can be there in the depth of human existence or as the indescribable nearness of the divine mystery. The revelation of Christ is thus wholly related to this 'revelation by grace', and this is wholly related to human creatureliness. Through Christian faith human beings become what they should be through God's creation. They come to themselves by coming to God, and they come to God by coming to themselves.

What Rahner represents here is radical existentialist interpretation. Bultmann also saw things in this way: 'There is no other light shining in Jesus than has always already shined in the creation. Man learns to understand himself in the

115

light of the revelation of redemption not a bit differently than he always already should understand himself in face of the revelation in creation and the law – namely as God's creature.'[13] If the revelation of Christ is only the disclosure of the truth of being human, then the Christian faith cannot be anything other than the awakening of the inner divine grace in human beings, and being a Christian is then an actualized form of being human. On the one hand, in this approach the specifically Christian threatens to disappear in the universally human, becoming its disclosure, awakening and mere confirmation. On the other hand, excessive demands are put on the specifically Christian if it is to be the truth about being human. Is that not the old claim to absoluteness through which so many Christians and also the churches became irrefutably aware of their incompletable incompleteness?

3. If being human is regarded as the presupposition of being Christian and being Christian is regarded as the expression and realization of being human, then between these two sides thought easily finds itself going round in circles: what has to be confirmed is presupposed and what was presupposed is confirmed. Being Christian and being human match like a picture and an appropriate frame. Being human becomes the universal of the particular, which is being Christian, and being Christian becomes the specific aspect of universal humanity. But in this way this particular and the universal are related to each other exclusively. There is really no room for the pluralism of religious freedom in an ideologically neutral state and for the pluralism of the world religions on earth. The mediaeval scheme of nature and grace is given a modern interpretation but not changed: 'Gratia praesupponit naturam': grace presupposes nature both passively and actively. 'Gratia non destruit sed perficit naturam': 'grace does not destroy but perfects nature'. The incarnation of Christ is the goal of creation. Therefore grace perfects nature and being Christian is the perfection of being human.

The old mediaeval scheme certainly related directly to the ontological stages of nature and supernature and the relationship between nature and grace in salvation history. But the scheme also reflected the church's claim to lordship over the world as the 'crown of society' and the perfect society. This claim by the church could only be sustained in a Christian empire. It can hardly be maintained in an open mission situation in six continents. Basically it has always proved too much for the church, since in a chiliastic way it identifies the church with the kingdom of God.

4. The extension of the scheme of 'nature and grace'

Down to the present, the theological tradition has preferred two-membered, dual thought. It has spoken of 'creation and redemption', of 'nature and grace', of 'necessity and freedom', of 'body and soul', and so on. In the context of this duality the principle was formed: *gratia non destruit, sed praesupponit et*

116

perficit naturam (grace does not destroy nature but presupposes and perfects it).

I think that the first half of this principle is correct but not the second, since it does not make an explicit distinction between grace and glory, history and new creation, the church and the kingdom of God, being a Christian and perfect humanity. Because this second differentiation is not made sufficiently clearly, this principle keeps leading to a triumphalism which has its foundation in eschatological enthusiasm: the glory which consummates nature is said already to lie in grace; the kingdom that transfigures nature is said already to exist in the covenant; the consummation of being human is said already to be given in being human. This enthusiasm leads to excessive demands constantly being made on grace, the church and Christians, since they are expected to provide something which has not yet been given them.

So I would reformulate the old theological principle in the second half as tripartite dialectic and say: *Gratia non perficit, sed praeparat naturam ad gloriam aeternam. Gratia non est perfectio naturae, sed praeparatio messianica mundi ad regnum Dei*: 'Grace does not perfect nature but prepares it for eternal glory. Grace is not the perfection of nature but the messianic preparation of the world for the kingdom of God.' The starting point of this principle is that the grace of God is manifest in the surrender and the resurrection of Christ, and its conclusion is that his resurrection is the beginning of the new creation of the world so that it becomes the realm of glory. The coming of Christ in the flesh is therefore not yet the goal of creation. The goal of creation is, rather, the kingdom for the sake of which Christ has come. It follows from this that talk of nature and grace and of the relationship between nature and grace must always be related to that future of God which perfects both nature and grace and therefore makes the relationship of nature and grace a relationship in history which is open to the future. It also follows that the historical covenant cannot be called the 'internal basis of creation'; that term can be used only for the coming kingdom of glory promised and guaranteed through the historical covenant.[14] Not least it follows that being a Christian cannot yet of itself claim to be the explicitation, the truth, the perfection of being human, but only represents a messianic way to a possible, future and shared perfection of humanity.

On this messianic way, Christian existence first of all finds Jewish existence alongside it as a travelling companion and witness to the same hope of a humanity which is finally freed and glorified and a humankind united in the righteousness of God. Christian existence does not displace Jewish existence but is directed towards it and enters into a historical companionship with it on the way.

According to its own promise, Christianity then discovers the other presences of the coming kingdom in the world, perhaps not immediately 'anonymous Christians', but certainly already the judge who will deliver the judgment to

117

come and who is already present in the anonymity of the poor, the hungry, the sick and the imprisoned (Mark 25).

The church of Christ is not identical with the kingdom of God, for the sake of which it has been called into life. Nor does it have any claim to be the sole representative of the coming kingdom. However, this recognition does not mean that it becomes dissolved in the randomness of religious confessions in a 'pluralistic society', but rather that it has an unambiguous place in relation to the presence of the kingdom of God in the world. In other words, it is assigned a place among the poor and its 'preferential option' is for the humiliated.

Mediaeval Judaism – for example in the person of Maimonides – was fond of seeing and assessing the Christianity which was evangelizing the nations as the messianic preparation of the Gentile world willed by God. I shall take up this estimation of Christian existence in Jewish theology and extend it beyond the world of nations to humanity and nature. Through the power of hope given to Christianity through Christ in the Spirit, humankind and nature receive a messianic preparation and are opened up to God's future.

If we think in terms of this messianic movement, then the great theological dualities are freed from merely being set over against each other and are made relative to something greater which is to come. They can then no longer be defined over against each other through a reciprocal negation, but with their multiple interconnections are defined in terms of a third element which they have in common. The historical mediations of grace and nature, covenant and creation, being Christian and being human, can then be recognized more precisely and understood in a more differentiated way.

5. Creation, incarnation and the kingdom of glory

Three remarks may serve to provide a basis for this extension of the scheme of 'nature and grace':

1. According to the first creation account the 'goal of creation' is not humankind as God's image on earth but God's sabbath. God 'completes' his creation by 'resting' from all his works. So he blessed and hallowed the seventh day.[15] This sabbath of God is the 'festival of creation', and as the festival of creation it is also the 'festival of completion'. Having so to speak gone out of himself in creation, God turns round on the sabbath and returns to himself in the sabbath rest. God is completely present as himself. In coming to rest he allows his creatures to be there. Before his face, in his presence and his rest, they are what they should be, and develop in their freedom.

The Creator has called into being from nothingness all that is created. All that exists is threatened by this nothingness. It can be annihilated again. Therefore, one can conclude, all that exists is restlessly in search of a place and time where the threat cannot reach it, a 'place of rest'. 'So then, a sabbath rest still remains for the people of God; for those who enter God's rest also cease

118

from their labours as God did from his' (Heb.4.9f.).

Not only is the human heart 'restless until it finds rest in you', as Augustine said, but all creatures whom God has created and made are filled with this unrest. According to the first creation story the 'rest' in which they come to themselves and their joy in existence is not heaven or the God of the other world, as Gnosticism and mysticism taught, but the sabbath of God in creation. In the resting, direct presence of God all creatures find their support and eternal protection from nothingness. The sabbath fills all creatures and the whole community of creation with the happiness of the eternal presence of God. From a biblical perspective, is not what Karl Rahner has described so convincingly in all his writings as the incomprehensible mystery of God, which is yet so near, the quietness and rest of the sabbath nearness of God? In it God shares himself not through speaking but through silence, not through action but through being there.

2. The incarnation of God in Christ is without doubt not only related to the Fall but also to the original creation of men and women in the image of God. Therefore Christ is called the visible image of the invisible God, and it is said that men and women come to their true and original determination as being in the image of God when they are 'conformed' to Christ, the firstborn among many (Rom.8.29). But the incarnation of God in Christ has to be related to more than the Fall and the original creation if its meaning is to be understood. It also has to be related to God's future: 'If anyone is in Christ there is a new creation. The old has passed away and behold everything is made new' (II Cor.5.17).

This eschatological reference of christology can all too easily be lost sight of if the incarnation is put at the centre of christology. But if one moves from the surrender of Christ to his suffering and death on the cross and his resurrection from the dead and the transfiguration of his new corporeality, then the eschatological horizon of christology immediately becomes clear. It also becomes clear that this eschatological horizon does not coincide with the protological horizon, since the redemption and transfiguration of creation is not identical with the restoration of the original creation. The 'new creation' is also new in comparison to the 'original creation', because it fulfils it. That can already be recognized in the humanity of Christ. In the perspective of its destiny to be in the image of God, Christ's humanity is the restoration of this original destiny and is to be seen as its true and complete fulfilment. But in the perspective of the transfiguration of creation in the realm of glory, the humanity of Christ is perfect participation in the divine nature.

Thus the humanity of Christ can be seen as the primal sacrament. According to the Thomistic theology of the sacraments, it is a *signum rememorativum* and is to be related to the original image of God in human beings; at the same time it is a *signum prognosticon* and to be related to the final glorification in God's eschatological sabbath: in the unity of both perspectives it is a sign of grace for

119

present-day human beings in their history. So however much the humanity of Christ points back to original universal humanity, and in this respect may also be regarded as a certain fulfilment of humanity, on the other hand it points beyond itself to a greater future for all men and women and in this respect is a way and a transition: Christ is the incarnate promise of God for the world.

If we keep these multi-level complexes in view, then to explain being human as the presupposition of being Christian and being Christian as the consummation of being human is too narrow an approach. Being Christian is not in itself already the consummation of being human, but only a historical course and a promise of the consummation of humankind. One is not a human being in order to become a Christian but becomes a Christian in order to be a human being. What universal and true humanity is can certainly be sought hypothetically in the origin of peoples, but in reality it lies in the historical future: it is the human person in a human world community. What have developed anthropologically from the Christian tradition are in fact projects for being human in a human way in that shared future of the nations. In this situation it is perhaps even more realistic to begin from the fact that at present there are Christians, Jews and other peoples, but not yet humane human beings as members of a human community. One could then go on to say that there are Christians, Jews and other peoples in order that a human society should come into being whose members really understand themselves as humane human beings, and that therefore Christians, Jews and peoples are to be regarded as promises of this human future and ways towards it.

However, that in itself already brings us to a rather different estimation of that theme which 'with all its urgency cannot be avoided . . . either by a theology of grace and of the church which has a true understanding of itself, or by an honest pastoral theology which looks at our times dispassionately'.[16] There is a universalism of being human, a particularism of being a Christian and a pluralism of religions – none of the angles of this triangle can be removed. I now have to describe what, according to eschatological theology, the inalienable particularism of the Christian church contributes to the universalism of being human and the pluralism of religions and thus justifies it.

6. The kingdom of God in history and the church

1. If we introduce the distinction between historical grace and eschatological glory seriously into discussion of the problem, the difference between the historical church and the eschatological kingdom of God must be stressed.[17] The church is *not yet* the kingdom of God, and in the kingdom of God there will no longer be a temple and therefore also no longer a church because 'God will be all in all'. Now if the church is not yet the kingdom of God, the historical church cannot claim and assume the character of the kingdom of God which is indicated by universality. The kingdom of the new creation is universal, but not the church.

This immediately becomes clear from the internal problem of the relationship of the Christian church to Judaism and the synagogue: if the church were universal in its intention and its tendency, it could not respect a Judaism alongside itself. The only future salvation of the Jews would then be baptism and entry into the church.

This triumphalism, which has been represented and practised in church history long enough, already came to grief on the biblical testimony of Romans 9-11. Israel has its abiding call to salvation alongside the church and shares with the church a common hope for the appearing of the Messiah in glory. In that future of God which alone can be called truly 'universal', the special existences of the church and Israel will cease because their special elections to special service will be fulfilled.

2. The apostolic gospel of the kingdom in the name of Jesus takes sides in an inhuman world in which human beings are humiliated, oppressed and exploited by other human beings: 'He has shown strength with his arm, he has scattered the proud in the imagination of their hearts, he has put down the mighty from their thrones, and exalted those of low degree; he has filled the hungry with good things, and the rich he has sent empty away' (Luke 1.51f.). That must also be evident in the church community itself: 'Consider your call; not many of you were wise according to worldly standards, not many were powerful, not many were of noble birth; but God chose what is foolish in the world to shame the wise, God chose what is weak in the world to shame the strong, God chose what is low and despised in the world, even things that are not, to bring to nothing things that are, so that no human being might boast in the presence of God' (I Cor.1.26-29). The partisanship of the apostolic gospel for the poor, weak and lowly against the rich, strong and exalted is to be understood as the concrete apostolic way towards the universality of the kingdom of God. Specific testimony to the universal kingdom in a violent world cannot be given in any other way. Christian partisanship for the poor, weak and humiliated is the historically necessary form of bearing witness to the universal kingdom. Jesus turned one-sidedly to the sinners, the sick and the lepers, in order also to save the righteous, the healthy and the despisers. Paul became the missionary to the Gentiles in order to save Israel, too, in this way.

The so-called particularism of the Christian church is not to be lamented in the perspective of its universal claim to salvation if it means the partisan support of the church of Christ for the poor in the name of the coming kingdom. The real problem of the church in today's world is not its particular and marginal existence in pluralistic societies with its universal claim to salvation, but the need to provide partisan support for the mass of poor people in violent societies, whether in ideological and religious terms these societies are 'pluralistic' or uniform.

If the church is to discover its universal significance in its particularity, then

121

it will hold to the presence of Christ in the poor, weak and oppressed of this world. It must discover his universal presence of judgment and the kingdom of God in the world and identify itself in that.

We thus return to Rahner's thematic question. Are there 'anonymous Christians' outside Christianity in the world? There are: they are the poor, the hungry, the thirsty, the sick and the imprisoned of Matt.25 whom Christ declares to be his 'brothers and sisters', whether they are Christians or not. There are the children of Matt.18 to whom Jesus promises the kingdom, whether they believe or not. So there are also 'anonymous Christians' where deeds of mercy and justice are done to them.

(ii) The Question of Compassion and God's Impassibility

(a) Karl Rahner

'But let us turn once again to the theology of the cross. If I were now to add anything over and above the reference already made to a basic conception of death, then I would have to know more precisely the nature of the inadequacy of my position. If I wanted to launch a counterattack, I would say that there is a modern tendency (I don't want to say a theory but at least a tendency) to develop a theology of the death of God that, in the last analysis, seems to me to be gnostic. One can find this in Hans Urs von Balthasar and in Adrienne von Speyr, although naturally much more marked in her than in him. It also appears in an independent form in Moltmann. To put it crudely, it does not help me to escape from my mess and mix-up and despair if God is in the same predicament. I know of course and I have emphasized that the classical teaching on the Incarnation and the theology of the hypostatic union included and must include, even while avoiding Patripassanism (a suffering and dying God the Father), a meaningful and serious statement to the effect that God died. I have no intention of denying or obfuscating this. But on the other hand, it is for me a source of confusion to realize that God, when and in so far as he entered into this history as his own, did it in a different way than I did. From the beginning I am cemented into its horribleness while God – if this word continues to have any meaning at all – is in a true and authentic and consoling sense the God who does not suffer, the immutable God, and so on. In Moltmann and others I sense a theology of absolute paradox, of Patripassianism, perhaps even of a Schelling-like projection into God of division, conflict, godlessness and death. To this I would say first of all: What do we know then so precisely about God? And second, I would

122

ask: What use would that be to me as consolation in the true sense of the word?'[18]

(b) Jürgen Moltmann

Dear Fr Rahner,

I discovered this interview too late, so I can only reply to it posthumously. I would love to have discussed this basic question of our faith personally with you. But if, as we believe, death brings an end to the limits of our finitude in space and time, at this moment before God you are more present to me than in the limited time of your life.

In the interview, which was about Hans Urs von Balthasar, you mentioned me only in passing, but you struck at the heart of my faith and my theology of the 'crucified God'. 'Only the suffering God can help,' wrote Dietrich Bonhoeffer in a Gestapo cell. Christ, the one who was tempted, the Son of God who died forsaken by God, helped me when I sat 'cemented' in a messy concentration camp in 1945, tormented and forsaken by God, and abandoned all hope. It is on the basis of this experience of God that I believe and think. So I am disturbed by your objection that God is 'in a consoling sense the God who does not suffer'. I find no connection between consolation and apathy and therefore find no way into your experience of God and self.

Of course God entered into our history of suffering in a divine way; he was not subjected to it against his will. For the theologians of the early church there was only the involuntary suffering of creation and the essential apathy of the Godhead. But there is a third form of suffering, the voluntary suffering of love for the beloved and in the beloved. That God does not suffer as finite creatures suffer does not mean that he is incapable of suffering in any way. God is capable of suffering because he is capable of love. His being is mercy. I developed this at length in my book *The Crucified God* (270ff.). An impassible God is capable of neither love nor feeling. Empathy is impossible for such a God. So such a God is not in a position to console people either. One can only console when one shares another's feelings. And one can only share another's feelings if one has empathy. And having empathy means being passible and not impassible. I cannot imagine an impassible God as a God who consoles in a personal sense. He seems to me to be as cold and as hard and unfeeling as cement.

What most disturbed and shocked me, though, was what you said about yourself. 'From the beginning I am cemented into its horribleness.' That sounds bitter, cut off, isolated and incapable of movement. Those who are 'cemented' in cannot be reached by anyone and do not reach anyone. That sounds like a life which is unloved and incapable of love. Indeed it sounds like a frozen, fossilized life, one which is already dead. Are these the pains of being cut off from natural relationships which celibacy imposes on a young man enthused by God? Is being 'cemented' in a special Jesuit experience of a complete lack of ties to the world so as to be available to God at any time? Or is it just the feeling of an old man for whom physical existence has become increasingly burdensome? But who at the end of a rich and blessed life would look only at its 'horribleness' and not at the same time at its fragile beauty and its finite goodness? And who, having taken this way by his own decision, would complain about the price of following Christ? There is more to it than that. 'From the beginning . . . ', you say, and by that evidently mean this human existence generally and what is determined by it for each of us. Is that the wicked world, or fate, or God himself? Because we do not belong among the 'damned of this earth', the feeling of hell that you express must come from the damnation of the *massa perditionis* by God. The phrase 'from the beginning' weighs heavily on any attentive reader because it sounds so hopeless and brings so little comfort.

How can the *Deus impassibilis* be God in a sense which comforts you? Perhaps in the sense that in God there is no more suffering, pain and crying and that in suffering, pain and crying we long for redemption in him. But certainly not in the sense that God for his part is 'cemented' into his inability to suffer or to be moved and his unloved lovelessness. With what right do we human beings say that God is 'incapable'? Do we not 'cement' God in with the negations of negative theology? If that is the case, then a personal experience of being locked in and the divine experience of the *Deus impassibilis* go closely together. In that case, would the God who is locked into his immobility and impassibility be a comfort for the person whose existence also seems to be like that? In that case God would be, as you put it, in the same predicament, and neither God nor human beings could find comfort in eternity.

I won't let my thoughts run on. You will now know more than you did then and than I know now. I remain here with great respect for you, having learned a great deal from you, and now having been deeply shocked by you,

Yours sincerely,

Jürgen Moltmann

3

Creation, Covenant and Glory

A Conversation on Karl Barth's
Doctrine of Creation

In engaging in an argument with Karl Barth I do not feel that I can dissociate myself from him: I owe Barth too much for that. But one does not honour a teacher by regurgitating his thoughts and quoting his texts or even blaming him for his thoughts, so as to be able get them from him again with greater authority. One honours a teacher by independently attempting to recognize and express an issue with which he too was concerned. If this issue is that of God, then it is always greater than our fragmentary knowledge and involves all our efforts in a fellowship of seeking and thinking in which we learn from one another and supplement one another by providing correctives. I do not mean this in the general sense that all knowledge is relative and therefore a matter of indifference, but have in mind the concrete difference between times and situations in which recognitions are disclosed and superseded. In the 'Third Reich' with its blood and soil cult of the Aryan race different demands were put on a Chrisitan theology of creation from those with which such a theology is confronted today in the face of a global ecological crisis. The different situations have no character as revelation, but they do have hermeneutical relevance. With this in mind, I shall attempt to take up the intentions of Barth's doctrine of creation and implement them in a different way from the one that he took. I do not believe that in principle he would have been opposed to this; indeed I imagine that he himself would not have expected a 'theology after Barth' to begin again any differently from the same beginning.

It is true that as one gets older one becomes biographical. But the reminiscences that I want to pass on are not a 'quest for lost time', but an early present which still moves me today, even if, chronologically speaking, for others it is part of the long distant past. For me Karl Barth is the present. As Göttingen students in the group around Iwand, Wolf and Weber, at an early stage I and my friends cast our longing eyes towards Basle. Others received a grant or could at

125

least live in Lörrach, but I had no chance of doing either. So I could only read the *Church Dogmatics*, not hear Barth in person. And that kept me at a certain distance. Still tormented at that time by Kierkegaard and struggling with the young Luther, I felt the stately, meditative and doxological style of the *Church Dogmatics* to be like a beautiful dream: too beautiful to be true on this earth, from the annihilation of which in the war we had just escaped. Only the doctrine of predestination with its theology of the cross (in II.2) touched my heart. Through the good offices of Helmut Traub I was then able to visit Barth twice, but in these brief periods I did not particularly warm to him because I was too preoccupied with my own problems. At that time I had turned to questions relating to the history of theology, especially seventeenth-century federal theology, since for a long time I had the impression that just as there could be no other philosophy after Hegel, so there could be no other theology after Barth. Arnold van Ruler and Ernst Bloch freed me from this misconception.

There was then an all too brief, but vigorous, exchange of letters when in 1964 I sent him my *Theology of Hope*. He must have read it and discussed it straight away. On 8 November he wrote to Richard Karwehl that the book was very 'stimulating and irritating, because the young author makes an energetic attempt to deal with the eschatological aspect of the Gospel better than the old man of Basel did in *Romans* and *CD*. I read him with great openness but hesitate to follow him because this new systematizing – though there is much to be said for it – is almost too good to be true.'[1] On 17 November, after some general and positive comments he conveyed a rather different view to me: 'My own concern relates to the unilinear way in which you subsume all theology in eschatology, going beyond Blumhardt, Overbeck and Schweitzer in this regard. To put it pointedly, does your theology of hope really differ at all from the baptized principle of hope of Herr Bloch? What disturbs me is that for you theology becomes so much a matter of principle (an eschatological principle). You know that I too was once on the edge of moving in this direction, but I refrained from doing so and have thus come under the fire of your criticism in my later development . . . But salvation does not come from the *Church Dogmatics* (I started out here when reading your book) but from knowledge of the "eternally rich God" with whom I thought I should deal. If you will pardon me, your God seems to me to be rather a pauper . . . '

This was indeed very pointed, since it was clear to Barth, too, that one cannot choose a 'rich' or a 'poor' God. But the real critical point lay in his 'three-dimensional' resolution of the 'one-dimensional' eschatological thought that he had detected in me: 'Would it not be wise to accept the doctrine of the immanent Trinity of God? You may thereby achieve the freedom of three-dimensional thinking in which the *eschata* have and retain their whole weight while the same (and not just a provisional) honour can still be shown to the kingdoms of nature and grace. Have my concepts of the threefold time (CD II.2, 47.1; II.1, 619-38)

126

and threefold parousia of Jesus Christ (CD IV.3, 69.4) made so little impact on you that you do not even give them critical consideration?'[2]

Here indeed is the crucial point: neither the three-dimensional unfolding of eternity in the modes of time – pre-temporality, supra-temporality and post-temporality – nor the doctrine of a threefold parousia of Christ deriving from Justin – 'he came in the flesh, comes in the Spirit and will come in glory' – made much impression on me. In the New Testament, *parousia* is in fact used only for the coming of Christ in glory, and in his doctrine of time Barth does not make a systematic distinction between future and advent. Basically he kept to the eschatology of eternity with which in the 1920s he had replaced the future eschatology of Blumhardt, from which he had started out.[3] But here we shall not be discussing eschatology and the reign of glory but with the 'equal honour' or the 'provisional honour' for the kingdom of grace and the kingdom of glory. Or is perhaps the kingdom of nature only honoured to the same degree when in respect of the covenant of grace and the kingdom of glory it is given not 'just' honour but an already prior honour.

I shall attempt to carry on a discussion with Barth in the realm of the doctrine of creation by posing some alternatives, but I shall also refer back to his other basic theological decisions which become relevant in the doctrine of creation. Here first of all are the key phrases:

1. An eschatological doctrine of creation develops a christological doctrine of creation: instead of the duality of 'creation-covenant' there is the dialectical movement of creation, covenant and that glory which fulfils covenant and creation, and *gratia non perficit, sed praeparat naturam ad gloriam Dei* (grace does not perfect nature but prepares it for the glory of God).[4]

2. A social doctrine of the Trinity goes beyond the monarchical doctrine of the Trinity and leads to a pneumatological doctrine of creation. What is normative for all relations in creation is not the structure of command and obedience within the Trinity but the eternal perichoresis of the triunity. From this there follows the presence of the Spirit in the fellowship of creation.[5] From this, too, there follows a perichoretic doctrine of creation: the essence of all things is the field of creation in which they live, move and have their being.

3. A fellowship of creation replaces hierarchical orders of creation. Order is not necessarily super- and subordination, but mutual fellowship held in a fluid balance. Barth's hierarchical parallels of Father-Son in the Trinity, God-world, heaven-earth, soul-body, man-woman are to be dissolved and brought to life in terms of mutuality and perichoresis.

4. In Barth's Scheleiermacherian doctrine of 'natural death', the hope of cosmic resurrection is given up and finitude is equated with mortality.

5. Is Barth a modern theologian?

1. The kingdom of glory as the basis and goal of creation[6]

The second part of the leading sentence of §41, 'Creation and Covenant', reads:

> But according to this witness the purpose and therefore the meaning of creation is to make possible the history of God's covenant with man which has its beginning, its centre and its culmination in Jesus Christ. The history of this covenant is as much the goal of creation as creation itself is the beginning of this history (42).

The fourth leading idea of my doctrine of creation runs:

> *Gratia non perficit, sed praeparat naturam ad gloriam aeternam: gratia non est perfectio naturae, sed praeparatio messianica mundi ad regnum Dei.* This principle proceeds from the assumption that the grace of God can be seen in the raising of Christ, and concludes that Christ's resurrection is the beginning of the new creation of the world. It follows from this that we have to talk about nature and grace, and the relationship between nature and grace, in a forward perspective, in the light of the coming glory, which will complete both nature and grace, and hence already determines the relationship between the two historically. It also follows that God's covenant in history cannot already be called the 'internal basis' of creation. We can give this name only to the coming kingdom of God's glory which his covenant in history promises and guarantees (8).

Barth relates God's covenant to human beings and only to them. In this way his doctrine of creation takes on an anthropocentric focus, as though the non-human world were created just for human beings. Jesus Christ is the beginning, middle and end of the covenant of God with humankind, as though Christ had come only for their sake and were only their reconciler and Lord. The creation of the non-human world is explained as the 'external basis of the covenant'. Barth sees in it only the 'enabling' of the history of God with humankind and its beginning.

It is surprising that at this point, in determining the relationship between covenant and creation, Barth did not already consider the Reformed federal theology which he knew so well. If only he had taken his bearings from G.Schrenk, *Gottesreich und Bund im älteren Protestantismus* (The Kingdom of God and the Covenant in Early Protestantism), Gütersloh 1922, he would inevitably have been struck by the way in which he differed from tradition. For Cocceius, creation is not just a work of God which makes the covenant possible but is itself a covenant with God, the covenant of creation. The history of the covenant then goes beyond the step-by-step dismantling of the covenant of works and the step-by-step construction of the covenant of grace, into the future of the kingdom of glory, for the sake of which – as theological tradition had always said since the early church fathers – God created the world: for the glory

128

of God. Human beings, too, are created 'to glorify God and enjoy him for ever', as the Westminster Catechism says. According to Phil.2, the humiliation and exaltation of Christ, his death on the cross and the universal cosmic hymn of praise take place 'to the glory of God the Father'. Together with the history of the covenant of God with men and women, the initial covenant of creation with all creatures is developed into the consummation of the new creation in the present glory of God. Orthodox theology calls the 'divinization of the cosmos' the goal of creation and the purpose of grace. The more time goes on, the less I understand why Barth connected creation and covenant together so exclusively as a pair, and why his impressive remarks on the sabbath as the 'crown of creation' (223) did not lead him to revise the anthropocentrism in pairing creation and covenant which he in fact shares with 'modern religion'.

If one wanted to revise his views in one's own interest one could well start from the last remark in his first sentence: 'creation itself is the beginning of this history' (viz. of the covenant). If that is the case, then the creation itself is already God's covenant, and not just the enabling of such a covenant with just one creature. If creation as a whole is God's covenant from the beginning, then all creatures live in this covenant, and not just human beings, and as 'centre of the covenant' Christ is the reconciler not only of human beings but of the whole cosmos, as Eph.1 and Col.2 say. In that case not only is the non-human world made for the sake of human beings (7ff.), but human beings are made for the sake of the earth. There is no one-sided purpose; the intention is reciprocity in the fellowship of all creatures. And if the creation itself is already the 'beginning' of this history, then within it there is obviously an unstoppable bias, a tendency and openness towards this history of the covenant. The honour of the realm of nature is therefore a provisional honour: the honour of the provisional, of that which points beyond itself, of the parable and the promise, is its true honour. However, for its part the history of God's covenant in Christ with human beings is full of promise, tendency and openness towards its consummation in the kingdom of glory. Grace is not yet glory, but its promise and beginning. That is the 'provisional honour' of grace, the end of its eschatological provisionality. In saying this I am in no way 'robbing the redemption in Christ which has already taken place' of its reality at the expense of 'eschatological redemption', as C.Link fears, but am respecting the reconciliation in Christ which has already taken place and which according to Barth himself is 'the anticipation' of eschatological redemption. At the end of the history of the covenant stands not the covenant, nor even the history or the historicity of existence and the world, but creation again: the new creation (Rev.21).

The creation, namely the creation transformed by the indwelling of God, is the goal of history. What can be described as the goal of creation is not the 'historicizing of nature' but the eschatological 'naturalizing of history'.

If we do not take seriously the difference between grace and glory, between

129

reconciliation and redemption, we make too many demands on grace because we expect of it what only glory can give. We make too many demands on the covenant and the history of God with men and women, because it is already meant to give what only *theosis,* the visible indwelling of God in his new creation, can give to all creatures.

However, if we take this difference seriously, then we may hope from God's future not only the redemption of human existence and the consummation of human history but also the redemption and consummation of non-human creation which is sighing here. What will redeem captive creatures is not the freedom of the children of God but the glory of God which reveals itself in the freedom of the children of God (Rom.8.21).

The eschatological doctrine of creation interprets the first in the light of the last and recollection in the light of hope. Just as Israel spelt out the significance of the creation 'in the beginning' in the light of the exodus, the covenant and the Torah, so Christianity interprets creation in the light of the risen Messiah and recognizes in the firstborn from the dead the firstborn of the whole creation (Col.1.15). The messiah takes the place of the Torah and expounds creation. He expounds creation in the light of the kingdom of God which has been announced to him and has begun. Any really christological doctrine of creation must therefore by that very fact become an eschatological doctrine of creation if it takes Jesus Christ seriously as the messiah of the coming kingdom. That means that it will seek to decipher the reality of the world in a messianic light, in both its need (Adorno) and its messianic enciphering (Bloch). The creation is the ontic promise and the ontological parable, the real promise and the real symbol of the coming kingdom of God.

The eschatological doctrine of creation leads to a cosmic hope: that calls for an eschatology related to the whole creation and not just to human destiny, but also related to the relationship between human culture and non-human nature, and a nature which is independent of human influence. What will become of the human world? What will become of the world which was there before human beings, which is there without human beings and which will possibly be there even after human beings?

2. The social doctrine of the Trinity surpasses the monarchical doctrine of the Trinity and leads to a pneumatological doctrine of creation

If one takes Barth at his word, then everything has its hidden beginning in the mystery of the immanent Trinity. At all events, Barth's doctrine of the Trinity is the blueprint of his doctrine of creation, which can be recognized everywhere. Anyone who thinks that this or that part of the structure of his doctrine of creation has to be changed must therefore be in a position to change his doctrine of the Trinity. In *The Trinity and the Kingdom of God* I set a 'social doctrine of the Trinity' over against the 'trinitarian monarchy' of God in Barth. Leonardo Boff took it up for liberation theology and Patricia Wilson-Kastner for feminist theology. Orthodox theology was already on this course.[7]

In his reinterpretation of the doctrine of the Trinity Barth began from the modern need to stop interpreting the Absolute as substance and to think of it as subject. Tertullian's principle *una substantia - tres personae* had therefore to be turned into 'one divine subject in three different modes of being'. Barth's starting point in the 'self-revelation of God' does not allow any other trinitarian principle than that of the subjectivity of God. In the 1927 *Christian Dogmatics* God is the 'one, personal God'. In *Church Dogmatics* I.I (1932), we have 'God the Lord'. God is the 'one, personal God' in the mode of being of the Father, the Son and the Spirit. Therefore Barth identifies the subjectivity, the nature and the rule of God with one another, and follows the neo-scholastic F.Diekamp in claiming that 'in God, as there is one nature, so there is one self-consciousness' (I.1, 358). The three divine modes of being can be understood only as three 'repetitions in God': *repetitio aeternitatis in aeternitate*. The Son is the eternal self-knowledge and the temporal self-revelation of the one God (I.1,480). On the presupposition of the one subjectivity of God, Trinity can only be understood as an internal process of self-differentiation and self-identification of the one God. 'In it (viz. the doctrine of the Trinity) we are speaking not of three divine I's, but thrice of one divine I' (I.1, 370).

The crucial test is the hermeneutics of the biblical history. Barth's monarchian doctrine of the Trinity does not express the 'personal encounter of the Father who loves the Son, the Son who prays to the Father and the Spirit which confesses the Father and the Son'.[8] The principle from which Barth develops his doctrine of the Trinity, 'God is Lord', is not the way the New Testament talks about God. The New Testament says, rather, 'God is the Father of our Lord Jesus Christ' and does not begin from one subject but two, the Father and the Lord. The explicit, trinitarian extensions to the 'fellowship of the Holy Spirit' are therefore not to be read apart from that.

In my theology of the Trinity I began from the biblical story of Christ and thus from the difference between the subjects and their fellowship: Jesus, the messianic Son; the Abba God, upon whom he calls; and the Holy Spirit, who binds Jesus to the Father and through him comes into the world. If we begin from the trinitarian history of the three subjects, then our questions must be about the unity of these three subjects in the history of Christ and must we look at them in trinitarian terms: we may not understand them monistically. So following the Gospel of John I have understood the unity of Jesus the Son with the Father as a perichoretic unity, i.e. as a social unity of 'I' and 'You' in 'We' and 'Us', in mutual giving and taking, and in communicating and participatory living. The term *perichoresis*, Latin *circuminsessio*, used by John of Damascus in the doctrine of the Trinity, best grasps the unity of the three persons. Through their reciprocal love they exist in one another in complete empathy, so that they

131

are wholly one. In the intensive exchange of their energies they mutually permeate one another in a perfect way and share themselves fully with one another.

Patricia Wilson-Kastner has understood *perichoresis* as *perichoreusis* and depicted it as a round dance. According to this metaphor the three persons are united in perfect movement. The unity of the trune God is intensive liveliness, vibrant movement and perfect rest in movement. The unity of the triune God is not complacently shut in on itself, but is an open, inviting unity, as John 17.21 says: 'that they may also be in us', just as this eternal liveliness of the triune God in the communication of the Spirit is an attractive, life-giving life, and the eternal love which the triune God is in himself is the love which communicates itself to all the world in the surrender of the Son. The perichoretic concept of unity surmounts the 'dangers' of both 'tritheism' and 'modalism', since it combines threeness and oneness without reducing the threeness to oneness or the oneness to threeness. The concept of mutuality is an ingredient in this perichoretic concept of the Trinity and its content is governed by that.[9]

Barth's approach entails that the structure of rule and obedience within the Trinity is normative for God's relationship as Creator and all the conditions in creation which correspond to God. I quote from the doctrine of reconciliation in IV.1, 200f.: 'We have not only to deny but actually to affirm and understand as essential to the being of God the offensive fact that there is in God himself a *prius* and a *posterius*, a superiority and a subordination . . . that it belongs to the inner life of God that there should take place within it obedience.' 'His divine unity consists in the fact that He is both One who is obeyed and Another who obeys.' By that Barth means the Father who rules and commands in exaltation and the Son who is obedient in humility (similarly 194, 164, 159). However he found this even 'hard', 'insidious' and 'offensive'. Why? Did he think that he had to assert these theses contrary to his own feelings?

The approach in terms of a perichoretic doctrine of the Trinity entails that the levels of relationship in *perichoresis* and mutuality within the Trinity, rather than the levels of constitution within the Trinity, are normative for the relationship of God to creation and all the corresponding relationships in creation. It is unclear and open to misunderstanding to describe the relationship of Father and Son as rule and obedience, for these are characteristic of any kind of relationship between master and servant. In my view, the mutual love in which Jesus and the Father are so one that the Son is 'in' the Father and the Father 'in' him describes the eternal life within the Trinity more clearly and in a way less open to misunderstanding.

This is not the first point at which a charge of projecting human images on to the Godhead along the lines of Feuerbach's critique of religion could be levelled. It already relates to the patriarchal concept of the God who is sovereign Lord. But given the foundation of the concepts in biblical history the charge cannot be levelled at either point, since according to the first commandment the statement 'God is the Lord' is a summary of Israel's exodus experience and not a projection of domination. Similarly, the social doctrine of the Trinity is a short version of Jesus' trinitarian experience of God and the community and not a social projection. Feuerbach's criticism of religion overlooks the historical communication of the experience of God and comes to grief on the facts of real experience.

A perichoretic understanding of the relation of God to creation sees God's creating, forming, sustaining, enduring, receiving, accompanying, moving and suffering as an expression of the liveliness of his love. The coexistence of Creator and creature is also their mutual life, their cohabitation and influence on each other. The Creator finds space in the fellowship of creatures. The creatures find space in God. So creation also means that we are in God and God is in us. 'In him we live, move and have our being' (Acts 17.28), and Barth himself (II.1,475) works this out in a very fine way. 'God in creation' and 'creation in God' is the perichoresis which is realized in the Spirit of creation. Always to stress only the distinction between God and the world and God's transcendence over the world in the doctrine of creation is to adopt a one-sided approach and a theology of secularization imitating the secularizing of the world. Rather, creation means fellowship between God and the world: 'You are the lover of life and your God is in all things' (Wisdom 12.1). Creation is 'God's immanence in the world' (III.1, 216) and the immanence of the world with God. In other words, the mystery of creation is best grasped philosophically by panentheism.

Here, however, there needs to be a theological discussion of the trinitarian concept of creation. We have two possibilities: modalistic pneumatology and trinitarian pneumatology. I called my pneumatological doctrine of creation 'creation in the Spirit', in order to indicate (a) that God the Father created this world in the power of his Spirit through his Daughter-Wisdom/Son-Logos, and (b) that therefore this world exists from God and through God – and in God :'*Sic in Spiritu Sancto sunt omnia*' ('Thus everything is in the Holy Spirit', Meister Eckhart, *Sermo* IV.1). If everything is created in the Spirit, then the Spirit also permeates everything that is and enlivens it through his power: 'The Spirit of the Lord fills the earth' (Wisdom 1.7). The Spirit is 'God who breathes through all creation', as an English hymn puts it. Because this Spirit lives in eternal perichoretic unity with the Son and the Father, there cannot be a dissolution of God in the world, as theologians fear, nor the divinization of evolution which some new age scientists (E.Jantsch, F.Capra) want. At this point Christian Link has asked critically (*EvTh* 47, 1987, 89) whether this is the Spirit of God or the 'God of the Holy Spirit'. According to the modalistic doctrine of the Trinity it is the Spirit (of the one God who transcends the world), and according to the perichoretic doctrine of the Trinity it is God the Spirit. 'The Holy Spirit is life-giving life, mover of all and the root of all that is created' (Hildegard of Bingen):

> I – fire of life –
> flash out over all the beauty of the fields,
> shine on the waters,
> burn in the sun;
> shine in the moon and stars,
> and awaken with a breath of wind
> each thing that is filled with life.
> This my breath is liveliness
> in all greening and blossoming
> . . . so in all this I am
> a hidden flaming power,
> through me the universe glows and burns.[10]

As *Spiritus animans, Spiritus suscitans, Spiritus patiens, Spiritus vivificans*, the creative Spirit (*Spiritus creator*) is present to each of his creatures and the fellowship of creation from which and in which they all live. In the Old Testament wisdom literature, 'Wisdom' and 'Spirit' are often identical and interchangeable. Because the trinitarian unity with the Father and the Son preserves the transcendence of the creative Spirit in respect of its workings, I see no reason not 'to draw the Spirit as deeply as possible into the flesh' and to identify his fellowship with all that is alive, makes alive and serves life. Why should not scientific descriptions also discover the complexes of life and thus also complexes of the Spirit? 'He who finds me finds life, and he who lacks me damages himself; all those who hate me love death' (Prov.8.35f.).

However, what serves life and leads to death can be recognized theologically only from the redeeming, justifying and sanctifying Spirit, because this is the 'breath of resurrection' and overcomes death. That is my answer to Ulrich Kühn's question whether a 'greater difference' should not be posited between the gift of earthly life and the gift of new, eternal life (*TLZ* 1987, 88), than I do? Any Christian natural theology is a secondary rediscovery of God in nature and presupposes the revelation of God in Christ. I observed this theological rule when I argued from the manifest experiences of the Holy Spirit in the fellowship of believers with Christ to the rediscovery of the activity of the creative Spirit in nature. C.Link overlooked this connection in his criticism.

Barth still assumed that the 'pneumatological doctrine of creation' was a 'special doctrine of Calvin's' (IV.3.1, 756). This is demonstrably not the case: rather, Calvin refers to the Cappadocian fathers' doctrine of the Trinity and its openness to the world, according to which the Father always acts through the Son in the Spirit and therefore creation itself is always brought about by the Spirit.[11] Only a narrow understanding of Augustine's doctrine of the Trinity, closed in on itself and always acting externally in a monotheistic way (*opera trinitatis ad extra sunt indivisa*), rules out this pneumatological doctrine of creation. A comparison with orthodox theology shows that Calvin did not produce any 'special doctrine'.

3. Community of creation instead of order of creation: a paradigm shift

Barth was evidently convinced from an early stage that order could exist only as superiority and subordination. His theological starting point in the sovereignty of God and his christological orientation on the relationship of Christ to the community in terms of the head and body of Christ do not allow him to deviate from this notion of order. If God corresponds to himself in the relationship of obedience to rule, the same must be true of all relationships in his creation which correspond to him. To describe relationships in creation Barth takes up Aristotle's old hierarchical doctrine of correspondence: as God corresponds to himself in himself, so God corresponds to himself in his relationship to the world. The cosmic relationships of heaven and earth and the anthropological relationships of soul and body and man and woman are ordered accordingly. III.2, 441: 'The antithesis of soul and body, like that of heaven and earth, is an antithesis within creation and immanent in the world . . . But the soul and body of man are the one man, as heaven and earth as a whole are one cosmos.' 'Man as preceding soul of his succeeding body is a picture of what Scripture describes in the relation of man and woman as the divine likeness of man's being fulfilled only in this duality, to the extent that even in this fulfilment ruling and serving are distinguished and yet wholly integrated as the work of the one man' (ibid., 427).

From this systematic picture of the hierarchical cosmos of correspondence and likeness I shall pick out only two points – though both of them are key ones: the relationships between soul and body and man and woman.

(a) According to the leading statement of §46, 'Through the Spirit of God, man is the subject, form and life of a substantial organism, the soul of his body – wholly and simultaneously both, in ineffaceable difference, inseparable unity and indestructible order.'

Order consists in being 'the ruling soul of a serving body'. The soul precedes and the body follows it; the soul is above, the body below; the soul is first, the body second; the soul rules and the body is ruled. Certainly the Spirit of God fills the soul as Spirit-soul and the body as Spirit-body and is present in both, but at the same time it is 'the principle that makes human beings subjects' and thus is present directly to the soul, but only indirectly to the body through the control of its ruling soul. In that human beings are their own lords and regents, they are 'spirit souls'. The real human act of living consists in the thought and will of the human subject, the soul. The dignity of the body consists in serving.

135

Barth does not once speak in so many words of any conversation with the body in the decisions of the soul, of any right of the body to resist against by the soul, of the body answering back to the soul, or of the desirability of some agreement between the two.

This is all the more surprising, since Barth was probably familiar with the ideas of the psychosomatic medicine of Victor von Weizsäcker and Ludolf von Krehl through his old friend Richard Siebeck. In 1956 Richard Siebeck even compared Barth's theological anthropology with anthropological medicine in a Festschrift for von Weizsäcker.[12] He found a parallel in the fact that psychosomatics had also introduced 'the subject' into medical science: the patient as person. However, he found it difficult to apply Barth's conception of order: 'But there is a tension and a bond in the unity between body and soul; there is no division of body and soul here, but the one which rules is at the same time the one which serves and vice versa . . . Careful clinical observation shows that not only the sick but even healthy people often cannot distinguish at all between serving and ruling . . . What is contentment, freshness and indeed weariness? Does the body rule the soul here, or the soul the body?' (59f.). So the phenomena of body and soul can take each other's place and represent each other: 'Anthropological medicine may draw the attention of theological anthropology to the fact that the order in the unity of body and soul, in which the soul rules and the body serves, wavers and changes.' It is an 'indissoluble interconnection' (63).

So is it not better to give up Barth's one-sided, monarchical image of the order of soul and body and use the image of mutual interrelationship, i.e. the *perichoresis* of body and soul? In human life and human life-style, body and soul, unconscious and conscious, voluntary and involuntary are always intertwined in such a way that they must be seen together and in their mutuality. As the soul speaks to the body, so the body speaks to the soul. The body has its own experiences, and its body language is full of a wisdom to which any sensitive soul knows how to listen. In the body we do not just have, as Barth thought, those 'dissipated lower urges' which must be self-consciously disciplined by the soul: 'To live as an authentic man would mean to keep oneself disciplined, to remain at the height to which one belongs as a man, to be what one is as a man even at the cost of severity against oneself' (IV.2, 454). I have therefore adopted theologically the concept of the Gestalt from Gestalt therapy in order to express the living, mutual relationship and perichoretic interaction of the energies of body and soul.[13]

Now Barth had theological reasons for his monarchical view of the ruling soul of a serving body: the prototype is Jesus Christ. Of him Barth says: 'He is not only his soul but also his body. But he is both soul and body in an ordered oneness and wholeness. His being is orderly and not disorderly. Nor is he this in such a way that the order is accidental and imposed from without. He is it in an order which derives from himself. He himself and from himself is both the

136

higher and the lower, the first and the second, the dominant and the dominated' (332).

But are this 'inner sovereignty' (397) and self-control and self-domination the pre-eminent characteristics of Jesus the human being? This image of the 'royal man' may correspond to the Schleiermacherian Jesus with the 'ever-dominant consciousness of God', but it is not the picture of Jesus to be found in the Synoptic Gospels. Everywhere in that picture, as feminist theology has shown, we find traces of reciprocity between Jesus and other people, between his bodily and his spiritual needs, between what he gives and what he receives, what he teaches and what he learns. For the Synoptic Gospels do not present Jesus as a human model but as the messianic prophet of the poor and the divine brother of the sick and the sinners.

(b) As a male, I can deal with Barth's picture of the order of man and woman briefly, because it has already been criticized often and from many sides. I do not understand Barth's hierarchy of the world, nor do I find any legitimation in Christian theology for the order according to which the man corresponds to the soul, heaven and Christ and the woman to the body, earth and the community. Nor do I understand those assignations of roles which always relate only to ruling and serving. Barth's concept of order does not bring any peace into the relationship between man and woman when all that he says is: 'A precedes B, and B follows A. Order means succession. It means preceding and following. It means super- and sub-ordination' (III.1, 169). That is simply the world order of patriarchy, and Barth was also well aware of that. In Henriette Visser 't Hooft, as early as 1934 he came up against a self-aware and free woman, indeed a feminist theologian[14]. She asked, 'Has not Christ made us free? Is not every human being, man or women, now in a direct relationship to God?' In his reply Barth claimed to be defending Paul: 'I am afraid that on the presupposition of the thesis about man and woman that you are considering (mutual interest, trust, responsibility), Paul would not have been able to say what he wanted, since between God and human there is no mutual interest, but only superiority.' The whole Bible, he claimed, presupposed 'in fact not matriarchy but patriarchy as the earthly temporal order of the relationship between man and woman'. It is the ordinance of God 'that Christ was a man and as such confirms the superiority of Adam'. Any 'mutualism' was excluded. Mrs Visser't Hooft replied: 'There is something quite different from superiority, namely love. Love knows no superiority or inferiority.' She ended her letter of 9 May 1934 with the remark: 'I hope that you have understood that I am only against being deprived of my head and my body' (19). I understand this wise statement to mean that she was against the woman's loss of head and man's loss of body which come about when the man is to be the 'head of the woman' and she is to be the body of the man. According to the basic notion of the perichoretic doctrine of the Trinity,

137

the true image of God lies in the mutual fellowship of man and woman. Only the mutuality of both of them, not the superiority of the man, leads the human life of men and women to full fruition in the powers of the shared spirit of God, which opens up community and brings both to life in mutual love and friendship. It is not super- and sub-ordination, but a shared common life in fellowship that corresponds to the triune God and is the incarnate promise of his kingdom.

4. Barth's doctrine of 'natural death' (III.2, §47.5) as an example of the unnatural division of person and nature, covenant and creation, end and body

According to the views of Paul and Augustine, death is 'the wages of sin': both the spiritual death of the soul and the physical death of the body. The universality of original sin is demonstrated by the unavoidability of death. The old Protestant orthodoxy maintained that spiritual death, physical death and eternal death are consequences of original sin and punishments for it. Schleiermacher was the first to dispute the causal connection between sin and physical death (*The Christian Faith,* §77): in itself death is neither an ill nor a divine punishment, but the temporal end of finite humanity. Only a consciousness of God disturbed by sin experiences death as evil and fears it as a punishment. We are not slaves of death, but of the fear of death. Consciousness of God fortified by grace no longer experiences death as evil and punishment, but as a natural end.

Barth took up Schleiermacher's view in his own way. Death is not 'in itself the judgment. It is not in itself and as such the sign of God's judgment' (632). In itself death has only the form of the limit of finite being and 'as such' is part of human nature. Just as human birth is a step from nothingness into being, so death is the 'step from being into nothingness'. For 'finitude means mortality' (625). Thus 'death in itself' is part of the limited existence of finite humanity and is something natural. Barth distinguishes 'actual death' from this 'death in itself'. It is in fact the death of the sinner, feared by the sinner as a curse and understood as punishment. Without Christ and faith, 'death in itself' and actual death coincide. But with Christ and in faith we are freed from the curse of death for 'natural dying': 'This liberation from unnatural death means that, as it is liberation to eternal life, so too it is liberation to a natural death' (638) which 'by divine appointment belongs to the life of the creature and thus is necessary for it' (639). In what, then, does redemption consist, if natural death remains? It consists in the fact that God himself becomes the beyond for human beings and that as 'one who has been' the human being will share in the eternal life of God, and 'his finite life will be eternalized and glorified in God' (632f.)

Barth gives this idea of 'natural death' a christological foundation: for Christ to be able to die a representative accursed death for sinners on the cross he must be a man 'without sin', but at the same time mortal. Were physical death in itself the wages of sin, then the sinless would have to be immortal also. So on the

138

cross Christ died not only the accursed death of the sinner but also his own natural death. Therefore, Barth concludes, finite human nature as such is already created mortal. By contrast, the old Protestant doctrine of two natures held the human nature of Christ to be intrinsically immortal.

Over against the Augustinian tradition and Barth I would like to make the following comments:

1. Finitude is not necessarily mortality. There are finite beings which are immortal, e.g. angels on the one hand and stones on the other. Physical mortality first came into the world through sexual propagation.

2. In the new creation, suffering, pain and crying will be done away with, and death will be no more (Rev.21.4). Because eternal life is to rule in it, any death – physical death, spiritual death and eternal death - is to be excluded from it. Hope for the 'resurrection of the dead' is always just the personal side of the cosmic hope for the annihilation of death (I Cor.15.26) and the new creation without death. Without a new earth there is no hope of resurrection. So it is an incomplete description of Christian hope to say that only human beings will 'be eternalized and glorified' in God.

3. In the present state of creation, death is neither a 'natural' ingredient of the original order nor just the wages of human sin. Sin is human, but death is the fate of human beings, animals and plants, in other words of all living beings. Have animals and plants also sinned? Do they die only because of human sins? I do not believe that Paul meant either the one or the other when in Rom.8.19ff. he spoke of the 'anxious longing of creation'. The anxiety of creation is neither 'natural' nor there only for the sake of human beings. Rather, Paul sees the human 'waiting for the redemption of the body' as being parallel to this universal sighing of creation (9), so that a comprehensive solidarity comes into being in the fellowship of creation, made up of human beings and all other living things, as it sighs and waits. Even beyond human sin and violence, a sadness lies on the whole of earthly creation which Annette von Droste-Hülshoff has grasped in an amazing way in her poem 'The Groaning Creation'.[15] In my view this sorrow goes back to the first, open and incomplete creation. The death of living beings is neither natural nor sinful, but the sign of a tragedy (if I may put it like that) which is bound up with the experiment of the original creation of the world by God. The death of living beings is therefore also a sign of the longing of all living beings for a new creation in glory, of which it is said, 'The former creation has passed away, and all things have become new' (Rev.21.4). The cosmic hope for glory (Rom.8.18) transforms this universal sorrow of all living beings into a hopeful longing. The new creation not only reveals the freedom of the children of God but also brings the 'deification of the cosmos', i.e. the unhindered participation of all creatures in the eternal life of God.

4. It follows from this for the understanding of the mortality and the death of

Christ that Christ died the accursed death of sinners and that at the same time he died in solidarity with all living beings which are subject to the fate of death. His resurrection from the dead therefore brings the righteousness of God to sinners and opens up to all living beings the prospect of the annihilation of death and the 'life of the world to come'. Without this cosmic dimension of his death and resurrection from the dead which is developed in Ephesians and Colossians, our understanding of creation remains anthropocentric and egocentric, and we find no access to the great fellowship of creation in sorrow and in hope.

5. *Faith* can liberate us from the religious fear of death which is always a fear of judgment, so that we can die comforted and confident. But *love* leads us to die in solidarity with the whole of creation as it waits anxiously. Finally, *hope* makes it possible for us to resign ourselves to the dying of living creatures but not to an individual death, so that we regard it as 'natural' and a matter of course. Death has only a transitory power, for so long as there is time. Its future consists in its annihilation, so that creation is completed and made new without death.

5. Is Karl Barth a 'modern theologian'?

Because Karl Barth and the other representatives of early dialectical theology distanced themselves so abruptly from nineteenth-century Protestantism and its 'liberal theology' and presented themselves as the alternative, for a long time some of those who followed that rise of dialectical theology have regarded Barth's theology as the overcoming of 'modern bourgeois religion', while others who have not been able to follow him have attempted to isolate him as a reactionary anti-modern and his theology as 'neo-orthodoxy'. That has changed since recently Trutz Rendtorff, his pupil F.W.Graf and Falk Wagner want to claim Barth and his theology for what they call 'modern religion'.[16] This is possible and can be demonstrated by the way in which his theology of the sovereignty of God can be derived from the thought-patterns of the modern philosophy of subjectivity: God thinks himself, so he is; God reveals himself, so he proves himself. Barth in fact uses thought-forms from the philosophy of subjectivity which were developed by Fichte and Hegel and had already been taken over for 'modern theology' by Richard Rothe and Isaak August Dorner. But those who see only the thought-forms overlook the way in which, by its intention and its own commitment, Barth's theology is exegesis of scripture, so that his thought-forms only act as aids to his theological exegesis. Now scripture is not a product of the nineteenth century. Those who set it above their own contemporary thought-forms find that the scriptural gospel changes and breaks the thought-forms applied to it. Any more detailed study of Barth will come upon such changes which are made by scriptural exegesis to the thought-forms of which Barth makes use. At these breaking points the gospel begins to speak its own language. The gospel is the dividing line between Christian faith and modern bourgeoisie, not only for Barth himself but also for Barth's own thought-forms.

By contrast, those who think that theology today must become a metatheory of the 'religion of modernity' in order to maintain the old claim of Christianity to universality regrettably overlook its own self-chosen antiquatedness. For those who want to get an intellectual grip of their time always arrive 'too late', as Hegel observed in the introduction to his *The Philosophy of Right*. They can only grasp that past which no longer determines the present. Only the owls in the ruins of bourgeois Christianity are still nostalgically hooting for a 'religion of modern times' which no longer exists. And if it did exist, it would be nothing but the final cadences of a bygone era and a form of Christianity which is no longer binding. Thus while that form can still recognize itself, it cannot 'rejuvenate' itself, as Hegel put it. The 'rejuvenation' of Christianity will come about only from the reformation of the church by the Word of God, and this in turn will come about only from the rebirth of faith from the spirit of the biblical promise of God. This insight is all the more important today, since the dialectic of modernity has already turned the boast of modernity into its opposite. What is called 'modernity' in the prophecy of history is in concrete terms the human project of technological scientific civilization. The basic elements in the paradigm of thought and will for this civilization are:

1. The human being becomes an 'individual' subject and is reduced to the subject of understanding and will;

2. The natural environment is reified and comes to consist of cosmic building blocks, 'atoms';

3. Both these developments make it possible for human beings to seize power over nature, to control its processes and to safeguard the power thus gained.

These three principles are nowadays referred to euphemistically as the 'will to freedom' and the 'history of freedom' in modern times.

However, today the great project of 'scientific and technological civilization' is leading to three constitutional crises:

1. This civilization has produced the injustice of the 'Third World ' and year by year is increasing it;

2. This civilization has produced the system of nuclear deterrence, allegedly to secure its power, and year by year is increasing its powers of self-destruction.

3. By its irreparable destruction of the regenerative powers of nature, this civilization has brought about the worldwide 'ecological crisis' which through the destruction of species of plants and animals year by year is leading further towards ecological catastrophe for the organic earth.

What Freiligrath, who coined the term, once celebrated at the beginning of March 1848 with messianic enthusiasm as 'modernity' has long since become the end-time of the human race and the earth – that is, if we take Günter Anders' definition of end-time as that time in which the end of the human race is possible at any moment.

The three fatal crises of modern scientific and technological civilization are compelling us to reverse our lives, and this reversal calls for more than mere corrections of course. Many alert people sense the need for change today and therefore are talking of a way into 'post-modernity', into a 'new age'. The new 'paradigm' of thought and will is becoming increasingly clear, even if its ways cannot yet be recognized very clearly. Here are some basic elements of the new paradigm.

1. Freedom can no longer mean gaining power and domination. The victims and the costs of such an understanding of freedom are incalculable and are becoming excessive. By contrast, true human freedom is to be represented as fellowship in justice and mutual recognition.

2. The holistic principles of mutuality, reciprocity and partnership must replace thought in terms of domination and subjection, separation and control, and do so socially, economically and politically in relationships between human beings as well as in the relationship between human culture and the organic earth.

3. The goal of history can no longer be the seizure of human power over nature; human culture must make a permanent home on an organic earth. Being at home with and holding a balance with nature are the aims which serve life and survival.

Karl Barth himself could not see the development of these crises as clearly as we who are affected by them today. But he clearly recognized the spiritual forerunners of the modern, eschatological 'exterminism' in the rise of European nihilism. Over against this eschatological nihilism of modern times, in his doctrine of creation he stressed the reliable YES of the Creator and the wonderful goodness of his creation. Therefore Barth is one of the great figures of the old paradigm of 'modernity', because in it and by means of it he has set out the beginnings of the new paradigm for life in this 'end-time'.

4

'Where There is Hope, There is Religion' (Ernst Bloch)

The Philosophy and Theology of Hope[1]

1. Ernst Bloch and theology

In Ernst Bloch, theologians, too, have found a philosopher to whom they owe a great deal. He was a friend in whose company one could breathe, take courage and learn to ask questions. In the last years before his death many theologians, young and old, from countless lands, made their pilgrimage to his home on the Neckar, sat and ate with him at his small table, asked and were asked questions (and how!), and then went their way more hopefully than before. He was so free from vanity and so unpretentious that anyone who got close to him detected an atmosphere of trust and brotherliness. At the same time he was so caught up in his cause and the questions of his time that no one who got close to him could just make light conversation. In his intellectual company even theologians began to rediscover their own biblical, i.e. Jewish and Christian, horizon of hope and learn their own critical praxis of hope.

I first got to know Ernst Bloch when he was the ripe old age of seventy-five. What impressed me up to our last conversation on the day before his death was his original thought and, if one may put it that way, his childlike nature. He had been able to retain something which others so quickly lose: simple questioning and boundless amazement. Since his *Geist der Utopie* (The Spirit of Utopia, 1918), he called that 'the darkness of the lived moment'. He questioned, thought and recounted on the basis of the creative and inexhaustible presence of this origin. In it he was authentic. He was struck by things which others passed over heedlessly. He noticed changes where others saw only the same thing. He heard tones where others found no notes at all. The world in which he lived was full of traces, signs and signals which he sought to decipher. And he could open the eyes and ears of others to them. Almost every chapter in each of his books begins with remarks about something simple, nearby, taken for granted, and with a deep wonderment at it. 'I am. But I do not have myself. So first of all we become.'

We find this on the first page of his *Spuren* (Traces, 1930): three sentences which span his whole philosophy, three sentences between which all human beings can tell of their life, their hope, their suffering, their loneliness and what they share. 'Who are we? Where do we come from? Where are we going?' *The Principle of Hope* (1959) begins with these age-old metaphysical questions and then continues, 'What do we await?' That is the question of human hope. And 'What awaits us?' That is the question about the advent of that which is wholly other, the eschatological question. Does anything at all await us in the future of the world, in our own death? Bloch went on asking where others thought it better not to go on asking. We find what is simple the most difficult because we ourselves have not remained simple, namely in asking what we would like to ask, and in hoping what we wish for. With Ernst Bloch one found this difficulty made easy again. That was what was liberating about him. 'The one who has thought most deeply loves most ardently.' In this respect he was akin to Hölderlin. And the fact that his *The Principle of Hope* ultimately seeks fulfilment in the category of the 'homeland', developed to the point of being a universal, points to that childlike light which Bloch had preserved.

'Ernst Bloch as a theologian' is a provocative theme for theologians, for himself, for his friends and his opponents. And yet it is an apt theme, which cannot be suppressed.[2] I remember our first meeting very well. It was in the winter of 1959, after a lecture which the Leipzig philosopher had given in Wuppertal. We sat together in a smoke-filled pub. I asked him, rather naively, 'Herr Bloch, are you an atheist?' Thereupon he beamed at me and declared cheerfully, 'I am an atheist for God's sake.' The long history of his struggle with God lies in this paradox. It contains both Prometheus and Job, the Mosaic prohibition of images and the cry of the crucified Jesus, the mystical theology of Meister Eckhart and the Marxist critique of religion, along with personal elements. Bloch did not engage in any official or even any church 'theology'. He remained faithful to the heretical piety of 'revolutionary gnosis' from the *Spirit of Utopia*. But as early as 1918 he wanted to bring 'Marxism and religion united in the will for the kingdom' into the 'harvest festival of the Apocalypse'. By that he meant the ultimately successful encounter of human beings with themselves: 'but now the glory of the Lord is reflected in all of us, with unveiled faces'. He happily quoted Paul's remark, to end his first book *The Spirit of Utopia* with the hallowing of the name of God, a name which in the hands of our philosophy 'conjures up God and the truth as prayer'. What philosopher ever said that his philosophy 'conjured up God' and ended his work with a prayer? Only theologians do such a thing: only a few of them at that, and then very seldom. This messianic passion for the kingdom of glory which has not yet appeared can be detected as a leading motif in all his works. Certainly at a later stage he was more restrained in giving positive expression to this messianic hope, and he became increasingly harsh in his criticism of the church of the

144

rulers and his criticism of religious resignation – his political experiences with the churches in the Third Reich gave him reason enough for that. But even in the book which he devoted particularly to Christians, *Atheismus im Christentum* (Atheism in Christianity, 1968), the early longing for a form of 'religion of the exodus and the kingdom' (to quote the subtitle), which would ultimately also be politically credible, remained predominant. Marxism as an analysis of class rule and criticism of the existing alienation of the people and eschatological hope for the apocalypse of the kingdom which is promised to the poor, as the power for overcoming that need, come to a community in which neither side must give itself up, but rather each side comes to itself.

So in the 1960s Bloch came to the theologians, and the theologians came to him. So from then on the Christians came to Socialists and Socialists to Christians. United in the will for the kingdom which is promised to the poor, to the annoyance of their flocks they left their pitched camp and drew upon themselves the wrath of the shepherds and camp-commandants of the time. The more they entered into the real problem which they had in common, the alienation of the people, the more they traced the spirit of the kingdom which alone gave them certainty. Honest and reciprocal criticism was a condition of that.

Bloch put it like this. 'Only an atheist can be a good Christian', because consistent atheism liberates one from the idols and gods of this world. At the time I replied, 'Only a Christian can be a good atheist', because belief in the crucified Christ brings liberation from substitute religions, personality cults and fear of the authorities. At that time Bloch immediately took up 'the offer', as he called it and then, with the two critical statements as a motto, in his *Atheism in Christianity* described what he had meant. He was attempting to establish a new marriage between Marxism and Christianity by a collage of the following texts: 'Marx said, "Being radical means grasping things by the roots. But man is the root of all (social) things." I John again says, taking man, the root, not as the cause of something but as a determination to something, "And it has not yet appeared what we shall be. But we know that when it is made manifest, we shall be like him, because we shall see him as he is . . "' Bloch remarked: 'Had these two passages read each other or had they had a meeting, then a light which was both detectivistic and utopian would have fallen on the real problem of universal alienation and its possible removal.'[3] This combination shaped European 'political theology' in the 1960s. It shaped the Latin American 'theology of liberation'. And not least it brought the Christians and the Sandinistas together in one common liberation front against the Somoza dictatorship in Nicaragua. The name Ernst Bloch stands for these combinations of Marxist criticism and Christian-messianic hope.

Ernst Bloch – the old man with the raised fist – remained a riddle to many of his contemporaries for whom the word 'socialism' was loaded with negative personal experiences or filled only with private daydreams. In divided Germany discussions of socialism were generally highly unpopular because of the repressions and obsessions which were expressed in them. The fact that Ernst Bloch had gone through various forms of socialism, enthusiastic and disappointed, welcomed and despised, always hoping anew, made it difficult for some people to get on with him. Nevertheless, there was no hidden ideological riddle here, but something very simple and also very clear: 'Socialism, and then communism, is what has been sought in vain for so long under the name *morality*' (*Politische Messungen* [Political Measurements], 1970). For the sake of morality, with Kant's categorical imperative and a simple concern for self-respect, Ernst Bloch became a pacifist in the First World War and a Marxist in the Weimar Republic. In 1961 he left the dictatorial socialism of the German Democratic Republic, and in the Federal Republic fought for democratic socialism and hoped for the one universal, natural communism which would bring human beings closer to encountering one another and the world closer to the homeland of identity. Bloch was a moralist before he made a commitment to socialism. In anger and in militant hope he always remained a moralist with integrity. For the sake of morality he imagined social utopias, for the 'weary and heavy-laden'. For the sake of morality he developed a natural law with a future, namely as a constitutional utopia for the 'humiliated and the injured'. For the sake of morality he outlined the symbolism which is still valid today, of the 'upright walk' and the 'raised head'. However, conversely morality also puts socialism, democracy and communism as questions of morality, human dignity and self-respect as a critical question to the socialism which really exists, the democracy which really exists and the communism which does not yet exist, but is only intended. It asks what is their 'human face'.

Ernst Bloch was often asked by theologians about his understanding of death, immortality and resurrection. He always reacted to them in his writings, interviews and personal conversations in a remarkably shy way. His own death had no terrors for him. Nor did he lay any veil over it (*idola mortis*). Rather, he repressed the idea of death. For him, as for Paul, death was the 'radical counter-utopia', but also a mystery: 'unimaginable nothingness which as yet has found no illumination.' And yet he was aware of a connection out there. He found in music as 'resounding silence' a connection with death as the 'absolute silence'. On the evening before his death, when my wife and I had visited him, he again listened to his favourite music, Beethoven's overture Leonore no.3, with its trumpet signal for the liberation of the prisoners, which always moved him deeply. In Beethoven it 'announces an advent of the messiah. So it resounds down into the prison: freedom, utopian recollection, the great moment is there, the star of hope fulfilled in the here and now . . . '

Ernst Bloch's own work is such a messianic overture for a future, with that trumpet signal for the prisoners, the humiliated and the dead. Bloch made those imprisoned in alienation, exploitation, humiliation and death 'prisoners of hope'. In the face of death he held firm to a *non omnis confundar* (*The Principle of Hope*, 1182). The phrase comes from the Christian canticle, the *Te Deum; 'In te, Domine, speravi, non confundar in aeternum'*: 'In thee, O Lord, have I trusted, let me never be confounded.'

2. Messianism, religion and atheism

In 1960, a year before Ernst Bloch moved from Leipzig to Tübingen, I tried to introduce his work *The Principle of Hope* to the Federal Republic under the title 'Messianism and Marxism'. Although it was his democratic socialism which in the 1960s set students and citizens, trade unions and parties, churches and schools on the road to a reform which brought more democracy, I personally was fascinated by his messianism. At that time I asked: 'In Bloch (in the *Principle of Hope*), has messianism triumphed over Marxism, or has it succumbed to it?' Nowadays I would no longer put this question as an alternative. The messianism seems to me to be the overarching perspective and the inner impulse for his socialism, and the democratic socialism the present historical form of messianism in the face of the present misery of capitalism. In 1919 Walter Benjamin reported to his friend Gershom Scholem: 'Bloch is now working on his main work, a system of theoretical messianism.' The messianic spirit brings both socialism and democracy out of its rigidity and opens both of them up both to greater perspectives on the future. It puts both 'in the balance' and mediates between opposites between which there has been no mediation hitherto – but it does just hold them 'in the balance'.

(a) Messianic interpretation of the history of religion
'Where there is hope there is religion, but where there is religion there is not always hope.'

In chapter 53 of *The Principle of Hope*, Bloch presented a messianic interpretation of the great religions, especially those which used to be called 'founder religions'. According to Bloch their special significance lies in the fact that alongside the religious mystery and together with it they revere that 'commitment of the founder to the religious mystery' which reveals the mystery. The exceptional human transcending with which each religious act begins is part of the divine transcendence. Therefore in the 'founder religions' the unique religious act of the founder is regarded as taking place for the first time, is set up as a model to be imitated, and is celebrated as a sacrament of mediation along with the transcendence which is experienced in it. Granted, the mediator is not himself what he mediates. But because this is mediated only through him, he takes on decisive significance for the goal, and guiding power for all who seek it.

In terms of the history of religion Bloch speaks of a 'growing' commitment

147

of the founder to the religious mystery. This notion of a religious development is of course a construct. It is constructed from that religion which depicted itself as 'absolute religion'. Bloch takes up this claim from Hegel. Though he does not – like Hegel – declare Christianity to be the 'absolute religion', he does ask about a 'consummation of the history of religion' which as such represents its 'sublation'. This longing for the consummation of the history of religion is typically 'messianic'. It leads both to the absolutizing of one's own religious experience and the relativizing of all other experiences, and also to the experience of the impossibility of consummating history and relativizing one's own experience.

This ambivalence can be recognized clearly in Bloch's account. However, that personal 'commitment to the religious mystery' first appears with Moses and is then 'consummated' with Jesus: through his religious action on Mount Sinai, Moses made the God of this volcano the 'spirit of the exodus' of his people. The 'God over us' became the 'God before us'. The lofty Lord of heaven becomes the future kingdom of his glory on earth.

Through his surrender Jesus penetrates the transcendent as a 'human tribune' and utopianizes it so that it becomes the kingdom.[4] Here Bloch still keeps to the lines of Hegel's 'absolute religion', but with the difference that for him the history of the human consciousness of God is in no way already automatically regarded as the history of the divine consciousness, but is first focussed on the final restoration of the messianic 'hope in totality'.

According to Bloch, a new 'anthropology of religion' fell due with Feuerbach. But going beyond Hegel and Feuerbach, Bloch calls for a new 'eschatology of religion'.[5] With Feuerbach he demythologizes religious symbolism 'for the sake of human beings'. But in contrast to Feuerbach, Bloch applies it not to existing human beings but to the real concern of existing human beings, that for which they hunger in the inexhaustible nucleus of their existence, that which shines on them in the darkness of the lived moment: their true future. Bloch's demythologizing of religion is not just 'for the sake of human beings'; it is similarly 'for God's sake'. In the way in which it combines the two, it is an eschatological demythologizing for the sake of what God and human beings really want, namely their fellowship in glory: according to the Jewish Kabbala the revelation of the ten Sephiroth, the *kabod*, the *doxa*, the glory of God. Thus what is believed messianically with the word 'God' is not done away with and settled any more than what is wanted with the word 'human being' and intended by the word 'nature'. It is preserved and brought out in hope.

Bloch's principle 'where there is hope there is religion' leads to his view of Christianity as the 'essence of religion', in so far as and to the extent that 'humane-eschatological, explosively posited messianism has emerged'.[6] At the same time the opposite is also the case: 'Where there is hope there is atheism', in so far as atheism and its criticism of religion has precisely the same intention, namely the humane-eschatological messianism which is placed explosively in it. That is the ambivalence in Bloch's 'inherited religion', his 'meta-religion'. For this 'inherited religion' can amount to a legacy of what has been condemned to death and in this respect can be irreligious. But it can also mean the fulfilment of what is only promised by religion, and in that respect it can be more than religious. So Bloch at one point calls that future 'without religion', and two pages earlier 'not simply no religion'.[7] This ambiguity is a typical sign of the solemnity of messianic consummation: it must both end and consummate at a stroke. As a result, if Bloch is to be consistent and not diverge into a substitute satisfaction, his atheism must argue for God against 'God', and for the still unknown appearance of God in glory against the images, names and concepts of God, which are all idols.

(b) Messianic hopes and concrete utopias

> In life all only repeats itself,
> Only fantasy is eternally young. What has never ever been,
> That alone never grows old (F.Schiller).

On what is Bloch's messianic hope focussed? The ideas of a goal which he uses change, fluctuate, alter and are uncertain. He talks about 'totality', 'explosive perfection', *ens perfectissimum,* 'homeland of identity', 'habitability in being', 'transfiguration of nature', and again and again of 'the kingdom', interpreted in astral-mythical terms as 'crystal' and seen biblically 'as glory'.

'Rebirth' and the 'leap into the wholly other' are the conditions of this future over against this world, its laws and customs. In this connection Bloch is fond of talking about the 'most unconditional utopia', the utopia of the unconditioned. It announces itself in changing signs and signals, but is not yet known to anyone. It is experienced mystically in the 'darkness of the lived moment', but it cannot be seen and grasped in a world which is still unchanged.

Bloch regards this messianism of the *Totum,* of the kingdom of glory or of identity, as the 'salt of the earth – and of heaven too'.[8] The messianism which proclaims such a future in history must also make its unattainability known through the best of all possible societies, by constantly applying its goad to the 'untranscended frailty of all creation' and the similarly 'untranscended immediacy of surrounding nature'. As is well known, Bloch in particular depicted social utopias of happiness and their realizations through democratic socialism, and constitutional utopias of human dignity and their political realizations through human rights and democracy. But he regarded these as partial utopias, which have been extracted from the *'Totum* of utopia' and have dropped out – wherever they have been regarded in isolation and marked out in a one-sided way.

Without the *'Totum* of utopia' they lose their connection and their best

149

intentions. In the '*Totum* of utopia' an absolute is anticipated 'in which yet other contradictions than social contradictions will cease and in which the understanding of all previous connections will also change'. So Bloch was in no way undertaking a reduction of the messianic utopia or even of religious images of hope to inner-worldly, social or political real utopias, but on the contrary was attempting to integrate these concrete partial utopias into the '*Totum* of utopia'. In this respect he remained religious.

Anyone who – out of fear or hope – had assumed that religion would be buried in a 'classless society' will be disappointed by the end of Bloch's book on *Natural Law and Human Dignity*: 'A society which is no longer antagonistic will hold fast to all worldly destinies; it presupposes an absence of any economic and political situation, an absence of destiny, but it is precisely for that reason that the indignities of existence emerge all the more tangibly, from the jaws of death down to the ebbing away of life in boredom or satiation. The messengers from nothingness have lost the credentials given them by class society; they bear a new and now largely unrecognizable face, but the series of purposes which is broken off in them now devours in a new way.'[9] So Bloch's utopian view of the 'classless society' ends with the vision of a new religion as the 'linking of a whole forward-looking dream through our paltry fragments', and the vision of a new church which will take friendliness, profundity, brotherliness, difficulties, seriously – a catholicity in solidarity with the neighbour and open to the morrow, 'so that it does not live for the day but beyond the day'; in other words, a 'church without superstition and on the way'.

Anyone who – again whether out of fear or hope – had assumed that Bloch would have to stylize Jesus of Nazareth as a social rebel or a political revolutionary will be no less disappointed. The messianic idea of the kingdom certainly began to be effective in Jesus' preaching as a social movement among the weary and heavy-laden, the humiliated and injured in Galilee, because it gave them impetus, a sense of value and hope, but in its intended content and hope it does not in any way coincide with any social utopia. As a historically necessary form among these intangibles the liberating gospel for the poor anticipates something that has not yet appeared, and will explode the whole system of earth and heaven, as the Apocalypse proclaims. This is the kingdom: 'What no eye has seen nor ear heard . . . ' (I Cor.2.9).[10]

The unconditional and total content of messianism is addressed in the symbols of God and the kingdom of God. It stimulates ever-new social and constitutional utopias which are related to reality, and spurs on liberation movements and the people's fight for justice. But in itself it goes beyond that and also takes people further through it. So here we have a concrete utopia and more than utopia. Here is real revolution and more than revolution. That is brought about by the surplus of messianic hope despite the transformations of the God hypostasis into the revolutionary impulse. Indeed it happens precisely because of this transformation of what does not disappear in any transformation, and therefore will in turn transform the transformations. Messianism is made concrete through its production of real utopias, linking them to what is subjectively and objectively possible. It always transcends its own immanence. It constantly puts its own realizations in the balance of the not-yet, which draws it on further.

(c) Messianic hope and atheism

'Without atheism messianism has no place.' So runs Bloch's thesis.[11] But what would 'theism' mean here? We read that 'the existence of God, indeed God generally as his own being, is superstition'. Religion itself is superstition if it is not hope, and its symbols are not symbols of that 'most unconditioned of utopias', nor are they an invitation to the movement of hope. Bloch's atheism is emphatically directed against the *Totum* as a symbol of hope when it is hypostatized as 'God', i.e. as its own 'being' existing for itself. If God is thought of as absolute and is worshipped as eternal, then hope is paralysed. So ideas of the creator and ruler of the world, of the power of heaven and the authority of the throne, fall under the judgment of hope. 'God becomes the kingdom of God, and the kingdom of God no longer contains a God: i.e. this religious heteronomy and its reified hypostasis are completely dissolved in the theology of the community but in one which has itself stepped beyond the threshold of the previously known creature, of its anthropology and sociology.'[12]

Bloch's atheism for the sake of the greater hope has at least three motives.

1. The first basis is the messianic hope which brings heaven to earth in order to find the future of the earth. Bloch's atheism is not a reductionist atheism, far less does it remain at a banal level. Nor, despite its proximity to Feuerbach, is it a merely futurized reductionist atheism. As in the best parts of Marx, Bloch is concerned only with a functional criticism of religion, not with a criticism of the essence of the religious, and therefore only with a functional reinterpretation of belief in God along the lines of messianism. Belief in God is superstition when it has the effect of superstition. Belief in God causes human alienation when it robs human beings of their freedom, when it fixes experiences in religious terms and thus gets in the way of messianic transcending into the future. But if experience, praxis and analysis show that belief in God has a liberating, stimulating and mobilizing effect on the real overcoming of real misery, this functional criticism fades away. The criticism of the praxis of belief in God is refuted by praxis. That is one level of the functional criticism of religion by Marx and Bloch.

2. Behind this we can see another level. It is the impulse of the Mosaic prohibition of images. In the Baalized religion of Yahweh the Old Testament prophets stressed the difference between Yahweh and the Baals by the prohibition of images. In the political religions of Christendom the theology of the cross

and the discipleship of the cross have similarly criticized the idolizations of Christian faith. Bloch's atheism is influenced by the Mosaic prohibition of images, given radical Jewish form in the prohibition against uttering the name of God and imaging the being of God. Though religious ideas are formed from religious experience, they may not prescribe this experience; if they did, they would fix the experience and thus bring the journey to an end. But as symbols they can be an invitation to further experiences. So they must remain open and mobile, if they are to be open and issue an invitation to the movement of transcending.

Myths of origin keep relating human beings to the same origin. They depict the *restitutio in integrum*, the restoration to the authentic state. Eschatological signals invite human beings to set out from what is always the same and to experience new life. So as signs of change these myths are themselves changeable signs. In Bloch's symbolism one can see a predilection for the symbol of the *incipit vita nova:* a new life begins. His demythologizing of religious symbols for the purpose of echatologizing them has support from the messianic traditions of Judaism: when the messianic time dawns, the oppressive idols and demons will disappear from the world; the earth will become human and habitable. It is the idea of messianism that the messianic time will fulfil the prohibition against images world-wide. The messianic time will so change the world that human understanding can leave its world, which is duplicated and alienated in the images, in order to feel at home in the world.

3. Behind these levels of the prohibition of images a third messianic level then emerges. According to kabbalistic tradition the messianic world will be a world without similitudes. In it the similitude and that of which it is a similitude will no longer need to be related, because in it a form of being will emerge which is no longer in need of being depicted and indeed is incapable of being depicted.[13] The distances between God and creation, between faith and experience, between consciousness and being, will then cease. Does not Pauline eschatology also contain this vision? When all powers are abolished and death is annihilated, then 'God will be all in all' (I Cor.15.28). But if God is 'all in all', the ontological distance between God and the world which had to be bridged by symbols, similitudes, ideas and hypostases disappears. In the glory of God, which indwells and penetrates all things, there is an end to the strangeness of God compared with this world and the alienation of human beings from God. So here, too, there is an end to all the symbols and similitudes of the other which in history participate in the strangeness of God and the alienation of human beings, because historically they point to that homeland. For the captive people of God they are 'the Lord's song in a strange land' (Ps.137.4). 'God all in all' can no longer be represented in images and does not need to be communicated by anything. This vision means a nearness of God which makes images,

symbols, signs and figures superfluous.

That also holds for theological concepts. What in the history of Israel is called 'God' has its foundation in the exodus experiences of history and points forward to the glory which will permeate all things, but still participates in the alienation and slavery from which the departure is being made. The glory itself shines out in a light which – according to the Jewish Kabbala – has not yet left its source. What no one yet has seen or heard is to change and transfigure the world in the kingdom. Compared with the conceptions of God which are necessarily alienated in history, the kingdom of God will be 'atheistic'. So those historically conditioned conceptions of God are to be interpreted messianically, i.e. expounded in terms of the fact that they themselves are made superfluous in the presence of God.

Bloch remains messianic precisely when his remarks in this area sound ambiguous and contradictory: 'God becomes the kingdom of God, and the kingdom of God no longer contains any God' – if one is not to accuse it of being thoughtless, this thesis is highly ambivalent in its contradictory use of the word 'God'. If mere reduction were meant, then the kingdom could no longer be called the 'kingdom of God'. If the messianic interpretation of this statement is correct, then in the coming kingdom 'God', the being existing outside the world for himself, becomes the glory dwelling in the world. In that case the 'kingdom of God' no longer contains any 'God' who is separated from the world and exists for himself outside it.

The following sentence also contains this ambivalence. 'This religious heteronomy and its reified hypostasis dissolve completely in the *theology* of the community . . . ' So they do not dissolve in human autonomy but in the 'theology of the community'. In that case, as is shown by the next sentence, which is about crossing the 'threshold of the creation as it has been hitherto', and by the allusion to Hegel, the only possible reference can be to the indwelling of God in his people in the power of the Holy Spirit, the 'God in us'. In the God who is present in the Spirit and the kingdom the religious heteronomies and the reified hypostases in fact dissolve.

In my view, the statement about the 'consummation of the exodus God so that it becomes that of the kingdom, the dissolution of Yahweh in this glory', is also to be understood in messianic terms. The God of the exodus consummates himself to be the God of the kingdom, and this 'consummation' is then the 'dissolution' of his historically manifest and historically conditioned Yahweh figure in the form of that glory of which, according to the vision of the prophets, 'all lands are full' (Isa.6.3).

3. The price of messianism

At the end of his tractate on 'The Messianic Idea in Judaism', Gershom Scholem mentioned the price that the Jewish people had to pay and still has to pay for this idea which it gave the world. The magnitude of the messianic idea corresponds to the weakness of the Jewish diaspora, which in exile was not prepared to commit itself on a historical level beause it dreamed in messianic terms of a homecoming. The messianic hope has kept the Jewish people alive dispersed among the peoples. From year to year they lived in the hope, 'Next year in Jerusalem'. Precisely for that reason, however, they did not live with their hearts fully in the present. The messianic idea has the weakness of the provisional and the transitory, which does not give itself up but preserves itself; which cannot die because it does not want to live. 'To live in hope is something great, but it is also something deeply unreal.'[14] In Judaism the messianic idea forced 'life in postponement', in which nothing can be done and achieved with any finality. Judaism found a readiness for irrevocable commitment in concrete terms only after Auschwitz, in the return to Zion. This was indeed accompanied by the messianic tones of Zionism, but did not write itself into a religious metahistory.

Bloch's philosophical messianism also holds the world in a balance: 'Such knowledge-conscience as the inherited substratum of religion cited above, i.e. as the mindfulness that it is *hope in totality*, at the same time grasps the essence of the world in tremendous suspense, towards something enormous which hope believes is good, which active hope workes to ensure is good.'[15] To denote this state of being-in-the-balance into which the messianic idea brings the world and the experiences of the world, Bloch uses rich variations on the symbols of the 'open world process', the 'material of process' and the *experimentum mundi*.

On the one hand that sounds encouraging: nothing is final, everything is open, 'Poland is not yet lost'. Hope can be disappointed, otherwise it would not be hope. Only hope can be disappointed, but it cannot be destroyed by any disappointment, because none is yet final.

But it also has the weakness mentioned by Gershom Scholem: nothing is done finally and everything remains provisional. Life in the 'balance', indeed in this 'tremendous balance' between hope and the 'tremendous', can only be a 'life in constant postponement'. Every word remains open, every idea remains fleeting, every action can be revoked. Everything is just an 'experiment'. The nucleus of existence does not give itself here because it is preserved for a better future and is holding back. But where and through what does the final, the unreserved commitment to the concrete, the complete surrender to the unconditional, come into this messianic life and thought which is always provisional, because it is hopeful?

Even if we describe the messianic life in hope not only in negative terms as a life in postponement but also in positive terms as a life in anticipation, and define life in the dynamic of the provisional, not only through the constant 'not yet real' but also through the 'now already possible', this question remains as a criticism of the theory and praxis of *The Principle of Hope*.

According to Jewish tradition the messianic times begin with the death agony of the old world and the birth pangs of the new. From a Christian perspective it has already begun representatively for all with the passion and resurrection of Christ in this one person. It is not Jesus's commitment of himself to a transcendent mystery of God but his commitment of himself to the immmanent mystery of this world, 'to death on the cross', which opens up the messianic time to sighing creation, and messianic life to alienated men and women. So this hope can only be put into practice through complete self-commitment. That is no state of being in the balance, no open process and no merely experimental attitude to life, but the paradox of living and dying in the light of the cross and resurrection of the Messiah. In that case there is no transcending of reality in hope for the future without the paradoxical counter-movement of the incarnation of love in this reality, no departure to new shores without the giving up of life. In the movement of the incarnation, the kingdom of God is already lived out here in a paradoxical way and not just hoped for. The real life of hope in fellowship with the crucified Messiah is manifested in no other way than 'as dying, and behold we live' (II Cor.6.9). Without this paradox of the real, the dialectic of the possible remains only a possible dialectic.

I am not saying this as a theological criticism of Bloch's philosophy of hope. I am saying it in respect of hope itself, whether hope has a philosophical or a theological foundation, especially in the changed world situation of 1985. At that time, at the beginning of the 1960s, we were convinced and enthused by hope in action, an active, militant hope, which could ally itself with the friendly tendencies in the world process, in the realm of unlimited possibilities, to lead to success. Today it has become irrefutably clear to us that we are living, and have to live, in the end-time (as Günter Anders put it), i.e. in the time in which the nuclear end of humankind is possible at any moment - within a few hours − , a time in which the ecological crisis has become a permanent crisis, and a time in which mass misery and famine has people in the countries of the 'Third World' in its grasp. Our possibilities have become objectively more limited and subjectively clearer: 'The end is near.' But that simply means that hope in action becomes hope in resistance. So hope in the wide range of possibilites must become a hope in the narrow sphere of danger. The dialectical hope for the possible must become a paradoxical 'hope against hope'. Today true hope, human and divine, says not only 'It is possible', but first of all *tamen −* nevertheless!'

5

'What God would he be who came only from outside . . . ?'

In Memory of Giordano Bruno

His monument stands at the ancient place of execution in Rome, which now bears the name Campo dei Fiore and is occupied by an Italian flower market. At the ceremony on 9 June 1889 at which it was unveiled Professor Bovio announced: 'Here he was burned, and his ashes do not lay dogma to rest. Here he rises again, and the religion of intellectual freedom calls for no vengeance. It calls for the toleration of all doctrines, all cults, and above all the cult of justice. Work instead of church prayers, research instead of mere faith, discussion instead of subjugation; its articles are the discoveries of science, its concordats the international congresses and world exhibitions of a joint work. This faith has no prophets, but thinkers. If you are seeking its temple, it is the universe. If you are seeking its haven, it is the human conscience . . . In Bruno's universe there is no excommunication, and the whole human race has access to this community.'

1. Prophet or heretic?

While many thousands were streaming to that place to honour the martyr of intellectual freedom and of the piety of the universe, and to celebrate their own faith in work, science and progress, Pope Leo XII spent the whole day in St Peter's on his knees before the bronze statue of the prince of the apostles, in prayer, fasting and concern for the salvation of the Roman Catholic church and the faith which brings bliss. He too had made a public statement on this occasion. In all churches his encyclical was be read out to the faithful, to warn them against the arch-heretic and heresiarch Giordano Bruno and to blacken him morally in the eyes of the faithful. In it we read: 'He did not have any scientific achievements to show, nor did he acquire any merits for the advancement of public life. His mode of action was dishonest, deceitful and completely self-seeking, intolerant of any opposed views, outspokenly malicious and full of a fawning flattery which caricatures the truth.'

This remarkable catalogue of personal invective can still be found in the first edition of the Catholic *Lexicon for Theology and the Church*, published in German in 1930. There we find: 'An unsteady itinerant life took the sick controversialist and backbiter to Geneva, Toulouse, Paris, London, Wittenberg . . . where he did not shrink from a change of confession and eternal argumentation . . . The more recent spirit of the time, hostile to the church, sees Bruno as its main hero and has set up monuments to him in Naples and in Rome.' In the meantime the excitement seems to have died down. In the second edition of the *Lexicon,* published in 1957, this personal invective was dropped in favour of an objective account.

Has the assessment of Bruno finally become unprejudiced? Has the trial really been reopened, or should people continue to be divided over Bruno: the free spirit with the hope of a humane world on the one hand, and the faith of the church with the recollection of the barbarism of that execution on the other? Are the heretics of that time the prophets of tomorrow simply because they were declared to be heretics? Did Giordano Bruno really so put in question the papacy of his time, the church and Christianity, that he became a deadly danger and of necessity had to fall victim – to put it in a friendly way – to the 'self-defence' of the church in Rome? Was he the herald of a new, post-Christian, cosmic world-view far ahead of his time?

The indictment against Bruno mentions a number of 'errors', some of which were taken from his cosmology of an immeasurable universe and some of which were found in his satires against the Pope and the church. Having heroically and without resistance withstood the cruel torture, he was condemned as an *'impertinente e ostinato eretico'*. The verdict was signed by the famous Jesuit Cardinal Bellarmine. Bruno was handed over to the secular authorities of Rome for them to burn him alive. And not only was the man burned, but – as the verdict says - also 'all his books and writings, on the steps of St Peter'.

No serious theological account was taken of his concerns either before or during his trial, or after his death. As far as I know there was no theological discussion of his cosmology, and those who took his cosmology seriously were not interested in its theological dimensions. If Bruno's world-view was pantheistic, materialistic and thus in the modern sense 'atheistic', why then did he talk of God at all, and why did the vision of the infinite cosmos become the central experience of God for him? But if his view of the cosmos led him to speak of God, from where was this concept of God derived and what is its relationship to the Jewish and Christian understanding of the presence of God in the world?

In this chapter I want to give a brief account of Bruno's life and describe the main features of his world-view and his picture of human beings, so that we can begin the necessary conversation which theology has owed him for four hundred years. That is the least that theology can do for this unfortunate victim of a church fanaticism which, though of its time, is not excluded even today, if it is to restore Bruno's dignity and salvage its own honour.

2. The life and death of a 'passionate hero'

Giordano Bruno (Filippo) was probably born in spring 1548 in Nola, at the foot of Mount Cicala near Naples. On 15 May 1565 he entered the Dominican convent of S.Domenico Maggiore in Naples. The Dominicans had a reputation for persecuting heretics and passing judgment on witches. As 'hounds of the Lord' (*domini cani*) – to use a derogatory term – during those centuries they ran the Inquisition. However, Thomas Aquinas had also lived and taught in that convent in Naples. Here Bruno was ordained priest in 1572; his comprehensive education in ancient and humanistic natural philosophy also dated from that time. Evidently he was provocatively entangled in rash debates by Montecalcini, the head of the Inquistion. At all events, a secret dossier was compiled against Bruno by the Inquisition, from which in 1576, when he was twenty-eight, an indictment 'in one hundred and thirty points' was levelled him, relating to doubts about the faith and a 'proclivity towards lascivious poetry', as the 1930 *Lexicon* claimed.

Bruno escaped the hopeless prospect of a trial by flight. There began what in the literature is called his 'itinerant life', though it was neither unsettled nor fugitive, but took him to the cultural centres of the then European world. He travelled through upper Italy, Venice, Brescia, Bergamo, got to know the famous English humanist Sir Philip Sidney in Milan, and in 1579 arrived in Geneva, the sanctuary for Protestant refugees from all over Europe. Calvin was already dead and the execution of Servetus lay twenty-five years in the past, but in Geneva, with Theodore of Beza, the period of Reformed (Aristotelian) orthodoxy had dawned on which the empiricist philosopher Petrus Ramus had already come to grief, a victim of the St Bartholomew's Day massacre in Paris in 1572. Bruno probably joined the reformed Italian community in Geneva. At all events, his name appears both on the list of this community and in the register of the Geneva academy. However, this was not a change of confession but rather a mistake: Bruno was a heretic of the late Renaissance, but not a supporter of the Reformation.

Bruno soon went on via Lyons to Toulouse, after Paris the most significant university city in France at that time. There he gained qualifications to teach theology with a thesis on Thomas Aquinas and Peter Lombard, and began a successful teaching career. It will have led to his work *Clavis magna,* which was concerned with the memorizing technique of Ramon Lull. The *ars memoriae* had always fascinated him, and he himself must have had an outstanding memory. However, there was more to it than that: specifically the idea of operationalizing all thought operations by the standards of mathematics and making the human brain a controlling thought-machine. In 1581 he went to Paris, became professor at the College of Cambrai, and gained a great reputation with his book on the art of memory, *De umbris idearum,* which he dedicated to Henry III. He also produced literary works here, including *Il candelaio.*

In April 1583 Bruno moved to London and lived as a guest in the house of the French ambassador. In summer 1583 he gave a course in Oxford on the cosmology of Copernicus. In the tolerant atmosphere of Elizabethan England and under the protection of Sir Philip Sidney, he wrote his main cosmological works, *Cena della cenire, De l'infinito, Universo et mondo* and *De la causa, principio et uno.* In his style he tried to imitate the dialogues of Plato, but what he achieved were more didactic poems than authentic dialogues. He also published rhetorical works, like the *Spaccio de la bestia trionfante* in 1584; composed as an attack on the Pope and the church, this later led to his condemnation. His praise of men inspired by God, *De gl'heroici furori,* appeared in 1585.

In 1585 he returned to France. Here a call reached him to go to Lutheran Wittenberg, where with a commendation from Gentili he lectured for two years on the writings of Aristotle. In an *Oratio valedictoria,* out of gratitude he praised the German *philosophica liberta* and Martin Luther. In 1589 he taught at the Lutheran High School in Helmstedt, which had become famous, and wrote his main works on cosmology, *De monado, numero et figura liber* and *De immenso et innumerabilibus seu de universo et mundis* (1591). In 1591 he taught in Reformed Zurich; he had become a European celebrity, a 'visiting professor', who was sought after internationally, like so many outcasts today.

However, then a late and disastrous invitation reached him from Giovanni Mocenigo to go to Venice. Mocenigo immediately denounced him to the Inquisition in Venice, which arrested him in 1592. Then began his years of suffering. At the beginning of 1593 he was handed over to the papal nuncio, sent to Rome and put in the prison of the Holy Office. His trial dragged on for more than seven years, which suggests a skilled defence and some inconclusiveness among the inquisitors.

The charges against him were wide-ranging, as it were on suspicion: denial of the Trinity, identification of the Holy Spirit with the world soul, denial of transubstantiation and the Virgin Birth, the claim that there was a plurality of worlds, an atheistic way of life, scorn for the papacy and the cult of the saints, and much else. His defence was that he was a philosopher, not a theologian, and so had argued according to the natural understanding and not according to faith: a doctrine of two kingdoms which was both Averroistic and Lutheran. In 1599 Pope Paul V, none other than the former Inquisitor-General C.Borghese, in whose hands the trial had been, intervened and called for the investigation to be speeded up; it was completed by Bellarmine. Bruno was condemned in the jubilee year of 1600. He replied proudly: 'You have made the judgment against me with perhaps greater fear than I who accept it.' The rest was cruel and utterly shameful: racked by torture and flayed, in the early dawn of 17 February he was

159

dragged to the place of execution and burnt alive. His last words are said to have been the remark of the dying Plotinus: 'I am attempting to assimilate that in the universe which is most exalted and nearest to God.' Bruno died as relaxed as Socrates and as sovereign as the Christian martyrs, in keeping with his own words: 'Anyone who fears bodily pain has never participated in the divine.'

3. The heavenly revolution

Up to the year 1543, the Aristotelian-Ptolemaic world-view dominated European thought and sensibility: the heavenly spheres circled like globes around a central, immobile earth; behind the sphere of the firmament lay the sphere of the *primum mobile*, the unmoved mover of the universe. Then Copernicus' work *On the Circular Movements of the Heavenly Bodies* appeared. With his mathematical calculations of the courses of the stars he attempted to break up the geocentric picture of the world. However, Giordano Bruno was the first to recognize the scope of Copernicus's discovery and to draw the consequences for cosmology. Bruno was the first really to carry through the 'heavenly revolution'. He did not set a heliocentric view of the world against the old geocentric view, but dissolved any kind of centrism and had the courage to think in terms of the infinity of the universe and the relativity of the centre and the limits: 'In the universe there is neither centre nor circumference; but, if you will, in everything there is a centre, and any point can be taken as the centre of any circumference' (*De l'infinito* 5.2). The universe is not built up of layers, like an onion, but all the stellar worlds move across immeasurable space. It is really only heaven, the immeasurable space, that is 'the universal womb', 'that which embraces all'. From this space and the bodies which are to be found in it there comes into being the universe as a connected whole. Now if this world is in the space which coincides with the magnitude of the world, there can also be other worlds in that space, and countless other worlds in countless other spaces. By 'world' (*mondo*) Bruno meant first of all just a planetary system, but his relativizing thought manifestly also dissolved the metaphysical ideas of the unity of the one world. And so he necessarily changed the concept of God.

What is the relationship of the absolute infinity of God to the newly discovered infinity of the immeasurable universe? What is the relationship of the unity of God to the newly discovered plurality of worlds? Bruno evidently attempted to clarify the differences between God and the universe: God is that which limits and the world is that which is limited. The world is infinite, and God is the one who embraces it in terms of perfect totality and fullness of being in all things. The universe does not have an absolute infinity but a dimensional infinity. 'I name God absolute and completely infinite, because he is everywhere whole throughout the world, and infinitely and fully present in each of its parts.' So divine and cosmic infinity do not contradict each other. Were God only another word for the universe, as the charge of pantheism claims, then the word

160

would be dispensable and atheism the logical consequence. For Bruno, though, God must be there, because otherwise the universe makes no sense. However, were God a merely abstract infinity, there would be no universe. The infinite would then have to be outside God and would have to be an infinity of nothingness, as Spinoza later said. The concept of the infinite, omnipresent God makes it impossible to think of a universe 'outside' God and God 'outside' the universe. A God who had an 'outside' to himself would not be God. So the universe can be rightly understood only 'in God'. Bruno therefore does not draw God into the world but brings the world to light in God. If this world is immeasurable and infinite in dimension, then the Godhead in which it is must be even greater (*semper major*). For Bruno, the concept of God is indispensable.

However, for Bruno the Godhead is not always the all-embracing One, but also fullness of Being in all individuals. God is maximum and minimum at the same time. If the geometrical minimum is the point and the physical minimum is the atom, then the metaphysical minimum is the monad. All things are made up of these basic units. They form the real unity of the world, for the Godhead is the *monas monadum*. Therefore Bruno says: *Deus est monas omnium numerum fons*. Just as the point as a centre expands to become the circle, so the divine *monas* multiplies into countless creatures. The multiform world is the *multiplicatio* of God. The greatest is included in the smallest and the world as a whole is reflected in the smallest thing. The nucleus of all things is in each thing, and the striving for *explicatio* and *multiplicatio,* development and multiplication, drives each individual being beyond itself: here is a true *coincidentia oppositorum* after the model of Nicolas of Cusa.

Bruno's universe is not, though, conceived of in mechanistic terms, as is Newton's, but organologically. He therefore takes up once again the old Stoic doctrine of the world-soul, which was also current among the church fathers: the world-soul which gives all things life and movement is the divine dynamic of the universe. 'Soul occurs in all things, and there is not even the tiniest particle that does not have such a share that it could not give itself life.' Like the Stoics and church fathers, Bruno could also call the world-soul the divine Spirit: the true reality and form of all things. In so doing he gave the universe a splendid subjectivity. From this follows the conception of a world which is a living organism. All things live with one another, for one another and in one another in the fellowship of the ensouled, organically formed and dynamically active world. The unity which is at work everywhere is God. The living power which permeates all things is divine: *physis optima deitas*.

In the face of the immeasurable universe, however, human beings lose all orientation. In immeasurable space there is no difference between above and below, right and left, before and behind. From Pascal to Nietzsche this shock was often described as the metaphysical homelessness of humankind: 'He who lost what you lost has no resting place.' Not so Giordano Bruno: man is certainly no longer the centre of a world which was made for his sake, but precisely for that reason he can and must choose the centre freely for himself and create his own orientation. Faced with the immeasurable universe, human beings are not lost; only now do they discover their own dignity and greatness. Bruno is, of course, part of Renaissance culture in calling the new man in the immeasurable universe the 'passionate hero'. But he is thinking of the heroes of the free spirit and their undeterred research into the universe, and also of the heroes of justice and truth. Their 'passion' is a *divina strazione*, is love for the divine in all things. Indeed, the divine Spirit itself lives and works in these heroes. They endure the experience of the Original: 'When God touches you, you become a flaming glow'. That is mystical rapture, but directed towards the divine universe itself, and not to a God beyond the universe. Therefore the 'passionate hero' feels a deep accord with the universe. In the finite he becomes one with the infinite. He becomes one with what holds the world together in its innermost depths.

4. 'It befits him to move the world inwarldy . . .'

Bruno's cosmological theses were discussed everywhere at the beginning of the Enlightenment. His writings were part of the great cosmological discussions of Newton, Leibniz, Wolff and others. However, his metaphysical world-view first gained influence through John Toland in England and Friedrich Heinrich Jacobi in Germany. Jacobi's *On the Teaching of Spinoza in Letters to Herr Mendelsohn* (1789), with a translation of Bruno's *De la causa* as an appendix, sparked off the famous dispute over pantheism in Berlin and deeply influenced theology at the time of Goethe. Goethe himself was not only an admirer of Bruno, this 'Faustian man', but also an independent student of his religious views. The finest example is the poem 'God and World'. In Bruno, *De immenso* I.11, we have: 'There is no divine intelligence which rotates outside the world and draws its circles, for it would be more worthy were it subject to an inner principle of movement, so that we have a nature, an idea and a soul of our own, which live just as much in that Innermost as in the body and are present to this in the universality of the mind, the body, nature and the soul.' In Goethe we find:

> What God would he be, who came only from outside,
> allowed the universe to run in a circle on his finger!
> It befits him to move the world inwardly
> to cherish nature in himself, himself in nature,
> so that what lives and moves and is in him,
> never misses his power or his spirit.

Goethe developed not only Bruno's metaphysical theory of monads but also his view of the world as an organism. Wherever Spinoza was present in German poetry and philosophy at the beginning of the nineteenth century, there too was Bruno. Bruno was more important than Spinoza for the attempts, as early as the beginning of the industrial revolution, to get beyond the mechanistic picture of the world on which the revolution was based and to find a human and organic relationship to nature.

The theological conversation with Bruno has to be carried on today, i.e. under the impact of the ecological crisis which has been brought about by the mechanistic view of the world and the scientific technological civilization which is grounded in it. The metaphysical presupposition for the development of the mechanistic world-view was the unsouling of the world. The old idea of a 'world soul' was rejected as being superstitious and animistic; the unsouled world was regarded as a machine which God the Lord has ordered by natural laws. 'God rules all things, not like a world soul, but like a Lord over the universe,' said Newton. The male conception of domination suppressed the old female image of the organic world with a soul. This also fundamentally changed the human attitude to nature: the goal is no longer the 'passionate hero' who in the divine spirit becomes one with the universe, but the man who makes himself the master and proprietor of nature through science and technology. But if the immanence of God in the world as a Spirit is given up in favour of the transcendence of the divine ruler over the world, the way is free for a completely spiritless and godless view of nature. In that case human beings drop out of the context of nature and the fellowship of creation. Their civilization becomes hostile to nature.

If nature and humanity are to survive on this earth, they must find the way together to a new fellowship. Human beings must once again integrate themselves and their culture into the cosmic framework of the earth. Human beings cannot integrate themselves into a 'world machinery' without surrendering their humanity. Therefore it is necessary and meaningful to develop new conceptions of 'earth' as an organism, of the kind that Lovelock has undertaken today in his Gaia hypothesis: human beings do not live 'on' the earth or 'over against' nature, but 'in' the earth as a total organism, which by constantly adopting and assimilating energy guarantees life in general and also human life.

The metaphysical basis for such a 'post-modern' organological view of nature is beyond question a new understanding of the working of the Spirit in all things, or more precisely in all complex and open systems of matter and life. The Cartesian reduction of the mind to human thought must be overcome, so that human thought becomes a communicative thought in respect of nature and no longer serves the one-sided human domination of nature.

The theological foundation for the overcoming of the one-sided human religion of domination in modern society is beyond question the rediscovery of the immanence of God in the world in the Spirit of creation, which calls all things into being and is life-giving life for all that lives. It was a one-sided and not particularly imaginative adaptation of theology to the modern world to claim that the 'distinction between God and the world' follows from the doctrine of creation in Judaism, Christianity and Islam. But creation is more than creating a work and differentiating oneself from it. Just as the artist puts his or her whole soul into a creation, so God the Creator puts his whole soul into each of his creatures and shares himself with all creatures in his boundless love. The Creator who communicates himself is present in all creatures by virtue of his Spirit (Wisdom of Solomon 12.1), so that they are all capable of loving and praising him. Of course this does not make God and world one in the sense that they are one and the same. But God is creatively present in creation in such a way that, like Goethe, one must see God in nature and nature in God if one is to understand creation. The justified anxiety about that pantheism which is only a courteous form of atheism, as Schopenhauer put it, must not lead to the destruction of the true pan-entheism that we find in Bruno and Goethe. Only if God remains God, does his immanence in the world bring about the self-transcendence of all open living systems which can be established everywhere, along with their evolution and their increasingly complex intertwining in communal relationships, because in it lies that 'more' which extends beyond any state.

If we were to say 'God *is* evolution', as for example the astrophysicist Erich Jantsch did in his impressive book *Die Selbstorganisation des Universum* ('The Self-Organization of the Universe', 1979), then we would sink below the level of Bruno and Goethe and would have declared evolution to be the dynamic of the world, but have left unexplained the dynamic of evolution. Negations lead only to reductions. Certainly we gain nothing if we say with Jantsch, 'While God is not the Creator, he is the Spirit of the universe', but we do gain immeasurably rich perspectives if we say, 'Because God is the creator he is also the Spirit of the universe'. 'Spirit', understood as the 'dynamic of self-organiz-ation' at the different levels of the universe, does not become divine if we coin a dynamic concept of God for it and call the dynamic 'God', but only if we have a concept of God with a trinitarian differentiation. Only when we have reached its horizons can we say with Meister Eckhart that all is 'from God', all is 'through God', all is 'in God'. Bruno's vision of the immeasurable universe in the infinite God, of the God who works within the world through the monads, and of the God who ensouls and is the spirit of the universe, also finds its legitimate place in these wider trinitarian contexts. Bruno wanted to be a philosopher and therefore did not use the Christian conceptions of the creation of the world, the incarnation and the gift of the Spirit. That is not to be held against him, since in his time those theological doctrines were not available to scientists and philosophers in a way which was open enough for them to be usable.

We often read that Giordano Bruno stood at the beginning of the modern age as a prophet of coming discoveries and as a forerunner of many.

It seems to me that Giordano Bruno is returning at the end of this age as the herald of a new 'paradigm' for a world in which human beings can survive in organic harmony with the Spirit of the universe.

III

MY THEOLOGICAL CAREER

The kind invitation to provide a 'profile of my theology' which prompted this article left me somewhat confused. One can know many things and describe them objectively, but how can one know oneself and the inner impulses of 'one's theology'? It is very difficult to keep objectivity and one's own interests apart even when studying theologians of former times and of the present day and giving theological profiles of them. How much more will objectivity and subjectivity get confused in a personal account of oneself! To give an objective profile of my own theology for discussion, I would really have already to be outside it. But if I were outside it, the profile would no longer be completely my own. I would already have distanced myself from it. So what I can say in all honesty about the profile of my own theology is very limited, coloured by my own identity, and therefore in the last resort not even particularly authentic. Others would presumably be much more suited to doing this. If we had personal accounts of their own theology in twenty to thirty pages from Augustine, Thomas Aquinas, Luther or Bultmann, no one writing a monograph about these theologians would spend much time on them. The author would presumably regard the accounts as one view of these theologians' thought among many others and work them into his or her own view. The only way in which I can free myself from the confusion which this invitation causes me is to attempt to describe how I came to theology, and then to the theology which I put forward in my books. I can only describe the course I have taken and intend to take in the future, the points at which the road came to an end and I had to look for a new way forward, and the goals that I have pursued on this course, with all its deviations.

I was also asked to stress my own individual approach. But such a request suggests something of the solitary individual, and that has never been my position. Only in normal times may individuals have the privilege of leading their lives in a way that suits them as individuals and fits in with their own plans. If that happens, they are not very aware of their social conditioning. The historical situation leaves them in peace to go their own way and to pursue their 'individual approach' in theology. I am not one of a generation thus favoured by history, who have been granted this individual freedom. My individual biography was shaped, interrupted and radically changed, in a very painful way, by the collective biography of the German people in the last years of the Second World War and by a lengthy imprisonment after it. The 'individual approach' of my faith and thought and therefore also of 'my theology' is embedded in the collective experiences of guilt and suffering in my generation. So even today it is governed by my participation in the social and collective 'approach' of the community in which I live.

I must explain this briefly in biographical terms. When I was sixteen, I wanted to study mathematics and nuclear physics. I came from a liberal Protestant home in Hamburg, and from the start knew Lessing, Goethe and Nietzsche better than the 'black book', the Bible. Christianity and the church were remote. At the age of seventeen, in 1943, I was conscripted, and experienced the destruction of Hamburg in the fireball of July 1943 while serving in an anti-aircraft battery in the inner city. In 1944 I was sent to the front; in 1945 I was made a prisoner of war and returned to Germany in 1948, after three years. In the camps in Belgium and Scotland I experienced the collapse of my certainties, and in this collapse found a new hope in the Christian faith, which brought me not only spiritual but also (I think) physical survival, because it rescued me from despair and from giving up. I returned to Germany a Christian and with the new 'individual approach' to study theology, in order to understand that power of hope to which I owed my life.

So I would like to say that for me Christian faith is fundamentally bound up with the experiences of a particular existential situation, and that this situation was not just a private matter but also a social situation. Seen from outside, whatever may seem to be my own particular individuality is from the start always related to collective experiences. Anyone who has had to cry out to God in the face of the mutilation and death of so many who were comrades, friends and relatives no longer has any withdrawn, individual approach in theology. The problem is how one can speak of God 'after Auschwitz'. But even more it is how one cannot speak of God after Auschwitz. What can one talk about after Auschwitz if not about God? Silence is no rescue, and any other kind of talk does not even relieve the severe oppression. This sense of no longer being able to talk of God and yet of having to talk of God in the face of the specific experiences of an oppressive burden of guilt and cruel meaninglessness in my generation is presumably the root of my theological concerns, for reflection about God constantly brings me back to that aporia.

Further 'conjectures' about my theological approach are rather easier to make. Because I did not grow up with the Bible and the catechism, to the present day I have had the feeling that in theology I have to discover everything afresh for myself. That is what happened to me over eschatology, the doctrine of hope, the theology of the cross and most recently over the doctrine of the Trinity.

After my studies in Göttingen, above all with Hans-Joachim Iwand, Ernst Wolf and Otto Weber, I was ordained, and for five years was pastor of the small Protestant community in Wasserhorst, a suburb of Bremen. In 1958 I willingly, yet reluctantly, became an academic teacher at the same time. For me that means that under the shell of the professor, who has to teach, there is always the pastor, who has to preach, advise, stimulate and comfort. If this assumption is correct, it explains to some degree why even in theological teaching I am concerned not so much with what is always right, but more with the word which is addressed to us here and now; not so much with correct doctrine but with concrete doctrine; and therefore not so much with pure theory but with a practical theory. Perhaps the strict separation between pulpit and teaching lectern has not worked so well with me as with colleagues to whom preaching and the work of a pastor have remained remote.

I have also found it difficult to keep theological study completely separate from political commitment, when I have attempted to abstain from politics. That certainly says nothing about my political wisdom, but anyone who was so messed around with by the government of their state as my generation, which was spurred on to senseless death in war, cannot rest easily in the ivory tower of an unpolitical academia. I was aware of the political conditioning and the political responsibility of theology from my earliest days in Göttingen. I certainly owe that to my first teacher, Hans-Joachim Iwand. But I also owe it to my wife, whom I first met when we were both studying theology in Göttingen. She came from a Confessing Church community in Potsdam and had been much closer to the political resistance than I had been with the naive idealism of my Hamburg family.

That brings me to the last argument against the well-meaning suggestion that I should present my 'individual approach'. Since I came to know my wife during our study together in Göttingen, I have ceased to feel that I am an 'individual'. Our shared life began with a theological dialogue, and our marriage since then has been accompanied by theological dialogue. This has brought a great depth of friendship to our marriage and has made it an exciting affair, in which we have made constantly new discoveries in each other, in our own selves and together. Of course that does not mean that I want to share the responsibility for 'my' theological publications and foist them off on a partner. But I do want to draw attention to the constant and fundamental conversation from which my theological work derives and without which it cannot be understood. Precisely in such sharing one becomes 'one's own person', to quote the German title of my wife's book about the women around Jesus, and develops one's own ideas. One respects the other's ways and goes along with the changes that take place in them. That, I imagine, is individuality in sociality and sociality by virtue of individuality.

167

I shall now attempt to describe the methods of my theology in three respects.

I. *The whole of theology in one focal point.*   I adopted this method in my books *Theology of Hope, The Crucified God*, and *The Church in the Power of the Spirit*.

II. *Theology in movement, dialogue and conflict.*   The Christian-Marxist dialogue of the 1960s in which I took part moved me deeply and led both me and Johann-Baptist Metz to 'political theology'. The ecumenical dialogue in which I have shared since 1963 as a member of the ecumenical 'Faith and Order' commission involved me intensively in Protestant-Catholic conversations, especially conversations in Rome, and conversations between the Western churches and Orthodoxy, especially in Bucharest. I was drawn into the Christian-Jewish dialogue through my encounter with Pinchas Lapide and then through the study of the works of Franz Rosenzweig and Gershom Scholem. Finally, through lecture tours, I became involved in the conflicts of Christian theology in this divided world. Conversations with theologians from the Second World in Hungary and Romania and with theologians from the Third World in Korea, Taiwan, the Philippines and Latin America, were particularly exciting, and deeply disturbed me and influenced me. Last but not least, as a result of visiting lectureships and professorships I have had experience of the theological community and theological trends in the USA and have attempted to share their thought.

III. *The part as a contribution to the whole.*   After a phase of self-critical and positive disengagement in 1977 and 1978 I concentrated on my own 'contribution to systematic theology'. I am no longer describing the whole of theology at a contemporary focal point, but presenting my part of theology as a contribution to a shared whole.

I. The whole of theology in one focal point

1. *The Theology of Hope* (1964)

I embarked on this course when I began to write the *Theology of Hope*, which was published in Germany in 1964. I had really wanted only to make a contribution to the discussion of 'promise and history' which at that time had been started in the journal *Evangelische Theologie*. It was about the connection between the 'theology of the Old Testament' as presented by Gerhard von Rad, Walter Zimmerli, Hans-Walter Wolff, Hans-Joachim Kraus and others, and the 'theology of the New Testament' which had been pioneered by Rudolf Bultmann and corrected and developed further above all by Ernst Käsemann. Whereas for the Old Testament scholars I have mentioned the focal point of interest was the history of the divine promises, Bultmann's theology was governed by the present eschatology of the promise fulfilled in Christ and the 'end of history' practised in faith. Ernst Käsemann had put that in question with his provocative thesis that 'apocalyptic is the mother of Christian theology'.

However, by 'apocalyptic' he did not mean the speculations about the events at the end of the world but the underlying question when God would really be God in his kingdom and when his righteousness would triumph in the world. But this question presupposes that this 'end of history' is still to come and is in no way already present.

My own theological thinking had already been guided in this direction by my study in Göttingen with Walter Zimmerli and Ernst Käsemann. Through the Dutch theologian Arnold van Ruler I had been made aware of the 'theology of the apostolate' and the messianic motivation of the Christian apostolate by what Walter Freytag called the 'perspective on the end'. In publications between 1958 and 1961 I discussed these connections between eschatological hope and historical praxis.

Then came my discovery of Ernst Bloch's philosophy of hope. It happened in 1960. I read *The Principle of Hope* in the East German edition during a holiday in Switzerland and was so fascinated that I did not even notice the beauty of the Swiss mountains. My immediate reaction was, 'Why has Christian theology neglected this theme of hope, which is so distinctively its own?' 'What is left of the earliest Christian spirit of hope in present-day Christianity?'

I began work on a 'theology' of hope, in which the biblical theology of promise and the apocalyptic hope, the theology of the apostolate and the kingdom of God, and the philosophy of hope with its materialistic elements and its orientation on historical, social and political praxis, all came together for me. I did not want to become heir to Ernst Bloch. Nor did I want to become a follower. Far less did I want to baptize his principle of hope into Christianity, as Karl Barth was complaining at that time from Basle. Rather, I wanted to achieve a parallel treatment in Christian theology on the basis of its own presuppositions. Whereas Bloch thought that only modern atheism could form a basis for hope, and put forward the thesis, 'without atheism messianism has no place', I began from the God who raised the executed Christ from the dead and made him Lord of the future of the world. Whereas Bloch restored to their place in philosophy the social utopias in which the 'weary and heavy laden' were to be made happy, and then brought in the constitutional utopias according to which those who had been humiliated and had suffered hurt had to be given their human dignity, for me hope 'for the resurrection of the dead and eternal life', and thus the expectation grounded in the biblical testimony to God, became important and was the foundation for accepting the social and constitutional utopias. Sometimes, however, our discussions ended up in the simplistic alternative of transcending without transcendence versus transcending with transcendence, hope against God versus hope with God.

When I began the 'theology of hope', after the 'theology of love' in the Middle Ages and the 'theology of faith' in the Reformation, I had first thought in terms of hope, its foundation and its future, its experience and its praxis – in other words in terms of an *object* of Christian theology, on which hitherto sufficient light had not yet been cast. 'What may I hope for?' is *the* religious question of modern times, as Immanuel Kant pointed out. So the theology of hope is modern theology. In the course of the work, however, hope increasingly became the *subject* of theology for me. I no longer theologized *about* hope, but *from* hope. To think theologically from hope means bringing the whole of theology together in this focus and then seeing it all anew in this light of hope: 'The eschatological is not one element *of* Christianity, but it is the medium of Christian faith as such, the key in which everything in it is set, the glow that suffuses everything here in the dawn of an expected new day . . . A proper theology would therefore have to be constructed in the light of its future goal. Eschatology should not be its end, but its beginning' (16). Not only eschatology – the doctrine of the last things – but all the doctrines of Christian theology, from creation through history to the consummation, then appear in a different light and must be thought through again. That is what I managed to do in *Theology of Hope* at that time, in connection with the experience of history, the understanding of history and the historical practice of Christianity, in the framework of my presuppositions and possibilities: 'Wherever it develops into hope, faith causes not rest but unrest, not patience but impatience . . . Those who hope in Christ can no longer put up with reality as it is, but begin to suffer under it, to contradict it' (21).

But I had not yet rethought the sphere of the doctrine of creation in relation to natural philosophy and the natural sciences. Apart from a remark on the need for a 'cosmic eschatology' (137), which Ernst Bloch very readily picked up, there is little about this in *Theology of Hope*. At that time I was thinking of the 'historicization of the cosmos' in apocalyptic eschatology. I wanted to construct the doctrine of creation from the new creation of heaven and earth, in other words from Rev.21, and no longer from Gen.1. In 1964 the 'ecological crisis' had not yet penetrated my consciousness. At that time we were more terrorized by the horrors of history and fascinated by its possibilities. Only in 1985 could I produce the doctrine of creation which had been on my agenda since 1964.

The theme of hope, of a new dawn, was as it were in the air in 1964. The Roman Catholic Church was opening itself up to the questions of the modern world in the Second Vatican Council; in the USA the Civil Rights movement had reached a climax; in the USSR 'socialism with a human face' was coming into being; and the ecumenical movement was making great progress. Much was becoming possible in that decade which had previously been thought to be impossible. The year 1968 then bitterly disappointed some of these hopes.

In the long run, however, one idea from the *Theology of Hope* proved effective. It was that historical liberation and eschatological redemption should be seen together in one perspective, the perspective of 'creative discipleship': 'Eschatology does not mean merely salvation of the soul, individual rescue from

170

the evil world, comfort for the troubled conscience, but also the realization of the eschatological hope of justice, the humanizing of man, the socializing of humanity, peace for all creation' (329). '"Creative discipleship" of this kind in a love which institutes community, sets things right and puts them in order, becomes eschatologically possible through the Christian hope's prospects of the future of God's kingdom and of man' (334). The political theology which Johann Baptist Metz developed in the Christian-Marxist dialogues of the 1960s was governed by this. The Black theology with which James Cone gave a Christian interpretation to the Black Power movement of the oppressed Blacks in the USA took over the idea. Gustavo Gutiérrez's *Theology of Liberation* also followed this line. In this perspective, the Korean Minyung theology discovered the people of Jesus (*ochlos*) as the people of the kingdom of God. In many areas, new practical contexts for this historical-eschatological perspective were discovered of which I myself had not been aware.

When Pope John Paul II was in Nicaragua in 1983, he admonished the priests not to become involved in the political liberation of their people, but to prepare the people for eternal life. At that time we said that this was a false alternative: because I believe in eternal life I will commit myself to the life of the people. Because I am taking part in the rebellion of the people against the deadly powers of oppression, I hope for the resurrection of the dead. Those who set up alternatives here put asunder what God has brought together in Christ, no matter whether in religious terms they are concerned for eternal life or in secular terms are interested only in changing this world.

2. *The Crucified God* (1972)

The theological foundation for the Christian hope is the resurrection of the crucified Christ. However, anyone who uses this as a starting point for theological thought will continually be reminded of the other side of that foundation: the cross of the risen Christ. So it was in accord with the logic of that christological approach of the 'theology of hope' to work on the recollection of the crucified Christ. This recollection arose from the praxis of the discipleship of Christ in which one becomes 'creative' only when one takes up the cross. So in 1970 I wrote: 'As well as working out a political theology I have resolved more strongly than ever to reflect on the significance of the cross of Christ for theology, church and society. In a culture which glorifies success and happiness and becomes blind to the suffering of others, the recollection that at the centre of Christian faith is an unsuccessful, suffering Christ, dying in shame, can open peoples' eyes to the truth. The recollection that God has raised up a crucified man and made him the hope for the world can help the churches to dissolve their alliances with the powerful and enter into the solidarity of the humiliated' (*Umkehr zur Zukunft*, 1970, 14).

What had happened with the *Theology of Hope* happened again for me: the whole of theology was brought together in a focal point, the cross, and in this perspective of the crucified Christ I saw many things in theology in a different way from before. For me, the cross of Christ became the 'foundation and criticism of Christian theology'. That which can stand firm before the crucified Christ is true Christian theology. That which cannot stand firm should disappear from theology. This is particularly true of Christian talk of God. Christ died on the cross with a loud cry, which Mark interprets with the words of Psalm 22, 'My God, my God, why have you forsaken me?' This cry of dereliction from Christ is either the end of all theology or the beginning of a specific Christian theology. Its criticism of theology consists in the fact that all theologians stand before the crucified Christ like Job's friends, because in one way or another they attempt to answer his last question by identifying theological reasons for his forsakenness on the cross. The foundation of a Christian theology then consists in making the crucified Christ's experience of God the centre of all its ideas of God.

At that time I began with an interpretation of the death of Christ on the cross which followed the *theologia crucis* that Luther had based on the theses of the Heidelberg Disputation of 1518: God reveals himself to the godless not through power and glory, but on the contrary in suffering and the cross, and in this way justifies the sinner. But then I found that the question turned itself round. I no longer asked what the cross of Christ means for human beings, but also asked what the cross of the Son of God means for God himself, whom he had called 'my Father'. I found an answer to this question in the perception of the deep *suffering* of God, which is bound up with the death of the Son on Golgotha and becomes manifest in him. It is the suffering of a boundless love. However, this conception of the suffering God ran counter to the Western theological tradition which along with the immortality of God also taught his essential impassibility.

When I began to grapple critically with this axiom of impassibility, which is more philosophical than biblical, I discovered parallels that I would never have dreamed of. My first discovery was the Jewish conception of the pathos of God with which Abraham Heschel had interpreted the message of the prophets, and the rabbinic and kabbalistic doctrine of the Shekinah, the indwelling of God in the persecuted and suffering of people of Israel, as it has been depicted by Franz Rosenzweig in the *Star of Redemption* and by Gershom Scholem. The development of the theology of the cross of the suffering God brought me close to the Jewish theology of the history of the passion of God in Israel. On occasions it has been said that *The Crucified God* is a 'christology after Auschwitz'. That is true in so far as I saw Golgotha in the shadow of Auschwitz which lay on my generation and sought counsel in 'Jewish theology after Auschwitz'.

I found further parallels in the Japanese theologian Kazoh Kitamori, who at the end of the Second World War discovered the 'pain of God' and thus went beyond Luther's 'theology of the cross'. At that time Dietrich Bonhoeffer, too,

172

had written in his prison cell: 'Only the suffering God can help.' Only years after the publication of my book did I find in the Spanish philosopher and poet Miguel de Unamuno the doctrine of the 'grief of God' and in the Russian philosopher of religion Nikolai Berdyaev the notion of the 'tragedy in God'. I took up these ideas critically in my book *The Trinity and the Kingdom of God*. But what was a greater surprise for me was the discovery that in the nineteenth and twentieth centuries there had aleady been extensive public discussion of the 'passibility of God' in England which continental theology had almost completely ignored. The exception here had been Ernst Troeltsch, whose attention had been drawn to it by his friend Baron von Hügel.

I found positive influences from my theology of the cross in the way in which a new depth was brought to Latin American liberation theology by Jon Sobrino. I learned from his theology of the cross, which had not only been learned but also suffered. The translation also brought me into closer contact with the theology of the church in Korea, which was fighting and suffering for freedom and human rights. Surprisingly, assent to my approach also came from the camp of Orthodox theology, in the persons of Dumitriu Staniloae and Geevarghese Mar Ostathios. This moved me very much. Links also came about with those orders of the Catholic church which are particularly associated with the mysticism of the cross. My interest in the experiences of God in the 'dark night of the soul' was aroused by them.

A widespread accusation made against *The Crucified God* is the same as that made against *Theology of Hope*. It is the charge of one-sidedness. According to B.Mondin, the book stresses 'arbitrarily only a singly mystery of Christ, the mystery of the cross'. According to Jan Milic Lochman, the 'God of Christian faith is not just the crucified God'. Because this 'one-sidedness' is evidently a matter of method, I attempted to explain it in a discussion volume on *Theology of Hope*. 'I understand the "one-sidedness" which is doubtless present in the book as an expression and recognition of the "communion of saints" with other theologians. Others should also be aware of this. No one begins with a blank sheet. So it is a contribution to an open conversation which renounces the unreal attempt to take all sides into account and therefore does not seek to have a totalitarian effect.' In the discussion volume on *The Crucified God* I returned to this accusation again, and said: 'Apart from the fact that this "one-sidedness" arises from the theme that I have chosen, I wanted to attempt to grasp the whole of theology from a particular focal point. Here of course one has to take overemphases into account, but at the same time a new light falls on the other points of theological doctrine.'

I did not attempt to write these books as theological textbooks, informative on all sides, balanced in judgment and reassuring in wisdom. In them I wanted to say something specific in a particular cultural, theological and political situation, and took sides. They were written from the time for the time, and are

173

thus to be understood as contextual theology, set within the conflict of contemporary life. I do not dispute the significance of a pure, balanced academic teaching which will last beyond its time. But that is no closer to eternity than theology in the context of the given *kairos*. In the last twenty years I have felt that I have been a participant in theological movements and controversies, and not a solitary worker at my own theological task. That may to some extent explain the variety of the influences on me and my reactions, which may have irritated some doctoral students concerned with my theology.

3. *The Church in the Power of the Spirit* (1975)

Relatively soon after *The Crucified God* I wrote my book on the church and the Holy Spirit. 'Was that necessary?', asked some friends and critics. I thought so, for two reasons.

1. Work on the theology of the cross had led me to a reconstruction of the doctrine of the Trinity, for I could only understand what happened on Golgotha between Jesus and the God whom he had addressed as Abba, beloved Father, in trinitarian terms. The way in which I summed it up at that time was: 'The cross is the material principle of the doctrine of the Trinity. The Trinity is the formal principle of the theology of the cross.' One can see that vividly from the well-known mediaeval pictures of the Trinity which are called 'God's distress' or 'the mercy seat': the Father is holding in his hands the crossbeam of the cross on which his dead Son is hanging, and the Holy Spirit is descending from the Father's face on to the dead Son in the form of a dove, to raise him up. That is an image of the trinitarian theology of the cross which I attempted to understand. In my book, however, I did not get further than seeing a binity of God the Father and Jesus the Son of God. Where was the Holy Spirit, who according to the Nicene Creed is to be worshipped and glorified together with the Father and the Son? What role does the Spirit play in the history of Jesus with God his Father and the history of this God with Jesus the Son? So after the trinitarian theology of the cross it was necessary to develop a pneumatology, so that the theology of the cross did not turn into a binitarian theology. At that time I was working intensively on the doctrine of the Holy Spirit in seminars and meetings. I set out some of the results in *The Church in the Power of the Spirit*.

2. The other reason was the contemporary context. After the student unrest throughout the Western world at the end of the 1960s, the Protestant church in West Germany had a crisis about its relevance. People in the traditions and institutions had been 'made insecure'. Nothing was taken for granted any more. Everything was questioned. I thought that these signs of crisis could also be the signs of a new opportunity to renew the church from its origin. We were standing at a crossroads and had to make a decision. It seemed to me to be this. Either the Protestant church would continue the course that had led to the crisis, from a state church to a people's church, and from a people's church to a church for

174

the people which offered them pastoral care, and from that to the organized religion of this society – or it would renew itself through forces from below and became a community church of the people of God in the people. At the same time the programme of the 'community church' was very much alive in the Catholic church in Germany and Austria under the slogan 'A parish becomes a community'. It could also be seen in another way in the renewal of the Catholic church from the base communities in Latin America. Not least, the free, gathered community had been the promise of the Reformation, which had not been fulfilled by the Protestant state churches and churches of the people. From my own experiences on visits to the free churches of the United States, the countries of the Third World and socialist countries, I attempted to lay the theological foundation for the transition of the Protestant church from a 'church of the people' to a 'community church'. This practical idea for the book was directly connected with the theological idea of a trinitarian pneumatology, since without a new experience of the Spirit in the communities it is impossible to arrive at a renewal of the church.

The book describes the doctrine of the church and the sacraments from the perspective of the Holy Spirit. But I did not succeed as 'one-sidedly' as in the two other books bringing everything into a single focus, because too many different themes had to be discussed in this doctrine of the church. It was important to me to develop the self-understanding of the church in the relation-ship of the church to Israel and not apart from it. It was also important to me to depict the self-understanding of the church of Christ in constant connection with the 'people of Jesus', i.e. in connection with the poor and humiliated, the sick and the handicapped. Not least, in the doctrine of the sacraments, of worship and of the ministries I attempted always to begin from the form of the church as community and to reformulate doctrine in the light of that.

Whereas after the two earlier books there had been lively discussion, with views for and against, the reaction to this book was not focussed enough to indicate the need for a further discussion volume. The book had a marked ecumenical orientation, so that it was taken up in other confessions and denomi-nations, and I entered into new conversations on pneumatology with both Baptists and Orthodox; the Evangelical, Protestant and Reformed evidently could no longer see the contours of a clear ecclesiology. Nor was I concerned with such confessional distinctiveness any longer.

After 1975 I discussed the practical basic ideas of the book at many conferen-ces, and in my small book *The Open Church* also attempted to speak directly as one church member to other church members. However, the general trend in the Protestant church in Germany was towards a modernizing of the old church of the people in the direction of a church which provided religious care for the people. Certainly the new approaches from the community for the community were taken up, but there was no reorientation of the kind indicated by the

175

watchword 'community church'. Rather, things stopped at the 'church communities' for which pastoral care was provided. However, more recent surveys show that the silent exodus from this institutional church is continuing, especially in the great cities. As an institution for providing religious care, as a resource for meaning, as a professional guide through life, the church (i.e. the church to which people belong and have at their disposal) is emptying and trickling away. In any case, the future of the church is the voluntary community which offers and calls for a personal decision and active participation, whether the church likes it or not. It would be good if church leaders recognized this and made a change in time. They would spare themselves and other people much frustration. They would make the church more credible in the light of the Lord whom it serves.

Though I had not planned it from the start, in retrospect I found that that these three books belonged together. They have therefore been called a 'trilogy', and I have nothing against that. If one looks at them together one can see that I have been evidently led from Easter and hope to Good Friday and suffering and then to Pentecost and the Spirit. The focal points for theological light changed, and changed in such a way as to supplement one another and correct the onesidedness in each instance which I found unavoidable.

However, I then decided not to go on using this method of summarizing theology in a focal point but by contrast to make my limited and fragmentary contributions to the whole of theology. This change was dictated not only by the subject matter but also by the contemporary situation and by my own personal situation.

II. Theology in movement, dialogue and conflict

For me, theology has come alive not so much in particular 'schools' like the 'Barth school', the 'Bultmann school', the 'Rahner school' and others of the past generation, as in movements, dialogues and conflicts. In those 'schools', the elements of the masters' thought was developed further. In the movements and dialogues of our generation we opened ourselves up towards others – strangers and often even hostile adversaries – , experienced our limitations, became aware of new problems and had to struggle for answers for which there was no basis in tradition.

1. The first great dialogue which was important for me was the Christian-Marxist dialogue at the great conferences in Salzburg (1965), Herrenchiemsee (1966) and Marienbad, Czechoslovakia (1967). These dialogues between leading Marxist philosophers from France, Italy, Yugoslavia and Czechoslovakia on the one hand, and Catholic and Protestant theologians from Western and Eastern Europe on the other, were unique, and for me were unforgettable. They were organized by the Catholic Paulus Gesellschaft, the last of them in Marien-

bad in collaboration with the Czech Academy of Sciences. At that time the political and cultural situation in Europe was generally favourable: in the Second Vatican Council the Roman Catholic Church was becoming more open to the questions of the modern world; in Czechoslovakia 'socialism with a human face' was coming into being; and in Western Europe Ernst Bloch and the Frankfurt school were disseminating so-called neo-Marxism. To the surprise of both sides, theologians with a revolutionary disposition and Marxists who asked religious questions came together in the dialogues. They were honest, and propaganda and missionary zeal were both absent. People learned to take one another's strong points seriously and not just to criticize weaknesses. We found ourselves in a community which asked questions openly, a community which was always wider-ranging than those with partisan and confessional answers. Certainly the representatives of the communist and church institutions feared the loss of their respective identities. So they had not come. But it was our experience that in dialogue with each other both sides tended to get a distinct profile. Each side's position was challenged. Abstract identity took on concrete form.

This hopeful Christian-Marxist dialogue was violently broken off by the invasion of Czechoslovakia by the Warsaw Pact troops in autumn 1968. Many of our Marxist partners lost their jobs, were expelled from the party and left their country. After that, in Eastern Europe for a long time there were only walls. Moscow had always been against 'ideological dialogue' with Christians; it seemed to fear such dialogues. So as late as 1977 a book appeared by W.I. Garadza, *A Critique of New Trends in Protestant Theology*, published by Snanije Publishing House, Moscow. It discussed *Theology of Hope* at particularly great length and breadth, with the aim of branding it 'anticommunist', and settled the argument by stating: 'Through so-called "ideological dialogue" Moltmann supported the counter-revolution in Czechoslovakia, the downfall of which he subsequently regretted repeatedly.' The author does not mention that this was not a counter-revolution and that of course one cannot carry on any ideological dialogue with tanks.

Political theology in Europe developed out of the Christian-Marxist dialogue of the 1960s. Johann Baptist Metz introduced this name for the new theology into the discussion in 1966. We had first met at a birthday party for Ernst Bloch in Tübingen, and we owe to Bloch our ecumenical friendship and shared work in developing the political dimension of Christian theology. For Metz it was important to get beyond the privatization of Christian faith and have a new perception of the critical and liberating function of the church. For me the most important thing was the Christian critique of bourgeois and political religion. We did not want to 'politicize' the church – something of which we have been constantly accused since then – but we did want to 'Christianize' church politics and the politics of Christians.

177

However, the 'new' political theology had to assert itself somewhat laboriously against the 'old' political theology which had been inaugurated by the constitutional lawyer Carl Schmitt in 1922 (1934). He sought to demonstrate that all political concepts in history in support of the state were secularized theological concepts and thus that there was always a parallel correspondence betwen the theological and the political paradigm of a time. Schmitt himself then developed his own constitutional theory from the 'state of emergency' to support the dictatorship thought necessary in the fight for political existence between friend and foe. The 'new' political theology rejected this form of religious politics and took its starting point from the subject of the church in society. The earlier theology of church politics had always been governed by an interest in preserving the status of the church in society and in extending church power and influence. We began with a critique of this church politics by asking about the origin and legitimation of the church in the name of Christ and making Jesus' message of the kingdom of God for the poor the starting point of a politics of consistent discipleship. This soon took us beyond the church as a community of believers to fellowship with the people of Jesus, the poor and the sick. Accordingly the church of Christ must find its social location in and among this people of Jesus if it claims to be the church of Christ. The 'faith which is active in love' can be found where this love is necessary and expected.

Political theology became a 'movement' in theology which extended far beyond the frontiers of Europe. At a very early stage an encounter with theology in Latin America, first with the 'theology of revolution', then with 'liberation theology', and then with 'people's theology', led to deeper insights on both sides. All over the countries of the Third World, local, contextual and political theologies came into being which are mobilizing communities and Christians for social justice, independence and human rights. Through this intensive exchange at the level of such political theologies, theologians in Europe and North America were made aware of the suffering and hopes of the people and churches of the Third World. The 'unity' of theology in this divided world can no longer be guaranteed from Eurocentric, Roman or secular power centres. New centres are coming into being in Asia, Africa and Latin America, and these decentralizations are likely to begin to influence one another and help in sustaining conflicts only through a new ecumenical network of relationships.

I shall consider the criticisms of political theology only briefly here. The criticism from traditional Protestant doctrine is directed at the very beginning of this theology in 'faith which is active in love' (*fides caritate formata*). Political theology is therefore accused of being a wide range of things, from a 'new righteousness of works' through a 'moralizing of faith' to the 'utopian attempt to establish the kingdom of God on earth'. Against political theology it is said the Protestant starting point is faith which is formed from the Word of God (*fides verbo Dei formata*). I believe that at an early stage I sensed the

178

pressure of a certain political moralism and a merely dispositional social pietism in political theology and the movements inspired by it. So as early as 1971 I attempted to balance my contribution to political theology by sketching out an aesthetic theology: *Theology and Joy*. In that book I described the freedom of a Christian in terms of justifying faith, but in such a way that there was no serious opposition between faith which owes itself to the Word and faith which is active in love. Love of neighbour without faith goes just as wrong as loveless faith which remains solitary. The unity of the two sides of faith is important to me because it alone guarantees the ecumenical character of the new political theology, liberation theology and people's theology.

2. The two other dialogues which have become important for my theology need only be mentioned briefly here. They are ecumenical dialogue in the Faith and Order commission of the World Council of Churches, in which I have been involved since 1963, and Jewish-Christian dialogue, which I entered into actively only at a late stage, in 1976.

Ecumenical dialogue, especially dialogue between the Western churches and Orthodoxy, has led me to the conclusion that the confessional theologies in which we engage for our confessionally divided churches can be seen only as stages towards a future common ecumenical theology. I have no dreams of a world church which is uniform in doctrine and praxis. But I do hear Christ's promise of a eucharistic fellowship between the different churches and also follow this invitation to the Lord's table in my personal life. On the way to this eucharistic fellowship my own theology enters into a conciliar fellowship with the theologies of the other churches. One no longer reads the texts and books of the other theological confessions to discover what separates us but to find out what we have in common. One brings one's own tradition into the developing ecumenical fellowship with the other traditions. One recognizes the distinctive totality of one's theology as just part of a greater whole, and goes beyond its limits. This process is particularly exciting for me in connection with Orthodoxy, and I am particularly grateful to Dumitru Staniloae, the father of Orthodox theology in Romania, for opening it up to me.

It has rightly been said that with the separation of Christianity from Judaism in the first centuries there opened up the first schism in the history of the kingdom of God on earth. The ecumenical movement and ecumenical theology will therefore ultimately return to the beginning and reshape and articulate themselves in dialogue with Israel and Jewish thought. One cannot undo this schism, but one can find fellowship on our separated but parallel ways through history. So in my theology I have attempted to consult not only Catholic and Orthodox texts but also Jewish texts, since, as Martin Buber aptly said, we have 'one book and one hope in common'.

3. 'Theology in movement' also has its limitations, since movements come, go

and change very quickly in history. Anyone who always wants to ride the last wave, like a surfer, will soon get stranded. 'Theology in context' is concrete and realistic, but it must set limits and draw lines. Those who pay heed only to their context lose sight of their text and then do not know how to go on. I felt at home in the political theology movement. In its dialogues and conflicts I learned to be open, to accept the experience of others – and to recognize my limitations. However, the more political theology in the different contexts of liberation became the theology of the oppressed, the more I became clear about these limitations. Inspired by eschatological and political theology, James Cone outlined a 'Black theology' for his people in the USA. I can support his concern and also make it known in Germany through translations and forewords, but I myself cannot become black.

It was the same for me with Latin American liberation theology. One can do much in Europe to make it heard, to draw attention to the outcry of the poor which is articulated in it, so that European theology may formulate that repentance which is required of the First World, but one does not become one of the oppressed oneself. One can show solidarity with them, but does not become identical with them. I felt that clearly after a conference with Black theologians and liberation theologians in Mexico City in 1977.

Not least, feminist theology shows the limitations of male theology. Again, a man one can do a good deal to get it a hearing, to make people aware of the limitations of male theology, so that once again these limitations can be overcome in a joint enterprise. But that does not make him a woman. This insight came home to me in the middle of the 1970s: it was first painful and then liberating. My reaction was what I hope proved to be a productive disengagement from the movements I have mentioned; in other words, I have continued to be concerned with them, have taken them seriously and done all I could to make their causes known, but I have not acted as though these were my own causes. I am not black, but white; I am not oppressed, but rather live on the other side; I am a male and my thought is also masculine. I must be honest with myself and my limitations, for only then will it become possible for me to overcome these limitations. However, one cannot overcome these limitations alone, to extend one's own part to the whole. One can only go beyond them by recognizing a wider fellowship of mutual hearing and speaking, receiving and giving, and enter into it. This is what I have attempted to do since 1980 in my series of contributions to theology.

III. The part as a contribution to the whole

My systematic contributions to theology set out to discuss in a definite systematic sequence complexes of important concepts and doctrines in Christian theology. In calling them contributions I want to indicate that I do not plan a total system or a dogmatics of pure and universal doctrine. This is not renunci-

180

ation on my part, but an expression of my involvement in the wider dialogue complexes of Christian theology. It is also meant to express a realistic estimation of the limitations of my own standpoint and personal context and the way in which it is conditioned. I am not claiming to say everything or depict the whole of Christian theology. Rather, with these books, as a whole, I seek to be part of the wider community of theology to which I want to make a contribution.

In the first volume of this series, *The Trinity and the Kingdom of God* (1980), I took up a long-standing problem of the Christian doctrine of God which has remained unresolved since the beginning of the logification of Christian theology in the Greek cultural sphere, the relationship between the triunity of God and the rule of God, *trinitas et monarchia*. The New Testament proclaims the history of the revelation of God and the salvation of human beings by telling the story of Jesus Christ with God, his Father, and the Holy Spirit. It is a history of deep unity and clear difference, as is shown for example by the Gethsemane story. It is a story of three different subjects in a living unity. Its unity is living because it represents an open and inviting unity for human beings, as is indicated in Jesus' high-priestly prayer (John 17.21). By contrast, the rule of God can be exercised only by one subject. So what is the relationship between the triunity of God and the uniqueness of the rule of God? I began from this question in order to enter into a critical discussion with the monotheistic and modalistic tendencies in the theology of the Western church, especially the newer attempts by Karl Barth and Karl Rahner to develop a perichoretic doctrine of the Trinity which stresses the 'oneness' of the divine persons, their mutual interpenetration and indwelling; which brings out the strata of the history of human freedom in the relationship with God: servant of God, child of God, friend of God.

Because in the systems and dogmatics of Christian theology the understanding of God was always normative for the understanding of human beings and the world, I began my contributions with this apparently abstract and remote theme of the doctrine of the Trinity and developed a social doctrine of the Trinity. That caused some head-shaking among practical and political theologians, but also attracted Orthodox and feminist theologians. For if the concept of community, mutuality, *perichoresis,* comes to the foreground in the understanding of God, and takes up, relativizes and limits the concept of one-sided rule, then understanding of the determination of human beings among each other and their relationship to nature also changes.

In the second volume of this series, *God in Creation* (1985), I drew the first consequences. The trinitarian concept of mutual perichoresis is matched by an ecological doctrine of creation: the triune God not only stands over against his creation but also at the same time enters into it through his eternal spirit, permeates all things and through his indwelling brings about the community of creation. That gives rise to a new view of the interconnection of all things which is no longer mechanistic. The world no longer consists of basic building blocks, 'elementary particles', but of the harmony of their connections. The trinitarian concept of mutual *perichoresis* is matched by a new view of the image of God in human beings. In the reciprocal community of male and female and in the community of parents and children a being and life in accord with God can be recognized. Finally, the relationship between the soul and body can no longer be understood as a one-sided relationship of ruling and serving. Soul and body mutually interpenetrate in the living human form and constantly speak to each other, even if they do not always listen to each other. The goal of this trinitarian and ecological doctrine of creation is the doctrine of the sabbath, that rest and that non-interventionary letting-be through which the creation is perfected by God and celebrated by human beings.

My further contributions to theology are a christology and an eschatology, and finally a reflection on the foundations and methods of theology.

If I were to attempt to sum up the outline of my theology in a few key phrases, I would have at the least to say that I am attempting to reflect on a theology which has:

- a biblical foundation,
- an eschatological orientation,
- a political responsibility.

In and under that it is certainly a theology in pain and joy at God himself, a theology of constant wonder.

Notes

Introduction: Some Questions about the Doctrine of the Trinity Today

1. Thus J.Hick and P.Knitter (eds.), *The Myth of Christian Uniqueness*, SCM Press and Orbis Books 1987. See J.Moltmann, 'Dient die "pluralistische Theologie" dem Dialog der Weltreligionen?', *EvTh* 49, 1989, 528-36.

2. P.Lapide and J.Moltmann, *Jüdischer Monotheismus – christliche Trinitätslehre. Ein Gespräch*, Munich ²1982.

3. M.Schmaus, *Katholische Dogmatik* I, Munich 1960, 491.

4. M.J.Scheeben, *Handbuch der Katholischen Dogmatik* I, Freiburg 1873, 884.

5. His work counts as 'Catholic', in that while he draws on Protestant authors, he quotes only Catholic ones.

6. C.Yannaras, in *Gregorios o Palamas* 65, Thessaloniki 1982, 687, 51-61. The most recent Orthodox doctrine of the Trinity is presented by B.Bobrinskoy, *Le Mystère de la Trinité. Cours de Théologie Orthodoxe*, Paris 1986.

7. D.Staniloae, *Orthodoxia* XXXIII.4, 1981, 629-31. Cf. also J.Moltmann, 'The Unity of the Triune God', with responses by J.B.Cobb, S.B.Thistlethwaite and J.Meyendorff, *St Vladimir's Theological Quarterly* 28, 1984, 3.

8. B.J.Hilberath, *Der Dreieinige Gott und die Gemeinschaft des Menschen. Orientierung zur christlichen Rede von Gott*, Mainz 1990.

9. J.Moltmann, *Sulla Trinità*, Naples 1982; B.Forte, *La chiesa icona della Trinità*, Brescia 1984.

10. Mary Daly, *Beyond God the Father. Towards a Philosophy of Women's Liberation*, Beacon Press 1973 and The Women's Press 1986. It is worth noting the criticism of the trinitarian concept of person as it was shaped by Boethius in Catherine Keller, *Der Ich-Wahn. Abkehr von einem lebensfeindlichen Ideal*, Stuttgart 1989, 214ff.

11. S.McFague, *Models of God. Theology for an Ecological, Nuclear Age*, Fortress Press and SCM Press 1987.

12. Virginia R.Mollenkott, *The Divine Feminine. The Biblical Imagery of God as Female*, Crossroad Publishing Company 1984.

13. G.Scholem, *Von der mythische Gestalt der Gottheit*, Frankfurt 1973, ch.IV ('Shekinah, the Passive-Feminine Element in the Deity'), 135-192.

14. Elaine Pagels, *The Gnostic Gospels*, Random House 1979 and Weidenfeld and Nicolson 1980, Chapter III, 'God the Father/God the Mother', 57-83. The term 'Gnostic' tended to be used by the patriarchally conditioned Roman church simply to label Christian communities as heretical. Cf. also Ron Cameron (ed.), *The Other Gospels*, Lutterworth Press

183

1982.

15. E.Hennecke, W.Schneemelcher and R.McL.Wilson, *New Testament Apocrypha* I, Westminster Press and Lutterworth Press 1963, reissued SCM Press 1973, 163f.

16. E.Godel, 'Die Heilige Geistin', *Radius* 3, 1989.

17. M.C.Bingemer, 'Reflections on the Trinity', in Elsa Tamez (ed.), *Through her Eyes*, Orbis Books 1989, 56-80.

18. See below I, 2.

19. H.D.Betz, *Galatians*, Hermeneia, Fortress Press 1979, 179ff.

20. For criticism of this see my *The Way of Jesus Christ. Christology in Messianic Dimensions*, 262f.

21. Thus C.Ullmann, *Die Sündlosigkeit Jesu. Eine apologetische Betrachtung* (1828), Gotha [7]1863, 52f.

22. Patricia Wilson-Kastner, *Faith, Feminism and the Christ*, Fortress Press 1983, 121ff.

23. The Council of Florence (1442), Denzinger 704.

24. Carter Heyward, *The Redemption of God. A Theology of Mutual Relation*, Washington 1982. For further literature on the subject see Mary Grey, 'The Core of our Desire. Re-imaging the Trinity', *Theology* XCIII, no.755, 1990, 363-73.

25. Dorothee Sölle, *Suffering*, Darton, Longman and Todd 1976; she follows H.Vorgrimler, *Theologische Gotteslehre*, Düsseldorf 1985, 168.

26. P.S.Fiddes, *The Creative Suffering of God*, Oxford 1988. Cf. also W.McWilliams, *The Passion of God. Divine Suffering in Contemporary Theology*, Mercer University Press 1985.

27. F.Buchheim, *Der Gnadenstuhl. Darstellung der Dreifaltigkeit*, Würzburg 1984.

28. L.Dabney, *Die Kenosis des Geistes. Kontinuität zwischen Schöpfung und Erlösung im Werk des Heiligen Geistes*, Tübingen dissertation 1989.

29. So also M.Luther, WA V, 58.18.

30. H.Urs von Balthasar, 'Mysterium Paschale', in *Mysterium Salutis. Grundriss heilsge-schichtlicher Dogmatik* 3.2, Zurich 1969, 133-326. Cf. also J.O'Donnell, *The Mystery of the Triune God*, Sheed and Ward 1988, 57ff.

31. E.g. M.H.Suchocki, 'The Diversity of God', *The Drew Gateway*, Spring 1990, 59-70.

I THE HISTORY OF THE TRINITY

1. 'I believe in God the Father.' Patriarchal or Non-Patriarchal Talk of God?

This article was first published in *Evangelische Theologie* 43, 1983, 397-413

1. E. and J.Moltmann, 'Becoming Persons in a New Community of Women and Men', in *God. His and Hers*, SCM Press and Crossroad Publishing Company 1991, 1-16. Cf. also W.A.Visser 't Hooft, *Gottes Vaterschaft im Zeitalter der Emanzipation*, Frankfurt 1982, and in particular his account of historical patriarchalism, though I cannot follow uncritically his theological and ethical ideas of the 'age of emancipation' and its dangers of a 'lack of ties'.

2. Catharina Halkes, 'The Themes of Protest in Feminist Theology against God the Father', *Concilium* 143, 1981, 103-10. However, it should also be noted that in Islam, prayer to the Father in particular can bring women to Christian faith and a sense of their value.

3. Y.Spiegel, 'God the Father in the Fatherless Society', ibid, 3-10: see the whole issue, which is entitled *God the Father?*.

4. Max Weber, *Economy and Society*, University of California Press 1979, called 'patriarchal rule' a 'pre-bureaucratic structural principle'.

5. S. Freud, *The Ego and the Id*, Hogarth Press 1974, p.27. On this see P.Ricoeur, 'Die Vatergestalt – vom Phantasiebild zum Symbol', in *Hermeneutik und Psychoanalyse*, Munich 1974, 315-53.

6. H.Lang, 'Psychiatrische Perspektiven zur Frage nach dem Vater', in H.Tellenbach (ed.), *Das Vaterbild im Abendland* I, Stuttgart 1978, 179-91.

7. Ibid., 185.

8. E.Bornemann, *Das Patriarchat,* Frankfurt 1975; A.Falaturi, J.H.Petuchowski and W.Strolz (eds.), *Universale Vaterschaft Gottes. Begegnungen der Religionen,* Freiburg 1987. J.J.Bachofen, *Das Mutterrecht,* Frankfurt 1975, is still important on matriarchy; cf. now Heide Göttner-Abendroth, *Die Göttin und ihr Heros,* Munich 1980.

9. E.Peterson, 'Monotheismus als politisches Problem', in *Theologische Traktate,* Munich 1951, 45-148. Cf. also F.K.Mayr, 'Patriarchalisches Gottesverständnis. Historische Erwägungen zur Trinitätslehre', *TQ* 152, 1972, 224-55.

10. M.de Ferdinandy, *Tschingis Khan,* Hamburg 1958, 153.

11. E.Neumann, *Die grosse Mutter. Eine Phänomenologie der weiblichen Gestaltungen des Unbewussten,* Zurich 1956; H.Zimmer, *Die indische Weltmutter,* Frankfurt 1980.

12. A.Dietrich, *Mutter Erde,* Berlin [3]1925.

13. P.Münch, 'Die "Obrigkeit im Vaterland" – zu Definition und Kritik des "Landesvaters" während der frühen Neuzeit', *Daphnis* 11.1-2, 1982, 15-40. This article has given me much food for thought.

14. A.Wlosok, 'Vater und Vatervorstellungen im römischen Kultur', in H.Tellenbach (ed.), *Das Vaterbild im Abendland,* 18-54, whom I follow here.

15. Ibid., 21.

16. Ibid., 39.

17. There is an exegesis by A.Wlosok in H.Kraft and A.Wlosok, Texte zur Forschung 4, Darmstadt 1974, 48ff.: the transference of Roman conception of the father to the Christian God.

18. Lactantius, 'On the Wrath of God', Ante-Nicene Christian Library, Vol.22, London 1876, p.46.

19. M.Luther, *Larger Catechism,* in *Luther's Primary Works,* ed. H.Wace and C.A.Buchheim, Hodder and Stoughton 1896, 58.

20. Gerda Scharffenorth and K.Thraede, *'Freunde in Christus werden . . . ' Die Beziehung von Mann und Frau als Frage an Theologie und Kirche,* Gelnhausen 1977, 183ff.

21. J.Calvin, *Institutes of the Christian Religion,* II, 8, 38. On this see Münch, '"Obrigkeit"' (n.13), 29.

22. Cf. the important but unfortunately unpublished dissertation by Gerda Scharffenorth, *Römer 13 in der Geschichte des politischen Denkens. Ein Beitrag zur Klärung der politischen Traditionen in Deutschland seit dem 15. Jahrhundert,* Heidelberg 1964.

23. Ibid., 213ff.

24. Thus G.Forster, J. von Sonnenfels, C.von Rotteck et al., quoted by Münch, '"Obrigkeit"' (n.13), 37f.

25. I.Kant, *Werke,* ed. W.Weischedel, VI, 145.

26. E.g. D.Bonhoeffer, *Letters and Papers from Prison. The Enlarged Edition,* SCM Press and Macmillan, New York 1971, 327: 'The question is: Christ and the world that has come of age.' Cf. the collections of articles *Mündige Welt* I, Munich 1956, and further volumes, edited by E.Bethge. Similarly also Visser 't Hooft, *Gottes Vaterschaft* (n.1), 105ff.

27. J.Jeremias, *The Prayers of Jesus,* SCM Press and Fortress Press 1967, 11-65. But see now the criticism of R.Feneberg, 'Abba – Father', in *Kirche und Israel* 3, 1988, 41-52.

28. Cf. my *The Trinity and the Kingdom of God,* SCM Press and Harper and Row 1980, 70f.

29. Isa.35.4: 'God who brings retribution will *come* and help you.'

30. Schalom Ben-Chorin, *Mutter Mirjam. Maria in jüdischer Sicht,* Munich 1982, 99ff. It is striking that in the Sermon on the Mount Jesus does not expound the fifth commandment.

Is he expounding only the 'second tablet', or is he deliberately avoiding it?

31. J.Lohfink, *Jesus and Community. The Social Dimensions of Christian Faith*, Fortress Press and SPCK 1984, 49.

32. Ibid., 45f.: 'The later church not only created a multiplicity of official designations and honorary titles, but even introduced the address "Holy Father" for the Pope, in direct disobedience to Matt.23.9.'

33. Ibid., 44.

34. Cf. R.Hamerton-Kelly, *God the Father. Theology and Patriarchy in the Teaching of Jesus*, Fortress Press 1979.

35. This process has been described impressively by C.Fabricius, 'Urbekenntnisse der Christenheit', *Reinhold Seeberg Festschrift*, Leipzig 1929, 21-41.

2. The Motherly Father and the Power of His Mercy

This article was first published in *Concilium* 143, 1981, 51-6, in a different translation.

1. E.Bornemann, *Das Patriarchat. Ursprung und Zukunft unseres Gesellschaftsystems*, Frankfurt 1975.

2. E.Bloch, *The Principle of Hope*, Blackwell 1986, 1200.

3. Thomas Aquinas, *Summa Theologiae* Ia Q 93, art 4 ad 1: '*Sed quantum ad aliquid secundarium imago Dei invenitur in viro secundum quod non invenitur in muliere; nam vir est principium mulieris, sicut Deus est principium et finis totius creaturae.*'

4. Denzinger, 276: '*Nec enim de nihilo, neque de aliqua alia substantia, sed de Patris utero, id est, de substantia eius idem Filius genitus vel natus esse credendus est.*'

5. H.-J.Stoebe, '*rhm*, sich erbarmen', *THAT* II, 761-8.

6. E.Neumann, *Die grosse Mutter. Eine Phänomenologie der weiblichen Gestaltungen des Unbewussten*, Olten 1974.

7. K.Kitamori, *Theology of the Pain of God*, John Knox Press and SCM Press 1966; H.Urs von Balthasar, 'Mysterium Paschale', in *Mysterium Salutis*, III.2, Einsiedeln 1969; H.Mühlen, *Die Veränderlichkeit Gottes als Horizont einer zukünftigen Christologie*, Münster 1969; J.Moltmann, *The Crucified God*; E.Jüngel, *The Doctrine of the Trinity*, T.&.T.Clark 1976; L.Boff, *The Trinity and Society*, Orbis Books and Burns and Oates 1988; B.Forte, *Trinität als Geschichte. Der lebendige Gott – Gott des Lebenden*, Mainz 1989; W.McWilliams, *The Passion of God. Divine Suffering in Contemporary Protestant Theology*, Mercer University Press 1985; P.S.Fiddes, *The Creative Suffering of God*, Oxford University Press 1988.

8. A.Heschel, *The Prophets*, Harper and Row 1962.

9. F.Rosenzweig, *Der Stern der Erlösung* III, Heidelberg [3]1954, 192f. Cf. also P.Kühn, *Gottes Selbsterniedrigung in der Theologie der Rabbiner*, Munich 1968; T.E.Fretheim, *The Suffering of God. An Old Testament Perspective*, Fortress Press 1984.

10. J.K.Mozley, *The Impassibility of God. A Survey of Christian Thought*, Cambridge University Press 1926; see especially C.E.Rolt, *The World's Redemption*, SPCK 1913; and further K.Woollcombe, 'The Pain of God', *Scottish Journal of Theology* 1967, 129-48.

11. C.A.Studdert-Kennedy, *The Hardest Part*, London 1918, 14.

12. M.de Unamuno, *The Tragic Sense of Life*, Dover Books 1976; see R.Gracia Mateo, *Dialektik als Polemik. Welt, Bewusstsein, Gott bei Miguel de Unamuno*, Frankfurt 1978.

13. N.Berdyaev, *The Meaning of History*, Geoffrey Bles 1925; see P.Evdikomov, *Christus im Russischen Denken*, Trier 1977.

14. Moltmann, *The Crucified God*, 244ff.

15. A.Greeley, *The Mary Myth*, Harper and Row 1977, ch.8.

16. J.Moltmann, 'Open Friendship', in *The Open Church*, 50-63.

17. D.Bonhoeffer, *Letters and Papers from Prison. The Enlarged Edition*, SCM Press and Macmillan, New York 1971, 360f.: 'God lets himself be pushed out of the world on to the

cross. He is weak and powerless in the world, and that is precisely the way, the only way, in which he is with us and helps us. Matthew 8.17 makes it quite clear that Christ helps us, not by virtue of his omnipotence, but by virtue of his weakness and suffering. Here is the decisive difference between Christianity and all religions. Man's religiosity makes him look in his distress to the power of God in the world: God is the *deus ex machina*. The Bible directs man to God's powerlessness and suffering: only the suffering God can help. To that extent we may say that the development towards the world's coming of age outlined above, which has done away with a false conception of God, opens up a way of seeing the God of the Bible, who wins power and space in the world by his weakness. This will probably be the starting point for our "secular interpretation".'

18. L.Boff, *The Maternal Face of God*, Harper and Row 1987, and id., *The Trinity and Society* (n.7), comes to similar conclusions to those I arrive at in my book *The Trinity and the Kingdom of God* and in this article.

3. The Question of Theodicy and the Pain of God

This article was first published in *Bildung - Glaube - Aufklärung. Festschrift für Karl-Ernst Nipkow*, Gütersloh 1989, 270-5.

1. Timothy Rees, *Hymns and Psalms*, Methodist Publishing House 1983, no.36, verse 2.

4. 'I Believe in Jesus Christ, the Only Son of God.' Brotherly Talk of Christ

Previously unpublished.

1. In this chapter, drawn from my lectures on the doctrine of the Trinity given in the winter semester of 1989/90, I go into some questions which I did not discuss in detail in my book *The Way of Jesus Christ*.

2. The latest advance in this old direction has been made by K.- J.Kuschel, *Geboren vor aller Zeit? Der Streit um Christi Ursprung*, Munich 1990.

3. E.Wolf, 'Die Christusverkündigung bei Luther', in *Peregrinatio* I, Munich 1954, 30ff., esp.72ff.

4. E.Vogelsang, *Der angefochtene Christus bei Luther*, Berlin 1932.

5. D.Bonhoeffer, *Letters and Papers from Prison. The Enlarged Edition*, SCM Press and Macmillan, New York 1971, 362, 370. Cf. also his poem 'Christians and Pagans', 348.

5. Justice for Victims and Perpetrators

Previously unpublished.

1. Here I am keeping to the form of the doctrine of justification which was presented by my Göttingen teachers H.-J.Iwand, E.Wolf and E.Käsemann: H.-J.Iwand, *Glaubensgerechtigkeit und Luthers Lehre*, ThEx 75, Munich 1941; E.Wolf, 'Die Rechtfertigungslehre als Mitte und Grenze reformatorischer Theologie', in *Peregrinatio* II, Munich 1965, 11ff.; E.Käsemann, '"The Righteousness of God" in Paul', in *New Testament Questions of Today*, SCM Press and Fortress Press 1969, 168-82.

2. The one-sided grounding of the righteousness of faith in the theology of the cross which can be found in paragraph 4 of the Augsburg Confession is un-Pauline. It reduces the justification of life to the forgiveness of sins. A.Schlatter already criticized that in *Luthers Deutung des Römerbriefes*, Gütersloh 1917, 53ff., and Käsemann, '"Righteousness"' (n.2), 168ff., has taken his criticism further by understanding the righteousness of God as 'power', as 'gift and service', and as 'freedom and obedience' (171).

3. L.Ragaz recognized that and brought it out with admirable clarity in *Die Gleichnisse Jesu*, 1944. Cf. also G.Eichholz, *Gleichnisse der Evangelien. Form, Überlieferung, Auslegung*, Neukirchen 1971.

187

4. Ragaz, *Gleichnisse* (n.3).

5. F.M.Dostoievsky, *The Brothers Karamazov*, Book 6 B 3: 'From the Discourses and Sermons of Father Zossima'. This idea of universal guilt is only the other side of the Russian Orthodox notion of universal forgiveness. It embraces not only the world of human beings but also the world of nature: ask the animals for forgiveness! The divine love is 'all-embracing', since the universe is 'like an ocean. It flows and comes into contact with everything else; touch it in one place and it reverberates at the other end of the world.'

6. Cf. the statement at the World Mission Conference in Bangkok in 1973 on 'Salvation and Social Justice', quoted in K.Viehweger (ed.), *Weltmissionskonferenz Bangkok. Sarmudhprakam – Kilometer 31*, Munich 1973, 146-9.

7. N.Greinacher, *Die Kirche der Armen, Zur Theologie der Befreiung*, Munich 1980, chapter 4 ('From Medellin to Puebla'), 79-109.

8. F.Herzog, *Justice Church. The New Function of the Church in North American Christianity*, Orbis Books 1980, is an honourable exception.

9. Cf.G.Gutiérrez, *A Theology of Liberation*, Orbis Books 1973 and SCM Press 1974, Chapter 13, 'Poverty: Solidarity and Protest', 287ff.; see also *Option for the Poor*, the issue of *Concilium*, 187, 1986.

10. J.H.Cone, *The Spirituals and the Blues*, Seabury Press 1972, 53f.: 'Because black slaves knew the significance of the pain and shame of Jesus' death on the cross, they found themselves by his side: "Were you there when they crucified my Lord?"'

11. E.Wolf, 'Die Christusverkündigung bei Luther', in *Peregrinatio* I, Munich 1954, 72ff.; E.Vogelsang, *Der angefochtene Christus bei Luther*, Berlin 1932.

12. D.Bonhoeffer, *Letters and Papers from Prison. The Enlarged Edition*, SCM Press and Macmillan, New York 1971, 361.

13. Ibid., 349.

14. For the question of forgiveness and atonement 'after Auschwitz' see S.Wiesental, *The Sunflower*, Schocken Books 1978; A. and M.Mitscherlich, *Die Unfähigkeit zu trauern*, Munich 1968.

15. R.Schwager, *Brauchen wir einen Sündenbock? Gewalt und Erlösung in den biblischen Schriften*, Munich 1978.

16. H.Gese, 'The Atonement', in *Essays on Biblical Theology*, Augsburg Publishing House 1981, 93-116; B.Janowski, *Sühne als Heilsgeschehen*, Neukirchen 1982.

17. That has been shown in an enlightening way by N.Hoffmann, *Sühne. Zur Theologie der Stellvertretung*, Einsiedeln 1981.

18. P.Stuhlmacher, *Versöhnung, Gesetz und Gerechtigkeit*, Göttingen 1981.

19. Thus rightly N.Hoffmann, *Kreuz und Trinität. Zur Theologie der Sühne*, Einsiedeln 1982, 30, much of which I can follow,

20. Vogelsang, *Der angefochtene Christus* (n.11), 30ff.; W.Maas, *Gott und die Hölle. Studien zum Descensus Christi*, Einsiedeln 1979, 211ff.

21. See Hoffmann, *Kreuz und Trinität* (n.19), 17ff.

22. That has been demonstrated by H.Gollwitzer, *Von der Stellvertretung Gottes*, Munich 1969, supplementing and criticizing Dorothee Sölle, *Christ the Representative. An Essay of Theology after the 'Death of God'*, SCM Press 1967.

23. E.-M.Bachmann, *Gebete der Ostkirche*, Neukirchen-Vluyn 1987.

24. U.Duchrow, *Schalom. Biblische Arbeitshilfe zum Konziliaren Prozess*, Stuttgart 1987.

25. J.Moltmann, *The Crucified God*, 'Ways towards the Political Liberation of Man', 317ff.

26. B.McKibben, *The End of Nature*, Viking Books 1989.

27. C.Gestrich, *Die Wiederkehr des Glanzes in der Welt. Die christliche Lehre von der Sünde und ihrer Vergebung in gegenwärtiger Verantwortung*, Tübingen 1989, 28ff., has investigated questions connected with 'collective guilt', but in his criticism of what he calls

'political theology' (294) has not noticed the asymmetry of unjust and just conditions. If he had studied the Christian-Marxist dialogue from which European 'political theology' developed in 1967, he would not have failed to notice this.

28. K.Barth, 'The Christian Community and the Civil Community', in *Against the Stream. Shorter Post-War Writings,* SCM Press 1954, 13-50.

6. 'The Fellowship of the Holy Spirit.' On Trinitarian Pneumatology

This article was first published in *Credo in Spiritum Sanctum*, Libreria Editrice Vaticana, Rome 1984, 921-37; *Theologische Literaturzeitung* 107, 1982, 705-15.

1. J.Moltmann, *The Trinity and the Kingdom of God.* Here I am developing the ideas expressed in my earlier book.

2. Cf. L.Vischer (ed.), *Geist Gottes – Geist Christi. Ökumenische Überlegungen zur Filioque-Kontroverse,* ÖR Beihefte 39, Frankfurt 1981.

3. Ibid., 22.

4. Ibid.

5. Gregory of Nazianzen, *Fünf theologische Reden,* Düsseldorf 1963, 239 (XXXI, Speech 11).

6. Augustine, *De Trinitate* XII, ch.5. Similarly Thomas Aquinas, *Summa Theologiae* I a q 93 n.4. There is criticism of this in the major article by F.K.Mayr, 'Trinitätstheologie und theologische Anthropologie', *ZTK* 68, 1971, 427-77.

7. M.Schmaus, *Die psychologische Trinitätslehre de hl.Augustinus,* Münster 1927, 199.

8. Ibid., 222f.

9. Augustine, *Quaestiones de trinitate et de Gen.1* (VIII, 1173): *'Opera Sanctae trinitatis ad intra sunt divisa, ad extra sunt indivisa.'* So too M.Luther, acording to R.Jansen, *Studien zu Luthers Trinitätslehre,* Frankfurt 1976, 209: 'The real distinctions of the persons are existent only in God himself, in the *opera ad intra,* which must be understood as relationships. Outwardly towards the creatures God is only one God.' For criticism of this with a new approach see my *The Trinity and the Kingdom of God,* 160f.

10. Cf.C.B.MacPherson, *The Political Theory of Possessive Individualism: Hobbes to Locke,* Oxford University Press 1962; M.D.Meeks, 'Gott und die Ökonomie des hl.Geistes', *EvTh* 40, 1980, 40-57.

11. This discussion is described very well by W.Krusche, *Das Wirken des Heiligen Geistes nach Calvin,* Göttingen 1957, 33ff.

12. Quoted from Krusche, *Heiligen Geistes* (n.11), 41.

13. For criticism of this see K.E.Borresen, *Subordination et équivalence. Nature et rôle de la femme d' après Augustin et Thomas d'Aquin,* Oslo and Paris 1968. Rosemary Ruether, *New Woman – New Earth. Sexist Ideologies and Human Liberation,* Harper and Row 1975.

14. D.Staniloae, 'The Holy Trinity. Structure of Supreme Love', in *Theology and the Church,* St Vladimir's Seminary Press 1980, 73-108; Mar Osthathios, *Theology of a Classless Society,* 1979, esp.92ff.

15. For the concept of the 'charismatic community' cf. G.Eichholz, *Charismatische Gemeinde,* ThEx 77, 1959, and my *The Church in the Power of the Spirit.* In ecumenical dialogue it is always only the reciprocal recognition of ministries that is discussed as a condition for the unity of the church. Why is not the fellowship of the community also discussed as a condition for the unity of the church at the same time?

16. Staniloae, 'Holy Trinity' (n.14), 45ff.; M.-D.Chenu, 'The New Awareness of the Trinitarian Basis of the Church', *Concilium* 146, 1981, 14-21.

17. Nikolaus Count Zinzendorf, *Hauptschriften* II, Hildesheim 1963, 33ff.: the first sermon in Pennsylvania.

18. Cf. the extensive historical work by H.Dörries, *Die Theologie des Makarios/Symeon,*

Göttingen 1978.

19. E.Hennecke, W.Schneemelcher and R.McL.Wilson, *New Testament Apocrypha* I, Westminster Press and Lutterworth Press 1963, reissued SCM Press 1973, 163.

20. Dörries, *Theologie des Makarios* (n.18), 161, 257ff.

21. Thus nowadays e.g. by Osthathios, *Classless Society* (n.14), 92f.

22. H.Schmid, *Die Dogmatik der Evangelisch-Lutherischen Kirche,* Gütersloh [7]1893, IV, *De scriptura sacra,* 18ff.

23. Cf. K.Barth, *Church Dogmatics* I.i, T.& T.Clark [2]1975, 4, 'The Word of God in its Threefold Form', 88ff.

24. J.Moltmann, 'Justification and New Creation', in *The Future of Creation,* 149ff.

25. Ibid., 80-97.

26. Krusche, *Heiligen Geistes* (n.11), 11.

7. *'Come Holy Spirit – Renew the Whole of Creation'*

This article was first published in *The Ecumenical Review* 40.2, 1990, 98-107. The title is inspired by the theme of the Seventh Assembly of the World Council of Churches in Canberra, 7-20 February 1991.

1. There is a good collection of the global data by the Worldwatch Institute, *The State of the World 1987/88. A Worldwatch Institute Report on Progress towards a Sustainable Society,* W.W.Norton 1989. There is a reliable evaluation by the Brundtland Report of the World Commission for Environment and Development: V.Hauff (ed.), *Our Common Future,* Oxford University Press 1987.

2. I have described this in detail in *God in Creation. An Ecological Doctrine of Creation.*

3. Basil, *On the Holy Spirit,* 31d, Migne, PG 32, 136B.

4. Cf. G.Schimanowski, *Weisheit und Messias,* Tübingen 1985.

5. J.Jeremias, *The Unknown Sayings of Jesus,* SPCK 1957, 95.

6. Timothy Rees, *Hymns and Psalms,* Methodist Publishing House 1983, no.36, verse 2: 'God who breathes through all creation, God is love, eternal Love.'

7. J.Calvin, *Institutes of the Christian Religion* I, 13,14.

8. Cf. J.Moltmann, *Creating a Just Future,* SCM Press and Trinity Press International 1989.

9. Moltmann, *God in Creation,* 206ff.

10. Cf. D.Staniloae, *Orthodoxe Dogmatik* I, Gütersloh 1985, 291ff.: 'The world as the work of the love of God is destined to be divinized.'

11. J.Moltmann, *The Way of Jesus Christ. Christology in Messianic Dimensions,* Chapter VI, 'The Cosmic Christ', 274ff.

12. United Nations General Assembly Resolution 37/7, 28 October 1982: The World Charter for Nature, paragraph 3.

8. *The Inviting Unity of the Triune God*

This article was first published in W.Breuning (ed.), *Trinität. Aktuelle Perspektiven der Theologie,* Quaestiones Disputatae 101, Freiburg 1984, 97-113.

1. Conversely, I came to take up the doctrine of the Trinity through 'political theology'. Cf. J.B.Metz, J.Moltmann and W.Oelmüller, *Kirche im Prozess der Aufklärung,* Mainz and Munich 1970, 35ff.

2. Cf. M.Schmaus, *Die psychologische Trinitätslehre des hl.Augustinus,* Münster 1927.

3. R.Rothe, *Theologische Ethik* I, Wittenberg [2]1867; C.I.Nitzsch, *System der christlichen Lehre* (1829), Bonn [6]1851; I.A.Dorner, *System der christlichen Glaubenslehre* I, Berlin 1879, 31 and 32. See I.Oeing-Hanhoff, 'Hegels Trinitätslehre', *ThPh* 52, 1977, 378-407.

4. K.Barth, *Christliche Dogmatik im Entwurf,* Munich 1927, §9; *Church Dogmatics* I.1, T.& T.Clark [2]1975, §8. K.Rahner, 'Der dreifaltige Gott als transzendenter Urgrund der

Heilsgeschichte', *Mysterium Salutis* II, 1967, 317-401, uses a similar argument. For criticism of both see my *The Trinity and the Kingdom of God*, 139ff., 144ff. My criticism relates to the speculative approach of their doctrine of the Trinity, but I would endorse the way in which they ground it in salvation history and take this further.

5. For criticism of Barth's thesis of 'one personal God in three modes of being' see also already E.Schlink, *RGG*[3] VI, 1037: it 'is a misconception in the direction of modalism. It does not express the personal encounter of the Father who loves the Son, the Son who prays to the Father, and the Spirit who confesses the Father and the Son.'

6. H.J.Iwand, *Nachgelassene Werke* I. *Glauben und Wissen,* Munich 1962, 290. Similarly also G.Söhngen, 'Natürliche Theologie', *LThK* VII, Freiburg 1962, 811ff., on the position of 'natural theology' in the philosophy of the Enlightenment.

7. For the concept cf. J.Moltmann, 'Gedanken zur "trinitarischen Geschichte Gottes"', *EvTh* 35, 1975, 208-23; M.D.Meeks, 'Gott und die Ökonomie des Heiligen Geistes', *EvTh* 40, 1980, 40ff.

8. F.Kronseder, *Im Banne der Dreieinigkeit*, Regensburg 1934, 45.

9. This is stressed by Orthodox theology. Cf. N.A.Nissiotis, *Die Theologie der Ostkirche im ökumenischen Dialog,* Stuttgart 1968, I.2: 'Die pneumatologische Christologie als Voraussetzung der Ekklesiologie', 64ff. So now also Y.Congar, *I Believe in the Holy Spirit,* Geoffrey Chapman 1983, vol. III, 165ff..

10. L.Vischer (ed.), *Geist Gottes – Geist Christ. Ökumenische Überlegungen zur Filioque Kontroverse,* Frankfurt 1981, 12ff., 153ff.

11. J.Moltmann, 'The Fellowship of the Holy Spirit', above, 64ff.

12. Barth, *Church Dogmatics* I.1 (n.4), 358, refers to F.Diekamp, who is also the starting point for K. Rahner. See L.Oeing-Hanhoff, 'Die Krise des Gottesbegriffs', *TQ* 159, 1979, 285-303.

13. Barth, *Church Dogmatics* I.1 (n.4), 370, also stresses the unity of subject in the Trinity ('God is the Lord'). For an interpretation of this see E.Jüngel, *The Doctrine of the Trinity. God's Being is in Becoming,* T.& T.Clark 1976, 33: 'The doctrine of *perichoresis* helps us to formulate the concrete unity of the being of God in that we think of the modes of God's being of God as meeting one another in unrestricted participation.' Instead of 'unity' he also uses the term 'harmony' (37). The ideas of *perichoresis* and mutuality have now also been taken up by feminist theology in order to break up patriarchal conceptions of authority in the concept of God. Cf. P.Wilson-Kastner, *Faith, Feminism and the Christ,* Fortress Press 1983, ch.6, 'The Trinity', 121ff.; R.Oxford-Carpenter, 'Gender and the Trinity', *Theology Today* XL, 1984, 7ff.

14. E.Schlink also stressed this in his own way in his major article 'Trinität III.Dogmengeschichtlich' and 'IV.Dogmatisch', *RGG*[3] VI, 1025-38.

15. D.Staniloae, 'Der dreieinige Gott und die Einheit der Menschheit', *EvTh* 41, 1981, 439-50; id., *Theology and the Church*, St Vladimir's Seminary Press 1980.

16. 'God is love' is the practical definition of God. Cf. J.Gerhard, *Loci theologici*, loc.2, ch.5, 94: '*Practicam Dei definitionem propuit Joh.1: Deus est caritas.*'.

17. Moltmann, '"Trinitarische Geschichte"' (n.7), 208-23.

18. See my *The Trinity and the Kingdom of God,* 288-90.

19. PG 44, 377.

II THE TRINITARIAN VIEW OF HISTORY

1. Christian Hope – Messianic or Transcendent?
A Theological Conversation with Joachim of Fiore and Thomas Aquinas

This article was first published in *Münchner Theologische Zeitschrift* 33, 1982, 241-60.

1. Cf. E.Benz, 'Thomas von Aquin und Joachim von Fiore. Die katholische Antwort auf die spiritualistische Kirchen- und Geschichtsauffassung', *ZKG* 1934, 52-116. The translation of the *quaestio* is that of the Blackfriars edition.

2. M.Grabmann, *Geschichte der scholastischen Methode* II, Berlin 1957, 278.

3. H.Grundmann, *Studien über Joachim von Fiore* (1927), Darmstadt 1966.

4. A.Dempf, *Sacrum Imperium. Geschichts- und Staatsphilosophie des Mittelalters und der politischen Renaissance* (1929), Darmstadt 1954.

5. E.Buonaiuti, *Gioacchino da Fiore, i tempi, la vita, il messagio*, Rome 1931.

6. E.Benz, *Ecclesia Spiritualis. Die Kirchenidee der franziskanischen Reformation*, Stuttgart 1934.

7. H.Mottu, *La manifestation de l'Esprit selon Joachim de Fiore*, Neuchâtel and Paris 1977.

8. A.Crocco, *Gioacchino da Fiori*, Naples 1960.

9. *Storia e Messaggio in Gioacchino da Fiore. Atti del Primo Congresso Internazionale di Studi Gioachimiti*, Naples 1980; *L'Età dello Spirito e la fine dei tempi in Gioacchino da Fiore e nel Gioachimismo medievale. Dell' II. Congresso Internazionale di studi Gioachimiti, S.Giovanni in Fiore 1986; Florensia. Bollettino del Centro Internazionale di Studi Gioachimiti*, 1987, 1988; B.McGinn, *The Calabrian Abbot. Joachim of Fiore in the History of Western Thought*, Macmillan, New York 1985.

10. Henri de Lubac, *La posterité spirituelle de Joachim de Fiore*, I, *De Joachim à Schelling*, Paris 1979; II. *De Saint-Simon à nos jours*, Paris 1980.

11. Karl Barth, *Letters 1961-1968*, Eerdmans and T.& T. Clark 1981, 348f.

12. H.U.von Balthasar, 'Zu einer christlichen Theologie der Hoffnung', *Münchner Theologische Zeitschrift* 32, 1981, 81-102.

13. Ibid., 81. He quotes E.Bloch, *Das Prinzip Hoffnung*, Frankfurt 1959, 712, but has evidently misunderstood lines 29f.

14. *Concordia Veteris et Novi Testamenti*, Venice 1519.

15. *Expositio in Apocalypsim*, Venice 1527.

16. Thomas of Aquinas also associated his theological doctrine of the church with a theology of history: in history there are only two kingdoms, the kingdom of the old law and the kingdom of the new law; the kingdom of glory does not come about in history, but only after the end of history. Cf. M.Seckler, *Das Heil in der Geschichte. Geschichtstheologisches Denken bei Thomas von Aquin*, Munich 1964.

17. With E.Benz, 'Thomas von Aquin' (n.1), I render the expression *evacuare* which Joachim uses for the sequence of salvation history with the Hegelian expression *aufheben*, 'sublate', because it is a better description than the term 'abolish' of the relationship between the final and the provisional which Joachim has in mind.

18. The discovery of the connection between the New Testament and the Old and the taking up of the prophetic and apocalyptic promises of the Old Testament by the New was always historically, and still is today, the reason for the development of a Christian, truly futuristic eschatology. The way in which the Old Testament history of promise is made present in the gospel is the foundation for eschatological expectations. Conversely, these eschatological expectations awaken the memory of the unfulfilled promises of God to Israel. There is always an interdependence between the understanding of the relationship of the New Testament to the Old and eschatology.

19. Cf. C.A.Bernard, *Théologie de l'Espérance selon Saint Thomas d'Aquin*, Paris 1961.

20. Thus in opinion E of 1318 on the commentary on the Apocalypse by Petrus Olivi, which is evaluated by Benz, 'Thomas von Aquin' (n.1), 84.

21. Against Balthasar, 'Christliche Theologie' (n.13), who thinks that this orientation is 'Jewish'; cf. J.B.Metz, 'Gott vor uns. Statt eines theologischen Arguments' (227ff.); W.Pannenberg, 'Der Gott der Hoffnung' (209ff.); and J.Moltmann, 'Die Kategorie Novum in der

christlichen Theologie' (243ff.), in the Festschrift *Ernst Bloch zu ehren*, Frankfurt 1965.

22. R.Wittram, H.-G.Gadamer and J.Moltmann, *Geschichte – Element der Zukunft, Vorträge an den Hochschultagen 1965 der Evangelische Studentengemeinde Tübingen*, Tübingen 1965.

23. Thus rightly Benz, 'Thomas von Aquin' (n.1), 85.

24. Unconsciously, J.Pieper, *Über die Hoffnung*, Munich 1949, shows this very clearly. He replaces the exodus of Abraham with the general transitoriness of life so that the *status viatoris* is not defined by the divine promise in history but as 'the inner structure of human creatureliness' (19). The *status comprehensoris* is then the 'beatifying vision of God' in eternity. In view of his interpretation of hope as a supernatural virtue, one wonders why he calls this virtue 'hope' at all, since this naming of the unending human struggle is the only biblical allusion which can be found in this brief study.

25. For the biblical and philosophical concept of time cf. G.Picht, 'Die Zeit und die Modalitäten', in *Hier und Jetzt. Philosophieren nach Auschwitz und Hiroshima* I, Stuttgart 1980, 362ff.

26. J.Moltmann, *Theology of Hope* and *The Future of Creation*; cf. especially, 'Theology as Eschatology', in *The Future of Hope*, ed. F.Herzog, Harper and Row 1970, 1-50, especially 13 n.19.

27. Here one can also introduce anticipation as a basic category of historical reason, as does W.Pannenberg throughout. But the anticipation presupposes a prior giving. Where nothing is given (in advance) nothing can be taken (in advance). Anticipatory thinking presupposes history as an element of promised future. Ernst Bloch makes that clear in his definition of the concept of anticipation in correlation to the tendency in the world process. Cf. *The Principle of Hope*, Blackwell 1986, Chapter 15.

28. That is the central thesis of my *Theology of Hope*.

29. I first indicated these differentiations in the experience of time in *Church in the Power of The Spirit*, IV.5, 'The kingdom of God in the future and the present', 189ff.

30. I have taken over Joachim's teaching of the ages (*aetas*) and the states (*status*) of the history of God with the world by understanding them as 'strata in the concept of freedom' and as 'transitions' which are present in every experience of freedom. Cf. *The Trinity and the Kingdom of God*, 203ff. I am developing the ideas further here. That is also suggested by Joachim's idea of the 'hiddenness' of the future in the present, which has been brought out by E.Benz, 'Religiöse Geschichtsdeutung Joachims', *ZKG*, 1931, 80ff.

31. Vatican II, Constitution on the Church, VII.48: '*Iam ergo fines saeculorum ad nos pervenerunt (cf.I Cor.10.11) et renovatio mundi irrevocabiliter est constituta atque in hoc saeculo reali quodam modo anticipatur: etenim Ecclesia iam in terris vera sanctitate licet imperfecta insignitur. Donec tamen fuerint novi caeli et nova terra, in quibus iustitia habitabit (cf. II Petr.3.13). Ecclesia peregrinans, in suis sacramentis et institutionibus, quae ad hoc aevum pertinent, portat figuram huius saeculi quae praeterit et ipsa inter creaturas degit quae ingemiscunt et parturiunt usque adhuc et exspectant revelationem filiorum Dei (cf.Rom.8.19-22).*'

32. Cf. Mottu, *Manifestation* (n.7), 204ff. In church history, the promise in Jer.31.31ff. of the 'new covenant' and the 'law written in the heart' were constantly interpreted in terms of the 'time of the Holy Spirit', e.g. by Lessing, *Education of the Human Race*, 88ff.: 'No longer shall they teach one another, or say to each other, "Know the Lord," for they shall all know me, from the least of them to the greatest, says the Lord' (v.34).

33. The apostle does not speak of a 'Christian, vertical triad of faith, hope and love', as von Balthasar, 'Christliche Theologie' (n.12), 86, puts it.

34. Here I am taking up the exegetical discussion which has been summarized by H.Conzelmann, *I Corinthians*, Hermeneia 1975, 230f., and in my own way following Bult-

mann's and Conzelmann's proposal that *nuni* should be taken with *menein*.

35. E.Benz, 'Joachimstudien III', *ZKG* 1934, 65ff. See also Mottu, *Manifestation* (n.7), 292ff.

36. Benz, 'Joachimstudien', 98.

37. G.Scholem, *Judaica* I, Frankfurt 1963, 72f.

38. Benz, 'Joachimstudien', 101.

39. On the cover of volume II, *La posterité spirituelle de Joachim de Fiore,* Paris 1980, one can read, 'The future of the Spirit without Christ'.

40. Joachim, like many mystics before him and after him, described this transition from being a child of God in faith to being like God in sight as 'friendship with God'. Cf. E.Peterson, 'Der Gottesfreund. Beiträge zur Geschichte eines religiösen Terminus', *ZKG,* 1923, 161-202.

41. Benz, 'Joachimstudien', 68.

42. This summary may be examined in the CHERCHI TRINITARI, reprinted from *Liber Figurarum*, Corpus Christi College, Oxford, MS.255A, fol.7v. (Bodleian Library).

43. For the theological and philosophical problems of this dichotomy see my *Trinity and the Kingdom of God*, VI.2, 'The Trinitarian Doctrine of the Kingdom', 202ff.

44. C.Thoma, *Theologische Beziehungen zwischen Judentum und Christentum,* Darmstadt 1986, 128f.

45. Benz, 'Joachimstudien', 71f., does not seem to have seen this distinction clearly enough. So at one point he speaks of the kingdom as the 'state of fulfilment' and at another of the Holy Spirit, 'the real Lord of the time of the fulfilment of the kingdom'.

46. There is detailed comment on this in B.Hirsch-Reich, 'Joachim von Fiore und das Judentum', in P.Wilpert (ed.), *Judentum im Mittelalter,* Berlin 1966, 228-63.

47. Quoted in Benz, 'Joachimstudien', 70.

48. Quoted in Benz, 'Joachimstudien', 60.

49. Quoted in Benz, 'Joachimstudien', 103.

50. I have made detailed comments on this in P.Lapide and J.Moltmann, *Israel und Kirche: ein gemeinsamer Weg?*, Munich 1980, 24ff.

51. Evidence for this is his antithesis against Joachim: 'What the Lord says in Matt.24.34: "I say to you that this generation will not pass away before all this takes place (is fulfilled)" tells against this. In Homily 78 on Matthew immediately after the beginning, Chrysostom interprets this saying in terms of the generation of those who believe in Christ. So the state of those who believe in Christ will last until the end of the world.' For Matthew, this saying meant that the kingdom of God, and with it the end of this age, would still come in the present generation. Chrysostom and Thomas are turning the saying upside down if they think that it means that the generation of believers will last until the end.

2. Being a Christian, Being Human and the Kingdom of God

This article was first published in *Stimmen der Zeit* 9, 1985, 619-31.

1. Karl Rahner, *Theological Explorations* 6, Darton, Longman and Todd and Seabury Press 1974, 390-8.

2. Karl Rahner, *Theological Explorations* 4, Darton, Longman and Todd and Seabury Press 1966, 105-20.

3. 6, 396.

4. Karl Rahner, *Schriften zur Theologie* VI, Einsiedeln 1965, 545 (this passage is not in the English translation).

5. 6, 390f.

6. 6, 391.

7. 6, 391f.

8. 4, 107.

9. 6, 393.

10. 6, 394.

11. Ibid.

12. Ibid.

13. R.Bultmann, 'The Concept of Revelation in the New Testament', in *Existence and Faith. Shorter Writings of Rudolf Bultmann*, ed. Schubert M.Ogden, Collins and World Publishing Company 1960, 86.

14. K.Barth, *Church Dogmatics* 3.1, T.& T.Clark 1958, 228ff.

15. For what follows see F.Rosenzweig, *Der Stern der Erlösung* 3.1, Heidelberg 1954, 63ff.

16. Rahner, *Theological Explorations* 6 (n.1), 396.

17. J.Moltmann, *The Church in the Power of the Spirit*, 289ff.

18. *Karl Rahner in Dialogue. Conversations and Interviews 1965- 1982*, edited by Paul Imhof and Hubert Biallowons. Translation edited by Harvey D.Egan, Crossroad Publishing Company 1986.

3. Creation, Covenant and Glory.
A Conversation on Karl Barth's Doctrine of Creation

This article was first published in *Dialektische Theologie* 3, 1987, 191-214; *Evangelische Theologie* 48, 1988, 108-27

1. K.Barth, *Letters 1961-1968*, Eerdmans and T.& T.Clark 1981, 174.

2. Ibid., 175f..

3. Cf. W.Schmidt, *Zeit und Ewigkeit. Die letzten Voraussetzungen der dialektischen Theologie,* Gütersloh 1927; Kim Myung Yong, *Der Gottesbegriff Karl Barths in der heutigen Diskussion*, Tübingen dissertation 1985.

4. Moltmann, *God in Creation*, 21ff.

5. C.Link, 'Schöpfung im messianischen Licht', *EvTh* 47, 1987, 92.

6. Where Barth is quoted the page numbers given in the texts refer to *Church Dogmatics* III.1; otherwise they refer to my book *God in Creation*. In this chapter I am engaged in a critical discussion only of Barth's theses and not of his work as a whole or his various other remarks about the themes discussed here. So my criticism is just criticism of detail, and does not claim to be an overall criticism of his work.

7. L.Boff, *Trinity and Society,* Orbis Books and Burns and Oates 1986; Patricia Wilson-Kastner, *Faith, Feminism and the Christ*, Fortress Press 1983; Mar Osthathios, *Theologie einer klassenlosen Gesellschaft*, Hamburg 1980.

8. E.Schlink, 'Trinität', RGG[3] IV, 1037.

9. On this see Letty M Russell (ed.), *Feminist Interpretation of the Bible*, Fortress Press 1985, 47ff.; Wilson-Kastner, *Faith, Feminism and the Christ* (n.7), 124ff.; M.Farley, 'New Patterns of Relationship', in W.Burkhardt (ed.), *Women – New Dimensions*, New York 1975, 51-70, and above all Carter Heyward, *The Redemption of God. A Theology of Mutual Relation*, University Press of America 1982; Elisabeth Moltmann-Wendel, *A Land Flowing with Milk and Honey. Perspectives on a Feminist Theology*, SCM Press and Crossroad Publishing Company 1985, 141-54. The concept of mutuality has an interesting pre-history. It was introduced programmatically by P.-J.Proudhon into the social sciences in order to communicate 'freedom' and 'equality', the principles of the French Revolution, without hierarchical order, i.e. anarchistically. Against Darwin and social Darwinistic capitalism (the right of the stronger, the survival of the fittest), P.Kropotkin (1902) argued for the principle of 'mutual help in the world of animals and human beings'. By contrast, Nietzsche regarded mutuality as a 'great meanness' and censured it as an idea of early Christianity. In his cynical way he was quite right: 'When one looks for the beginnings of Christianity in the Roman world, one finds

associations for mutual aid, associations for the poor, for the sick, for burial, evolved among the lowest strata of society in which this major remedy for depression, petty pleasure produced by mutual helpfulness was consciously employed: perhaps this was something new in those days, a real discovery?'(*On the Genealogy of Morals*, Ch.III, ed. W. Kaufmann, Vintage Books, New York 1967, 135). Cf. 'Gegenseitigkeit', *Historische Wörterbuch zur Philosophie* III, 120ff.

10. Hildegard of Bingen, *Wisse die Wege*, Salzburg 1954, 156ff.; ead., *Lieder*, Salzburg 1969, 233.

11. Basil, *On the Holy Spirit*, Migne, PG 32.

12. R.Siebeck, 'Die Einheit von Leib und Seele in der theologischen Anthropologie und in der anthropologischen Medizin', in *Viktor von Weizsäcker. Arzt im Irrsal der Zeit. Eine Freundesgabe zum 70.Geburtstag*, Göttingen 1956, 54-65. See also R.Siebeck, *Medizin in Bewegung. Klinische Erkenntnisse und ärtzliche Aufgabe*, third edition with introductions by H.E.Bock and D.Rössler, Stuttgart 1983; and D.Rössler, 'Krankheit und Geschichte in der anthropologischen Medizin', in *Medicus Viator. Fragen und Gedanken am Wege Richard Siebecks*, Tübingen 1959, 165-80. See C.Frey, 'Zur theologischen Anthropologie K.Barths', in H.Fischer (ed.), *Anthropologie als Thema der Theologie*, Göttingen 1978, 39-69. Cf. also S.McLean, *Humanity in the Thought of Karl Barth*, Edinburgh 1980.

13. Moltmann, *God in Creation*, Chapter X, 2.

14. The correspondence was partially published in *Eva – wo bist Du? Frauen in der Ökumene*, Kennzeichen 8, Gelnhausen 1981, 11ff.

15. Annette von Droste-Hülshoff, *Gedichte*, Reclam 7662, 154-6. For Schelling, too, a 'veil of melancholy' hung over contemporary nature. The 'time of nature' is the 'winter of creation' which is waiting for its spring. F. Baader said that those who are reborn may even now conjure up fleeting blossoms from the 'paradisal state of nature' by 'anticipating' outside themselves what the Holy Spirit already gives out abidingly in advance in it. Cf. E.Bloch, *Das Materialismusproblem, seine Geschichte und Substanz*, Frankfurt 1972, 263ff.

16. T.Rendtorff, 'Karl Barth und die Neuzeit', *EvTh* 46, 1986, 298-314; F.W.Graf, 'Der Götze wackelt?', ibid., 422-41; F.Wagner, 'Theologische Gleichschaltung. Zur Christologie bei K.Barth', in T.Rendtorff (ed.), *Die Realisierung der Freiheit. Zur Kritik der Theologie K.Barths*, Gütersloh 1975, 522ff., 10ff.; T.Rendtorff, 'Der Freiheitsbegriff als Ortsbestimmung neuzeitlicher Theologie am Beispiel der Kirchlichen Dogmatik Karl Barths', in M.Welker et al.(eds.), *Gottes Zukunft – Zukunft der Welt. Festschrift für J.Moltmann*, Munich 1986, 559-78.

4 'Where There is Hope, There is Religion' (Ernst Bloch). The Philosophy and Theology of Hope

Previously unpublished.

1. This chapter was originally given as an exchange lecture in the Philosophical Faculty of the University of Tübingen in the Winter Semester of 1985/6.

2. Cf. J.Moltmann, *Im Gespräch mit Ernst Bloch*, Munich 1976; H.Deuser and P.Steinacker (eds.), *Ernst Blochs Vermittlungen zur Theologie*, Munich and Mainz 1983.

3. E.Bloch, *Atheismus im Christentum*, Frankfurt 1968, 351.

4. E.Bloch, *The Principle of Hope*, Blackwell 1986, 1191.

5. Ibid., 1202.

6. Ibid. 1193.

7. Ibid., 1203, 1201.

8. Ibid., 1201.

9. E.Bloch, *Naturrecht und menschliche Würde*, Frankfurt 1963, 310f.

10. Bloch, *Principle of Hope* (n.4), 1289.

11. Ibid., 1200.

12. Ibid., 1196.

13. Gerschom Scholem, *Judaica* I, Frankfurt 1963, 72f.

14. Ibid., 73.

15. Bloch, *Principle of Hope* (n.4), 1197.

5. 'What God would he be who only came from outside . . . ?' In Memory of Giordano Bruno

First published in H.Häring and K.-J.Kuschel (eds.), *Gegenentwürfe. 24 Lebensläufe für eine andere Theologie. Festschrift für Hans Küng,* Munich 1988, 157-68.

III MY THEOLOGICAL CAREER

First published in J.B.Bauer (ed.), *Entwürfe der Theologie,* Graz, Vienna and Cologne 1985, 235-57.

Abbreviations

Denzinger	H. Denzinger, *Enchiridion Symbolorum*
EvTh	*Evangelische Theologie*
LThK	*Lexikon für Theologie und Kirche*
ÖR	Ökumenische Rundschau
PG	Patrologia Graeca
RGG	*Die Religion in Geschichte und Gegenwart*
THAT	*Theologisches Handwörterbuch zum Neuen Testament*
ThEx	Theologische Existenz
ThPh	*Theologie und Philosophie*
TQ	*Theologische Quartalschrift*
TLZ	*Theologische Literaturzeitung*
WA	Weimarer Ausgabe
ZKG	*Zeitschrift für Kirchengeschichte*
ZTK	*Zeitschrift für Theologie und Kirche*

Index of Biblical References

200

Index of Names

Abelard, 52
Adorno, T.W., 130
Adrienne von Speyer, 81,
122
Albrecht, B., 30
Anders, G., 142, 155
Anselm of Canterbury, 52,
98
Aristotle, 88, 135, 159
Arnold, G., 64
Augustine, xi, 28, 60, 61,
62, 65, 81, 92, 98, 102,
103, 107, 109, 114,
134, 138, 139, 165, 189
n.6

Baader, F., 196 n.15
Bachmann, E.-M., 188 n.23
Bachofen, J.J., 185 n.8
Balthasar, H.U., xvii, 92,
122, 123, 184 n.30, 186
n.7, 192 nn.12, 23
Barth, K., xii, xviii, 55, 81,
82, 85, 92, 125, 142,
169, 176, 181, 189
n.28, 190 nn.23, 4, 191,
192 n.11, 195 nn.14, 1
Basil the Great, 73, 190
n.3, 196 n.11
Bauer, J.B., 197
Beethoven, L.von, 146
Bellarmine, R., 159
Ben-Chorin, S., 12, 185
n.30
Benjamin, W., 147
Benz, E., 92, 97, 99, 102,
192 nn. 6, 17, 192, 193
nn.23, 30, 194
Berdyaev, N., 24, 173, 186

n.13
Bernard, C.A., 192 n.19
Betz, H.-D., 184 n.19
Bethge, E., 185 n.26
Beza, T.von, 185
Biallowons, H., 195 n.18
Bingemer, M.C., 184 n.17
Bloch, E., xviii, 92, 126,
130, 143-55, 169, 170,
177, 186 n.2, 192 n.13,
193 n.27, 196, 197 n.15
Blumhardt, C., 79, 126, 127
Bobrinskoy, B., 183 n.6
Bock, H.E., 196 n.12
Bodin, J., 8, 9
Boethius, 183 n.10
Boff, L., xiii, 130, 186 n.7,
187 n.18, 195 n.7
Bonhoeffer, D., 37, 48,
123, 172, 185 n.26, 186
n.17, 187 n.5, 188 n.12
Borghese, C., 159
Bornemann, E., 185 n.8,
186 n.1
Borresen, K.E., 189 n.13
Breuning, W., 190
Bruno, G., xviii, 156-64
Buber, M., xvi, 179
Buchheim, F., 184 n.27,
185 n.19
Bultmann, R., 109, 165,
168, 176, 193 n.34, 195
n.13
Buonaiuti, E., 92, 192 n.5
Burkhardt, W., 195 n.9

Calvin, J., 8, 13, 40, 62,
134, 158, 185 n.21, 190
n.2

Capra, F., 133
Catherine of Siena, 29
Chenu, M.-D., 189 n.16
Cobb, J.B., xviii, 183 n.7
Coleridge, S.T., xii
Cone, J.H., 171, 180, 188
n.10
Congar, Y., 191 n.9
Crocco, A., 92, 192 n.8

Dabney, L., xvii, 184 n.28
Daly, M., xiii, 183 n.10
Darwin, C., 195 n.9
Dempf, A., 92, 192 n.4
Denzinger, D., 186 n.4
Deuser, H., 196 n.2
Dietrich, A., 185 n.12
Dörries, H., 189 n.18, 190
n.20
Dorner, I.A., 140, 190 n.3
Dostoievsky, F.M., 45, 187
n.5
Droste-Hülshoff, A.von
139, 196 n.15
Duchrow, U, 188 n.24

Eckhart, Meister, 133, 144,
164
Eichholz, G., 187 n.3, 189
n.15
Evdokimov, P., 186 n.13

Fabricius, C. 186 n.35
Falaturi, 185 n.8
Feneberg, R., 185 n.27
Ferdinandy, M.de, 185 n.10
Feuerbach, L., 132, 133,
148, 151
Fichte, J.G., 59, 140

201